Berlit®

Romanian

phrase book & dictionary

Berlitz Publishing
New York Munich Singapore

Contacting the Editors
Every effort has been made to provide accurate information in this publication, but changes are inevitable. The publisher cannot be responsible for any resulting loss, inconvenience or injury. We would appreciate it if readers would call our attention to any errors or outdated information by contacting Berlitz Publishing, 193 Morris Avenue, Springfield, NJ 07081, USA. Fax: 1-908-206-1103, email: comments@berlitzbooks.com

Satisfaction guaranteed—If you are dissatisfied with this product for any reason, send the complete package, your dated sales receipt showing price and store name, and a brief note describing your dissatisfaction to: Berlitz Publishing, Langenscheidt Publishing Group, Dept. L, 36-36 33rd Street, Long Island City, NY 11106. You'll receive a full refund.

Printed in Singapore by Insight Print Services (Pte) Ltd.,

Cover photo: © Imagesource.com
Map: HAMMOND World Atlas Corporation

Travelling around 65

Sightseeing 80

Relaxing 86

Making friends 92

Shopping guide 97

Contents

Acknowledgements

We are particularly grateful to Ani Price, Isabella Preoteasa and Irina Paladi for their help in the preparation of this book.

Pronunciation

This chapter is intended to make you familiar with the phonetic transcription we have devised, and to help you get used to the sound system of Romanian.

Note that Romanian uses some diacritical letters—letters with accent marks—which we don't use in English.

The imitated pronunciation should be read as if it were English (based on Standard British pronunciation), except for any special rules set out below. It is based on Standard British pronunciation, though we have tried to take account of General American pronunciation also.

Letters written in **bold** should be pronounced louder, though in Romanian stress is not as marked as in English.

The Romanian language

Romanian is relatively easy to read and write since it is a phonetic language in which all letters are pronounced. With the exception of the two typical sounds â and î, all the other sounds are easy to identify with English approximations.

Originating in the Latin language brought by Roman colonists in 101–275 AD, Romanian has much in common with French, Italian, Spanish and Portuguese.

Through the centuries the Romanian territories have been crossed by migrating tribes of Germanic, Slav and Magyar origin, each contributing words of their own vocabulary to the Romanian language.

Some words of Greek and Turkish origin are a reminder of the political dominance exercised by these two powers from the Middle Ages until Romanian independence in 1877.

Consonants

Letter	Approximate pronunciation	Symbol	Example	
b, d, f, l, m, n, p, t, v, w, x, z	are pronounced as in English			
c	1) like **c** in **cake**	c	**cartofi**	car**tof**^{y}
	2) followed by **e or i** like **ch** in **ch**eese	ch	**ceas** **cineva**	cheas **chee**neva
ch	like **k** in **k**ettle	k	**chibrit**	ki**breet**
g	1) like **g** in **g**irl	g	**rog**	rog
	2) when followed by **e** or **i,** like **g** in **g**ender	j	**ginere**	**jee**nereh
gh	like **g** in **g**irl	gh	**ghete**	**ge**teh
h	like **h** in **h**and	h	**hartă**	**har**ter
j	like **s** in plea**s**ure	zh	**jucărie**	zhu**ce**ree-eh
r	rolled consonant similar to the Scottish **r**	r	**roată**	**rwa**ter
s	like **s** in **s**un	s	**student**	stoo**dent**
ş	like **sh** in **sh**ort	sh	**şiret**	**shee**ret
ţ	like **ts** in bi**ts**	ts	**ţară**	**tsa**rer

Vowels

a	like the vowel sound in c**u**t	a	**alfabet**	**al**fabet
ă	like **er** at the end of teach**er**; but the **r** should not be pronounced	er	**masă**	**ma**ser
â	pronounced exactly like î below; it only occurs in the middle of the words	uh	**româneşte**	romuh**ne**shteh

e	1) like the **e** in ten; this is also pronounced at the end of the word, but to avoid confusion is represented **eh**	e eh	**elev** **carte**	elev **car**teh
	2) at the beginning of certain words, like **ye** in **yes**	ye	**este**	**yes**teh
i	1) like **ee** in b**ee**	ee	**intrare**	een**tra**reh
	2) If unstressed at the end of a word, **i** may be scarcely audible, softening the preceding consonant	^{y}	**bani**	ban^{y}
î	there's no exact equivalent in English; it resembles the **o** in less**o**n, kingd**o**m	uh	**înţeleg**	uhntse**leg**
o	like vowel sound in sp**o**rt, without pronouncing the **r**	o	**copil**	ko**peel**
u	like **oo** in b**oo**k	oo	**munte**	**moon**teh

Diphthongs

Diphthongs are combinations of a vowel and a semi-vowel, pronounced as one syllable. Practically all vowels in Romanian can act as semi-vowels in diphthongs. The following dipthongs are the most frequent.

ai	like **igh** in h**igh**	igh	**mai**	migh
au	like **ow** in c**ow**	a^{oo}	**stau**	sta^{oo}
ău	like **o in go**	oh	**rău**	roh
ea	1) no exact equivalent in English; sounds almost like **a** in b**a**t	a	**dimineaţa**	deemee**na**tsa
	2) at the end of the word like **aye** in **layer**	eh-a	**prea**	preh-a

* Hyphens are sometimes inserted between sounds to avoid confusion.

ei	like **ay** in b**ay**	ay	**lei**	lay
eu	no equivalent in English; start pronouncing the **e** of bed then draw your lips together to make a brief **oo** sound	e^{oo}	**leu**	le^{oo}
ia	like **ya** in **ya**rd	ya	**iarbă**	**yar**ber
ie	like **ye** in **ye**llow	ye	**ieftin**	**yef**teen
io	like **yo** in **yo**nder	yo	**chioşc**	kyoshc
iu	like **ew** in f**ew**	yoo	**iubire**	yoo**beer**eh
oa	like **wha** in **wha**t	wa	**poate**	**pwa**teh
oi	like **oy** in b**oy**	oy	**doi**	doy
ua	like **wa** in **wa**tch	wah	**ziua**	**zee**-wa
uă	similar to **ue** in infl**ue**nce	wer	**două**	**do**-wer

Pronunciation of the Romanian alphabet

A ah	**G** geh	**N** neh	**Ţ** tseh
Ă er	**H** hah	**O** oh	**U** oo
Â uh	**I** ee	**P** peh	**V** veh
B beh	**Î** uh	**R** reh	**W** dooblu-veh
C cheh	**J** zheh	**S** seh	**X** eeks
D deh	**K** kah	**Ș** sheh	**Y** eegrek
E eh	**L** leh	**T** teh	**Z** zeh
F feh	**M** meh		

Basic expressions

Yes.	**Da.**	da
No.	**Nu.**	noo
Please.	**Vă rog.**	ver rog
Thank you.	**Mulţumesc.**	mooltsoo**mesc**
Thank you very much.	**Mulţumesc foarte mult.**	mooltsoo**mesc fwar**teh moolt
That's all right/ You're welcome.	**Nu aveţi pentru ce.**	noo a**vets**y **pen**troo cheh

Greetings *Formule de salut*

Good morning.	**Bună dimineaţa.**	**boo**ner deemee**na**tsa
Good afternoon.	**Bună ziua.**	**boo**ner **zee**wah
Good evening.	**Bună seara.**	**boo**ner **sa**ra
Good night.	**Noapte bună.**	**nwap**teh **boo**ner
Goodbye.	**La revedere.**	la reve**de**reh
See you later.	**Pe curând.**	peh coo**ruhnd**
Hello/Hi!	**Bună!**	**boo**ner
This is Mr./Mrs./ Miss …	**Vă prezint pe domnul/doamna/domnişoara …**	ver pre**zeent** peh **dom**nool/**dwam**na/ domni**shwa**ra
How do you do? (Pleased to meet you.)	**Încântat de cunoştinţă.**	uhncuhn**tat** deh coono**shtee**ntser
How are you?	**Ce mai faceţi?**	cheh migh **fa**chetsy
Very well, thanks. And you?	**Mulţumesc bine, şi dumneavoastră?**	mooltsoo**mesc bee**neh shee doomna**vwas**trer
How's life?	**Cum vă merg treburile?**	coom ver merg **tre**booreeleh
Fine.	**Bine.**	**bee**neh
I beg your pardon?	**Poftim/Poftiţi?**	pof**teem** pof**teets**y
Excuse me. (May I get past?)	**Pardon, vă rog.**	par**don** ver rog
Sorry!	**Scuzaţi-mă, vă rog.**	scoo**za**tsee-mer ver rog

Questions *Întrebări*

Where?	**Unde?**	**oon**deh
How?	**Cum?**	coom
When?	**Când?**	cuhnd
What?	**Ce?**	cheh
Why?	**De ce?**	de cheh
Who?	**Cine?**	**chee**neh
Which?	**Care?**	**car**eh
Where is …?	**Unde este …?**	**oon**deh **yes**teh
Where are …?	**Unde sunt …?**	**oon**deh soont
Where can I find/ get …?	**Unde pot găsi/ de unde pot lua …?**	**oon**deh pot ger**see**/ deh **oon**deh pot loo-**a**
How far?	**Este departe?**	**yes**teh de**par**teh
How long?	**Cât timp durează?**	cuht teemp doo**ra**zer
How much/ How many?	**Câţi/câte?**	cuhts^y/**cuh**teh
How much does this cost?	**Cât costă?**	cuht **cos**ter
When does … open/ close?	**Când se deschide/ închide …?**	cuhnd seh des**kee**deh/ uhn**kee**deh
What do you call this/ that in Romanian?	**Cum se zice asta în româneşte?**	coom seh **zee**cheh **a**sta uhn romuh**nesh**teh
What does this/ that mean?	**Ce înseamnă asta?**	cheh uhn**sam**ner **a**sta

Do you speak …? *Vorbiţi …?*

Do you speak English?	**Vorbiţi englezeşte?**	vor**beets**ʸ engle**zesh**teh
Does anyone here speak English?	**Vorbeşte cineva aici englezeşte?**	vor**besh**teh cheene**va** a-**eech**ʸ engle**zesh**teh
I don't speak Romanian.	**Nu vorbesc româneşte.**	noo vor**besc** romuh**nehsh**teh
Could you speak more slowly?	**Puteţi să vorbiţi mai rar, vă rog?**	poo**tets**ʸ ser vor**beets**ʸ migh rar ver rog
Could you repeat that?	**Puteţi să repetaţi asta?**	poo**tets**ʸ ser repe**tats**ʸ **a**sta
Could you spell it?	**Cum se scrie?**	coom seh **scree**-eh

How do you pronounce this?	**Cum se pronunţă asta?**	coom seh pro**noon**tser **as**ta
Could you write it down, please?	**Vreţi să-mi scrieţi asta?**	vrets^{y} serm^{y} **scree**-ets^{y} **asta**
Can you translate this for me?	**Puteţi să-mi traduceţi, vă rog, asta?**	poo**tets**^{y} serm^{y} tra**doo**chets^{y} ver rog **asta**
Can you translate this for us?	**Vreţi să ne traduceţi asta, vă rog?**	vrets^{y} ser neh tra**doo**chets^{y} **asta** ver rog
Could you point to the … in the book, please?	**Puteţi să ne arătaţi … în carte, vă rog?**	poo**tets**^{y} ser neh arer**tats**^{y} … uhn **car**teh ver rog
word	**cuvânt**	coo**vuhnt**
phrase	**frază**	**fra**zer
Just a moment.	**Un moment.**	oon mo**ment**
I'll see if I can find it in this book.	**Să văd dacă-I pot găsi în această carte.**	ser verd **da**cerl pot ger**see** uhn a**chas**ter **car**teh
I understand.	**Înţeleg.**	uhntse**leg**
I don't understand.	**Nu înţeleg.**	noo uhntse**leg**
Do you understand?	**Înţelegeţi?**	uhntse**le**jets^{y}

Can/May …? *Pot/Îmi permiteţi …?*

Can I have …?	**Pot avea …?**	pot a**veh-a**
Can we have …?	**Putem avea …?**	poo**tem** a**veh-a**
Can you show me …?	**Puteţi să-mi arătaţi …?**	poo**tets**^{y} serm^{y} arer**tats**^{y}
I can't.	**Nu pot**	noo pot
Can you tell me …?	**Puteţi să-mi spuneţi …?**	poo**tets**^{y} serm^{y} **spoo**nets^{y}
Can you help me?	**Puteţi să mă ajutaţi?**	poo**tets**^{y} ser mer azhoo**tats**^{y}
Can I help you?	**Vă pot ajuta cu ceva?**	ver pot azhoo**ta** coo che**va**
Can you direct me to …?	**Puteţi să-mi spuneţi cum să ajung la …?**	poo**tets**^{y} serm^{y} **spoo**nets^{y} coom ser a**zhoong** la

Do you want …? *Vreţi să …?*

I'd like …	**Aş vrea …**	ash vreh-a
We'd like …	**Am dori …**	am do**ree**
What do you want?	**Ce doriţi?**	cheh do**reets**^{y}
Could you give me …?	**Puteţi să-mi daţi …?**	poo**tets**^{y} serm^{y} dats^{y}
Could you bring me …?	**Vreţi să-mi aduceţi …?**	vrets^{y} serm^{y} a**doo**chets^{y}
Could you show me …?	**Puteţi să-mi arătaţi …?**	poo**tets**^{y} serm^{y} arer**tats**^{y}
I'm looking/ searching for …	**Caut …**	ca^{oo}t
I'm hungry.	**Mi-e foame.**	myeh **fwa**meh
I'm thirsty.	**Mi-e sete.**	myeh **se**teh
I'm tired.	**Sunt obosit(ă)**	soont obo**seet**(er)
I'm lost.	**M-am rătăcit.**	mam rerter**cheet**
It's important.	**Este important.**	**yes**teh eempor**tant**
It's urgent.	**Este urgent.**	**yes**teh oor**jent**

It is/There is … *Este/Există …*

It is …	**Este …**	**yes**teh
Is it …?	**Este …?**	**yes**teh
It isn't …	**Nu este …**	noo **yes**teh
Here it is.	**Aici e.**	a-**eech**^{y} yeh
Here they are.	**Aici sunt.**	a-**eech**^{y} soont
There it is.	**Acolo este.**	a**co**lo **yes**teh
There they are.	**Acolo sunt.**	a**co**lo soont
There is/There are …	**Există …/Sunt**	eg**zees**ter/soont
Is there/Are there …?	**Există …?**	eg**zees**ter
There isn't/aren't …	**Nu există …**	noo eg**zees**ter
There isn't/ aren't any.	**Nu există nici unul/una.**	noo eg**zees**ter neech^{y} **oo**nool/**oo**na.

It's … *Este …*

beautiful/ugly	**frumos/urât**	**froo**mos /**oo**ruht
better/worse	**mai bine/mai rău**	migh **bee**neh/migh roh
big/small	**mare/mic**	**ma**reh/meec
cheap/expensive	**ieftin/scump**	**yef**teen/scoomp
early/late	**devreme/târziu**	dev**re**meh/tuhr**zyoo**
easy/difficult	**uşor/greu**	oo**shor**/gre^oo
free (vacant)/ occupied	**liber/ocupat**	**lee**ber/ocoo**pat**
full/empty	**plin/gol**	pleen/gol
good/bad	**bun/rău**	boon/roh
heavy/light	**greu/uşor**	gre^oo/oo**shor**
here/there	**aici/acolo**	a**eech**^y/a**co**lo
hot/cold	**fierbinte/rece**	fyer**bin**teh/**re**cheh
near/far	**aproape/departe**	a**prwa**peh/de**par**teh
next/last	**următorul/ultimul**	oormer**to**rool/ **ool**teemool
old/new	**vechi/nou**	vek^y/no^oo
old/young	**bătrân/tânar**	ber**truhn**/**tuh**ner
open/shut	**deschis/închis**	des**kees**/uhn**kees**
quick/show	**repede/încet**	**re**pedeh/uhn**chet**
right/wrong	**bine/rău**	**bee**neh/roh

Quantities *Cantităţi*

a little/a lot	**puţin/mult**	poo**tseen**/moolt
few/a few	**puţini/câţiva**	poo**tseen**^y/cuhts^y**va**
much	**mult**	moolt
many	**mulţi**	moolts^y
more/less (than)	**mai mult/mai puţin (decât)**	migh moolt/migh poo**t seen** (**de**cuht)
enough/too	**destul/prea**	des**tool**/pra
some/any	**nişte/oricare**	**neesh**teh/oree**car**eh

A few more useful words *Alte cuvinte utile*

above	**deasupra**	da**soo**pra
after	**după**	**doo**per
and	**şi**	shee
at	**la**	la
before (time)	**înainte**	uhna**een**teh
behind	**înapoi**	uhna**poy**
below	**dedesubt**	dede**soobt**
between	**între**	**uhn**treh
but	**dar/însă**	dar/**uhn**ser
down	**jos**	zhos
downstairs	**la parter**	la par**ter**
during	**în timpul**	uhn **teem**pool
for	**pentru**	**pen**troo
from	**de la**	deh la
in	**în**	uhn
inside	**înăuntru**	uhner-**oon**troo
near	**lângă**	**luhn**ger
never	**niciodată**	neechyo**da**ter
next to	**lângă/aproape**	**luhn**ger/**aprwa**peh
not	**nu**	noo
nothing	**nimic**	nee**meec**
now	**acum**	a**coom**
on	**pe**	peh
only	**numai**	**noo**migh
or	**sau**	sa^{oo}
outside	**afară**	a**fa**rer
perhaps	**poate**	**pwa**teh
soon	**curând**	coo**rind**
then	**atunci**	a**toonch**^{y}
through	**prin**	preen
to	**până la**	**puh**ner la
too (also)	**de asemenea**	deh-a**se**meneh-a
towards	**spre**	spreh
under	**sub/dedesubt**	soob/dede**soobt**
until	**până**	**puh**ner
up	**sus**	soos
upstairs	**la etaj**	la e**tazh**
very	**foarte**	**fwar**teh
with	**cu**	coo
without	**fără**	**fer**rer
yet	**încă**	**uhn**cer

Arrival

Whether you come by train, plane or car you will have to go through customs. If you did not obtain a visa in advance through your travel agency or Romanian Consulate, you can get one at road crossing points or the airport. Those travelling to Romania by train or car can get a visa at the border without a problem.

GHIȘEUL DE PAȘAPOARTE
PASSPORT CONTROL

The Romanian international airport Otopeni (*otopen*^{y}) is situated 18 km from the centre of Bucharest. A regular bus service links the airport to the centre and there is also an excellent taxi service. Allow plenty of time for the journey to and from the airport, as this is a very busy route and has frequent traffic jams.

Here's my passport.	**Poftiţi paşaportul.**	pof**teets**^{y} pasha**port**ool
I'll be staying …	**O să stau …**	o ser sta^{oo}
a few days	**câteva zile**	**cuh**teva **zee**leh
a week	**o săptămână**	o serpter**muh**ner
two weeks	**două săptămâni**	**do**-wer serpter**muhn**^{y}
a month	**o lună**	o **loo**ner
I don't know yet.	**Nu ştiu încă.**	noo shtee^{oo} **uhn**cer
I'm here on holiday.	**Sunt (aici) în vacanţă**	soont (a-**eech**^{y}) uhn va**cant**ser
I'm here on business.	**Sunt/Am venit în interes de serviciu.**	soont/am ve**neet** uhn eente**res** deh ser**vee**chee-oo
I'm just passing through.	**Sunt în trecere doar.**	soont uhn **tre**chereh dwar

If things become difficult:

I'm sorry, I don't understand.	**Regret, nu înţeleg.**	re**gret** noo uhntse**leg**
Does anyone here speak English?	**Vorbeşte cineva engleza aici?**	vor**besh**teh cheene**va** eng**le**za a-**eech**^{y}

LA VAMĂ
CUSTOMS

After collecting your baggage at the airport (*aeroport*) you have a choice: use the green exit if you have nothing to declare, or leave via the red exit if you have items to declare (in excess of those allowed).

bunuri de declarat goods to declare	**nimic de declarat** nothing to declare

The import and export of Romanian currency is prohibited, but there is no restriction on the amount of foreign currency visitors can bring into the country.

I have nothing to declare.	**Nu am nimic de declarat.**	noo am nee**meec** deh decla**rat**
I have …	**Am …**	am
a carton of cigarettes	**un cartuş de ţigări**	oon car**toosh** deh tsee**gerr**ʸ
a bottle of whisky	**o sticlă de wisky**	o **stee**cler deh **wees**kee
It's for my personal use.	**E pentru mine.**	yeh **pen**troo **mee**neh
It's a gift.	**Este un cadou.**	**yes**teh oon ca**do**ᵒᵒ

YOU MAY HEAR:

Paşaportul, vă rog.	Your passport, please.
Aveţi ceva de declarat?	Do you have anything to declare?
Vă rog să deschideţi acest sac.	Please open this bag.
Trebuie să plătiţi vamă pentru acest obiect.	You'll have to pay duty on this.
Mai aveţi bagaje?	Do you have any more luggage?

Baggage—Porter *Hamal*

Baggage-porters are available only at the airport. Luggage trolleys are available at the airport and Central Bucharest Railway Station (Gara de Nord). Don't hesitate to ask a taxi driver to help you.

Porter!	**Hamal!/Alo!**	**ha**mal/**a**lo.
Please take (this) …	**Vă rog luaţi (acest) …**	ver rog lwats^{y} (a**chest**)
luggage	**bagaj**	ba**gazh**
suitcase/traveling bag	**valiză/sac de voiaj**	val**ee**zer/sac de vo**yazh**
That one is mine.	**Aceea este a mea.**	**ache**-a **yes**teh a meh-a
Take this luggage …	**Duceţi acest bagaj …**	**doo**chets^{y} **achest** **bagazh**
to the bus	**la autobuz**	la aooto**booz**
to the luggage lockers	**la çabinele de bagaje**	la ca**bee**neleh de baga**zh**eh
to the taxi	**la taxi**	la ta**xee**
How much is that?	**Cât costă?**	cuht **co**ster
There's one piece missing	**Lipseşte un bagaj.**	leep**sesh**teh oon ba**gazh**
Where are the luggage trolleys (carts)?	**Unde sunt cărucioarele de bagaje?**	**oon**deh soont cerroo**chy wa**releh deh ba**ga**zheh

Changing money *Schimb valutar*

Foreign currency can be changed at airports, banks, most hotels and currency exchange offices in major cities. Avoid changing a large amount of money at the beginning of your visit as you may not easily be able to change it back. Never change money with street dealers; you're only likely to be cheated.

Where's the nearest currency exchange office?	**Unde este un birou de schimb prin apropiere?**	**oon**deh **yes**te oon bee**ro**^{oo} deh skeemb preen apropee-**e**reh
Can you change these traveller's cheques (checks)?	**Pot încasa nişte cecuri de voiaj?**	pot uhnca**sa** **neesh**teh **che**coor^{y} deh vo**yazh**
I want to change some dollars/pounds.	**Vreau să schimb nişte dolari/ lire sterline.**	vra^{oo} ser skeemb **neesh**teh do**lar**^{y}/ **lee**reh ster**lee**neh

BANK—CURRENCY, see page 129

Can you change this into lei?	**Puteţi schimba aceşti bani în lei?**	poo**tets**ʸ skeem**ba** a**chesht**ʸ banʸ uhn lay
What's the exchange rate?	**Care este cursul de schimb?**	**ca**reh **yes**teh **coor**sool deh skeemb

Where is ...? *Unde este ...?*

Where is the ...?	**Unde este ...?**	**oon**deh **yes**teh
booking office	**agenţia de voiaj**	ajent**see**-a deh vo**yazh**
newsstand	**chioşcul de ziare**	kyoshcool deh zee-**a**reh
restaurant	**restaurantul**	restaᵒᵒ**ran**tool
How do I get to ...?	**Cum se ajunge la ...?**	coom seh a**zhoon**jeh la
Is there a bus into town?	**Ce autobuz merge în oraş?**	cheh auto**booz mer**jeh uhn o**rash**
Where can I get a taxi?	**De unde pot lua un taxi?**	deh **oon**deh pot lwa oon ta**xee**
Where can I hire (rent) a car?	**Unde pot închiria o maşină?**	**oon**deh pot uhnkeeree-**a** o ma**shee**ner

Hotel reservation *Rezervare la hotel*

Do you have a hotel guide (directory)?	**Aveţi un ghid al hotelurilor?**	a**vets**ʸ oon geed coo ho**te**looreelor
Could you reserve a room for me?	**Puteţi să-mi rezervaţi o cameră?**	poo**tets**ʸ sermʸ rezer**vats**ʸ o **ca**merer
in the center	**în centru**	uhn **chen**troo
near the railway station	**lângă gară**	**luhn**ger **ga**rer
a single room	**o cameră cu un pat**	o **ca**merer coo oon pat
a double room	**o cameră cu două paturi**	o **ca**merer coo **do**-wer **pa**toorʸ
not too expensive	**nu prea scumpă**	noo preh-a **scoom**per
Where is the hotel/ guesthouse?	**Unde este hotelul/ hotelul- pensiune?**	**oon**deh **yes**teh ho**te**lool/ ho**te**lool pensee-**oo**neh
Do you have a street map?	**Aveţi o hartă a oraşului?**	a**vets**ʸ o **har**ter a o**ra**shoolooʸ

HOTEL/ACCOMMODATIONS, see page 22

Car hire (rental) *Închirieri auto*

There are car rental facilities at the airport and in major cities. The main rental offices are the National Tourist Office (ONT) and the Romanian Automobile Club (ACR). You must be at least 21 years old and have held a full driving licence for more than one year. Your hotel can help you with further information, or contact The National Tourist Office.

I'd like to hire (rent) a car.	**Aş vrea să închiriez o masină.**	ash vreh-a ser uhnkeeree-**ez** o ma**shee**ner
small	**mică**	**mi**cer
medium-sized	**de capacitate medie**	deh capachee**ta**teh **me**dee-eh
large	**mare**	**ma**reh
automatic	**automată**	aooto**ma**ter
I'd like it for a day/ a week.	**Pentru o zi/ o săptămână.**	**pen**troo o zee/ o serpter**muh**ner
Are there any weekend arrangements?	**Ce tarife aveţi pentru sfârşit de săptămână?**	cheh ta**ree**feh av**ets**ʸ **pen**troo sfuhr**sheet** deh serpter**muh**ner
Do you have any special rates?	**Ce reduceri faceţi?**	cheh re**doo**cherʸ **fa**chetsʸ
What's the charge per day/week?	**Cât costă locaţia pe zi/săptămână?**	cuht **cos**ter lo**ca**tsee-a peh zee/serpter**muh**ner
Is mileage included?	**Kilometrajul este inclus?**	keelome**tra**zhool **yes**teh een**cloos**
What's the charge per kilometre?	**Cât costă pe kilometru?**	cuht **cos**ter peh keelo**me**troo
I'd like to leave the car in …	**Aş vrea să las maşina în …**	ash vreh-a ser las ma**shee**na uhn
I'd like full insurance.	**Doresc o asigurare casco.**	do**resc** o aseegoo**ra**reh **cas**co
How much is the deposit?	**Ce avans trebuie să las?**	cheh a**vans tre**boo-yeh ser las
I have a credit card.	**Pentru plată am carte de credit.**	**pen**troo **pla**ter am **car**teh deh **cre**deet
Here's my driving licence.	**Poftiţi carnetul de conducere.**	pof**teets**ʸ car**ne**tool deh con**doo**chereh

CAR, see page 75

Taxi *Taxi*

Metered vehicles, both state owned (GETAX) and private, are available in Bucharest and all larger towns and are still an inexpensive means of travel. Taxi drivers can issue a receipt for the fare on request. It is customary to give a tip in addition to the amount shown on the meter. Taxis are easily identified by a light on top of the vehicle.

Where can I get a taxi?	**De unde pot lua un taxi, vă rog?**	deh **oon**deh pot lwa oon tax**ee** ver rog
Where is the taxi rank (stand)?	**Unde este staţia de taxi?**	**oon**deh **yes**teh **sta**tsya deh tax**ee**
Could you get me a taxi?	**Puteţi să-mi comandaţi un taxi, vă rog?**	poo**tets**ʸ sermʸ coman**dats**ʸ oon tax**ee** ver rog
What's the fare to …?	**Cât costă până la …?**	cuht **cos**ter **puh**ner la
How far is it to …?	**Este departe până la …?**	**yes**teh de**par**teh **puh**ner la
Take me to …	**Vreau să merg la …**	vraᵒᵒ ser merg la
this address	**adresa aceasta**	a**dre**sa a**cha**sta
the airport	**aeroport**	a-ero**port**
the town centre	**în centru**	uhn **chen**troo
the … Hotel	**la hotelul …**	la ho**te**lool …
the railway station	**la gară**	la **ga**rer
Turn at the next corner.	**Cotiţi la colţul următor.**	co**teets**ʸ la **col**tsool oormer**tor**
left/right	**la stânga/la dreapta**	la **stuhn**ga/la **drap**ta
Go straight ahead.	**Mergeţi drept înainte.**	**mer**jetsʸ drept uhna**een**teh
Please stop here.	**Vă rog, opriţi aici.**	ver rog o**preets**ʸ a-**eech**ʸ
I'm in a hurry.	**Mă grăbesc.**	mer grer**besc**
Could you drive more slowly?	**Aţi putea să conduceţi mai încet?**	atsʸ poo**teh-a** ser con**doo**chetsʸ migh uhn**chet**
Could you help me carry my luggage?	**Vreţi să mă ajutaţi la bagaje?**	vretsʸ ser mer azhoo**tats**ʸ la ba**ga**zheh
Could you wait for me?	**Puteţi să mă aşteptaţi?**	poo**tets**ʸ ser mer ashtep**tats**ʸ
I'll be back in 10 minutes.	**Mă întorc peste zece minute.**	mer uhn**torc pes**teh **ze**cheh mee**noo**teh

Hotel—Other accommodations

You are advised to book ahead if you intend to stay during the peak holiday season. Romania is not yet well equipped for independent tourists. Much is now being done to change this, and many hotels, motels and boarding-houses have been built. The so-called "Agroturisme" offers private accommodation in the country, and is becomming inceasingly popular for its clean rooms and home-cooked meals. Large hotels tend to cater to business travellers or to package tours to the Black Sea resorts, spa towns or cities linked with the life of Count Dracula.

hotel
(ho**tel**)

Hotels in Romania are classified from five-star to one-star, or de luxe. Few offer full or half board, or even bed and breakfast, though this is changing. Most rooms in three-star hotels have en-suite bathrooms and toilets. In two-star and one-star hotels, the bathroom and toilet might be shared, and visitors are advised to bring their own essentials, like soap and toilet paper. Breakfast is usually included in the price, but it is still advisable to query this in lower category cheaper hotels.

It is unwise to leave valuables in hotel rooms of any category.

motel
(mo**tel**)

There are an increasing number of motels in Romania, catering specifically for the motorist.

cameră mobilată
(**ca**merer mobee**la**ter)

Rented accommodation in private flats and houses is becoming increasingly available to visitors. Details may be available at the local tourist office; otherwise taxi drivers can be a useful source of information.

camin de studenţi
(ca**meen** deh stoo**dents**ʸ)

Youth hotels, run by the student travel service, CTT, are situated in major towns; these give preference to large groups and are open only in July and August, but are inexpensive if booked directly at the hostel.

cabane (ca**ba**neh) — A network of chalets for hikers in the mountains; cheap and friendly, though not necessarily comfortable, these cabins are listed in the official *Cabane Turistice* map.

Can you recommend a hotel?	**Puteţi să-mi recomandaţi un hotel?**	poo**tets**ʸ sermʸ recoman**dats**ʸ oon ho**tel**
Are there any self-catering flats (apartments) vacant?	**Ce apartamente aveţi libere?**	cheh aparta**men**teh a**vets**ʸ **lee**bereh
I'd like a private room.	**Vreau o cameră particulară.**	vraᵒᵒ o **ca**merer parteecoo**la**rer

Checking in—Reception *La recepţie*

My name is …	**Mă numesc …**	mer noo**mesc**
I have a reservation.	**Am o rezervare.**	am o rezer**va**reh
We've reserved two rooms/ an apartment.	**Am rezervat două camere/un apartament**	am rezer**vat do**-wer **ca**mereh/oon aparta**ment**
Here's the confirmation.	**Aceasta este confirmarea.**	a**cha**sta **yes**teh confeer**ma**reh-a
Do you have any vacancies?	**Aveţi camere libere?**	a**vets**ʸ **ca**mereh **lee**bereh
I'd like a …	**Aş vrea …**	ash vreh-a
single room	**o cameră cu un pat**	o **ca**merer coo oon pat
double room	**o cameră cu două paturi**	o **ca**merer coo **do**-wer **pa**toorʸ
We'd like a room …	**Am dori o cameră**	am do**ree** o **ca**merer
with twin beds	**cu două paturi**	coo **do**-wer **pa**toorʸ
with a double bed	**cu pat dublu**	coo pat **doo**bloo
with a bath	**cu baie**	coo **ba**yeh
with a shower	**cu duş**	coo doosh
with a balcony	**cu balcon**	coo bal**con**
with a view	**cu vedere la stradă**	coo ve**de**reh la **stra**der
It must be quiet.	**Trebuie să fie liniştită.**	**tre**booyeh ser **fee**-eh leeneesh**tee**ter
Is there …?	**Este/Există …?**	**yes**teh/eg**zees**ter
air conditioning	**aer condiţionat**	**a**-er condeetsee-o**nat**
a conference room	**o sală de conferinţe**	o **sa**ler deh confe**reen**tseh
a laundry service	**serviciu de spălătorie**	ser**vee**chyoo deh sperlerto**ree**-eh

CHECKING OUT, see page 31

a private toilet	**toaletă individuală**	twa**le**ter eendeeveedoo-**aler**
a radio/television in the room	**un radio/un televizor în cameră**	oon **ra**dee-o/oon televee**zor** uhn **ca**merer
a swimming pool	**o piscină**	o pees**chee**ner
hot water	**apă caldă**	aper **cal**der
room service	**servicii la cameră**	ser**vee**chee la **ca**merer
running water	**apă curentă**	aper coo**ren**ter

How much? *Cât costă?*

What's the price …?	**Cât costă?**	cuht **co**ster
per day	**pe zi**	peh zee
per week	**pe săptămână**	peh serpter**muh**ner
for bed and breakfast	**pentru cazare şi micul dejun**	**pen**troo ca**za**reh shee **mee**cool de**zhoon**
excluding meals	**fără mese**	**fer**rer **me**seh
for full board (A.P.)	**pensiune completă**	pensee-**oo**neh com**ple**ter
for half board (M.A.P.)	**demi pesiune**	**de**mee pensee-**oo**neh
Does that include …?	**Aceasta include şi …?**	a**chas**ta een**cloo**deh shee
breakfast	**micul dejun**	**mee**cool de**zhoon**
service	**serviciul**	ser**vee**chyool
Is there any reduction for children?	**Faceţi reduceri de tarif pentru copii?**	**fa**chets^{y} re**doo**cher^{y} deh ta**reef** **pen**troo co**pee**
That's too expensive.	**E prea scump.**	yeh preh-a scoomp
Do you have anything cheaper?	**Aveţi ceva mai ieftin?**	a**vets**^{y} che**va** migh **yef**teen
Is electricity included in the rental?	**Electricitatea este inclusă în chirie?**	electreechee**ta**ta **yes**teh een**cloo**ser uhn kee**ree**-eh

How long? *Cât timp (vreţi să staţi)?*

We'll be staying …	**O să stăm …**	o ser sterm
overnight only	**numai o noapte**	**noo**migh o **nwap**teh
a few days	**câteva zile**	**cuh**teva **zee**leh
a week (at least)	**o săptămână (cel puţin)**	o serpter**muh**ner (chel poo**tseen**)
I don't know yet.	**Nu ştiu încă.**	noo shtee^{oo} **uhn**cer

NUMBERS, see page 147

Decision *Decizie*

May I see the room?	**Pot să văd camera, vă rog?**	pot ser verd **ca**mera ver rog
That's fine. I'll take it.	**E în ordine, o iau.**	yeh uhn **or**deeneh o ya[oo]
No. I don't like it.	**Nu-mi place.**	noom[y] **pla**cheh
It's too …	**Este prea …**	**yes**teh preh-**a**
cold/hot	**rece/caldă**	**re**cheh/**cal**der
dark/small	**întunecoasă/mică**	uhntoone**cwa**ser/ **mee**cer
noisy	**zgomotoasă**	zgomo**twa**ser
I asked for a room with a bath.	**Am cerut o cameră cu baie.**	am che**root** o **ca**merer coo **ba**yeh
Do you have anything …?	**Aveţi ceva …?**	a**vets**[y] che**va**
better	**mai bun**	migh boon
bigger	**mai mare**	migh **ma**reh
cheaper	**mai ieftin**	migh **ye**fteen
quieter	**mai liniştit**	migh leeneesh**teet**
Do you have a room with a better view?	**Aveţi o cameră cu vedere mai bună?**	a**vets**[y] o **ca**merer coo ve**de**reh migh **boo**ner

Registration *Înregistrare*

Upon arrival at a hotel you'll be asked to fill in a registration form (*formular*).

Numele/Prenumele	Name/First name
Oraşul/Strada/Numărul	Home town/Street/Number
Naţionalitatea/Ocupaţia	Nationality/Occupation
Data/Locul naşterii	Date/Place of birth
Sosit din … /Cu destinaţia …	Coming from … / Going to …
Numărul de paşaport	Passport number
Locul/Data emiterii	Place/Date
Semnătura	Signature

What does this mean?	**Ce înseamnă asta?**	cheh uhn**sam**ner **as**ta
What's my room number?	**Ce număr are camera mea?**	cheh **noo**merr **a**reh **ca**mera meh-a

YOU MAY HEAR:

May I see your passport, please?	Paşaportul, vă rog!
Please sign here.	Vă rog să semnaţi în locul acesta.
How long will you be staying?	Cât doriţi să staţi?

Will you have our luggage sent up?	**Vreţi să ne trimiteţi bagajul în cameră?**	vrets[y] ser neh tree**mee**tetsy ba**ga**zhool uhn **ca**merer
Where can I park my car?	**Unde pot parca maşina?**	**oon**deh pot par**ca** ma**shee**na
I'd like to leave this in the hotel safe.	**Aş vrea să las aceasta în seiful hotelului.**	ash vreh-**a** ser las a**chas**ta uhn **sey**fool ho**te**looloo[y]

Hotel staff *Personalul hotelului*

hall porter	**valet**	va**let**
maid	**cameristă**	came**rees**ter
manager	**director**	dee**rec**tor
porter	**portar**	por**tar**
receptionist	**recepţionist(ă)**	recheptsyo**neest**(**er**)
switchboard operator	**telefonist(ă)**	telefo**neest**(**er**)
waiter	**chelner/ospătar**	**kel**ner/osper**tar**
waitress	**chelneriţă**	kelne**ree**tser

If you want to address members of staff, use a general introductory phrase: *Fiţi amabil, vă rog …* —feets[y] a**ma**beel ver rog.

General requirements *Servicii—Informaţii*

The key to room …, please.	**Daţi-mi vă rog, cheia de la camera numărul …**	**dat**seem[y] ver rog **key**a deh la **ca**mera **noo**merrool
Could you wake me at …, please?	**Puteţi să mă sculaţi la ora …, vă rog?**	poo**tets**[y] ser mer scoo**lats**[y] la **o**ra … ver rog
When is breakfast/ lunch/dinner served?	**Când se serveşte micul dejun/ prânzul/cina?**	cuhnd seh ser**vesh**teh **mee**cool de**zhoon**/ **pruhn**zool/**chee**na

NUMBERS, see page 147/TELLING TIME, see page 153

May we have breakfast in our room, please?	**Putem avea micul dejun în cameră, vă rog?**	poo**tem** a**veh-a** **mee**cool de**zhoon** uhn **ca**merer ver rog
Is there a bath on this floor?	**Există o baie pe palierul acesta?**	eg**zees**ter o **ba**yeh peh palee-**er**ool a**ches**ta
What's the voltage?	**Ce voltaj are circuitul electric?**	cheh vol**tazh** **a**reh cheercoo**ee**tool e**lec**treec
Where's the shaver socket (outlet)?	**Există o priză pentru aparatul de ras?**	eg**zees**ter o **pree**zer **pen**troo apa**ra**tool deh ras
Can you find me a …?	**Puteţi să-mi găsiţi …?**	poo**tets**ʸ sermʸ ger**seets**ʸ
babysitter	**o îngrijitoare de copii/o baby sitter**	o uhngreezhee**twa**reh deh co**pee**/o ´babysitter´
May I have a/an/ some …?	**Aveţi …?**	**a**vetsʸ
ashtray	**o scrumieră**	o scroomee-**er**er
bath towel	**un prosop de baie**	oon pro**sop** deh **ba**yeh
(extra) blanket	**o pătură (în plus)**	o **per**toorer (uhn ploos)
(more) hangers	**(câteva) umeraşe**	(cuhte**va**) oome**ra**sheh
hot-water bottle	**o buiotă cu apă fierbinte**	o boo**yo**ter coo **a**per fyer**been**teh
ice cubes	**cuburi de gheaţă**	**coo**boorʸ deh **gya**tser
needle and thread	**ac şi aţă**	ac shee **a**tser
(extra) pillow	**(încă o) pernă**	(**uhn**cer o) **per**ner
reading lamp	**lampă de citit**	**lam**per deh chee**teet**
soap	**săpun**	ser**poon**
writing paper	**hârtie de scris**	huhr**tee**-eh deh screes
Where's the …?	**Unde este …?**	**oon**deh **yes**teh
bathroom	**baia**	**ba**ya
dining-room	**sala de mese/ sufrageria**	**sa**la deh **me**seh/ soofraje**ree-**a
electricity meter	**contoarul**	con**twa**rool
emergency exit	**ieşirea de incendiu**	ye**shee**reh-a deh ccn**chen**dyoo
hairdresser's	**coaforul/frizeria**	cwa**fo**rool/freeze**ree**a
lift (elevator)	**liftul**	**leef**tool
Where are the toilets?	**Unde este toaleta?**	**oon**deh **yes**teh twa**le**ta

BREAKFAST, see page 40

Telephone—Mail — Internet *Telefon—Poştă — Internet*

Can I access the internet here?	**Pot să mă connectez la internet aici?**	pot ser mer conec**tez** la eenter**net** a**eechy**
Do you have any stamps?	**Aveţi timbre?**	**avets^{y} teem**breh
Would you post this for me, please?	**Fiţi amabil, puteţi să-mi puneţi acest plic la postă?**	feets^{y} **am**a**beel** **pootets^{y}** serm^{y} **poo**nets^{y} **achest** pleec la **posh**ter
Are there any letters for me?	**Am vreo scrisoare?**	am vro scree**swa**reh
Are there any messages for me?	**Am vreun mesaj?**	am vroon me**sazh**
How much is my telephone bill?	**Cât vă datorez pentru convorbirile telefonice?**	cuht ver dato**rez** **pen**troo convor**bee**reeleh tele**fo**neecheh

Difficulties *Dificultăţi—Probleme*

The … doesn't work.	**Nu funcţionează …**	noo foonctsyo**na**zer
air conditioning	**aerul condiţionat**	**a**-erool condeetsyo**nat**
bidet	**bideul**	bee**de**-ool
fan	**ventilatorul**	venteela**to**rool
heating	**încălzirea**	uhncerl**zee**reh-a
light	**lumina**	loo**mee**na
radio	**radioul**	**ra**dee-o-ool
television	**televizorul**	televee**zo**rool
The tap (faucet) is dripping.	**Robinetul curge.**	robee**ne**tool **coor**jeh
There's no hot water.	**Nu este apă caldă.**	noo **yes**teh **a**per **cal**der
The washbasin is blocked.	**Chiuveta este înfundată.**	kyooveta **yes**teh uhnfoon**da**ter
The window is jammed.	**Fereastra este blocată.**	fe**ras**tra **yes**teh blo**ca**ter
The curtains are stuck.	**Perdelele sunt blocate.**	per**de**leleh soont blo**ca**teh
The bulb is burned out.	**Becul s-a ars.**	**be**cool sa ars
My bed hasn't been made up.	**Patul nu a fost făcut.**	**pa**tool noo a fost fer-**coot**

POST OFFICE AND TELEPHONE, see page 132

The … is broken.	**Nu functionează …**	noo foonctsyo**na**zer
blind	**jaluzelele**	zhaloo**ze**leleh
lamp	**lampa**	**lam**pa
plug	**ştecherul**	**shte**kerool
shutter	**oblonul**	o**blo**nool
switch	**butonul/ întrerupătorul**	boo**to**nool/ uhntreroopertorool
Can you get it repaired?	**Îl puteţi da la reparat?**	uhl poo**tets**ʸ da la repa**rat**

Laundry—Dry cleaner's *Spălătorie—Curăţătorie*

There are laundry services in most big towns. Look for the sign *Nufărul*—**noo**ferrool.

I'd like these clothes …	**Aş vrea să las aceste rufe …**	ash vreh-a ser las a**ches**teh **roo**feh
cleaned	**pentru curăţat**	**pen**troo coorer**tsat**
ironed	**pentru călcat**	**pen**troo cerl**cat**
pressed	**pentru călcat**	**pen**troo cerl**cat**
washed	**pentru spălat**	**pen**troo sper**lat**
When will they be ready?	**Când vor fi gata?**	cuhnd vor fee **ga**ta
I need them …	**Am nevoie de ele …**	am ne**vo**yeh deh **ye**leh
today	**azi**	azʸ
tonight	**deseară**	de**sa**rer
tomorrow	**mâine**	**muhy**neh
Can you … this?	**Puteţi …?**	poo**tets**ʸ
mend	**repara asta**	repa**ra** **as**ta
patch	**pune un petec**	**poo**neh oon **pe**tec
stitch	**coase asta**	**cwa**seh **as**ta
Can you sew on this button?	**Puteţi coase acest nasture?**	poo**tets**ʸ **cwa**seh a**chest** **nas**tooreh
Can you get this stain out?	**Puteţi scoate pata aceasta?**	poo**tets**ʸ **scwa**teh **pa**ta a**chas**ta
Is my laundry ready?	**Sunt gata rufele mele?**	soont **ga**ta **roo**feleh **me**leh
This isn't mine.	**Aceasta nu este a mea.**	a**chas**ta noo **yes**teh a meh-a

There's something missing.	**Lipseşte ceva.**	leep**sesh**teh che**va**
There's a hole in this.	**Asta are o gaură.**	**as**ta areh o **ga**-oorer

Hairdresser—Barber *Coafor—Frizer*

Is there a hairdresser/ beauty salon in the hotel?	**Există un salon de coafură/un salon de cosmetică în hotel?**	eg**zees**ter oon sa**lon** deh cwa**foo**rer/oon sa**lon** deh cos**me**teecer uhn ho**tel**
Can I make an appointment for Tuesday?	**Pot să-mi fixez o oră pentru marţi, vă rog?**	pot serm^{y} feex**ez** o **o**-rer **pen**troo marts^{y} ver rog
I'd like a cut and blow dry.	**Aş vrea o tunsoare şi un pieptănat.**	ash vreh-a o toon**swa**reh shee oon pyepter**nat**
I'd like a haircut, please.	**Aş vrea o tunsoare, vă rog.**	ash vreh-a o toon**swa**reh ver rog
blow-dry	**un pieptănat**	oon pyepter**nat**
colour rinse	**un şampon colorant**	oon sham**pon** colo**rant**
dye	**un vopsit**	oon vop**seet**
face pack	**o mască**	o **mas**cer
hair gel	**un gel de păr**	oon jel deh perr
highlights	**un decolorat**	oon decolo**rat**
manicure	**o manichiură**	o maneek**kyoo**rer
(perm)anent wave	**un permanent**	oon perma**nent**
setting lotion	**un fixativ**	oon feexa**teev**
shampoo and set	**şampon şi bigudiuri**	sham**pon** shee beegoo**dee**-oor^{y}
with a fringe (bangs)	**cu breton**	coo bre**ton**
I'd like a shampoo for … hair.	**Un spălat cu şampon pentru …**	oon sper**lat** coo sham**pon** **pen**troo
normal/dry/greasy (oily)	**păr normal/uscat/ (gras)**	perr nor**mal**/oos**cat**/ gras
Do you have a colour chart?	**Aveţi o paletă de culori?**	a**vets**^{y} o pa**le**ter deh coo**lor**^{y}
Don't cut it too short.	**Nu tundeţi prea scurt.**	noo **toon**dets^{y} preh-a scoort
A little more off the …	**Puţin mai scurt …**	poo**tseen** migh scoort
back	**la spate**	la **spa**teh
neck	**pe gât**	peh guht
sides	**în părţi**	uhn perrts^{y}
top	**în creştetul capului**	uhn **crash**tetool **ca**poolooy^{y}

DAYS OF THE WEEK, see page 151

I don't want any hairspray.	**Nu vreau fixativ.**	noo vra^{oo} feexa**teev**
I'd like a shave.	**Vreau un ras.**	vra^{oo} oon ras
Would you trim my …, please?	**Vreţi să-mi aranjaţi … vă rog?**	vrets^{y} serm^{y} aran**zhats**^{y} … ver rog
beard	**barba**	**bar**ba
moustache	**mustaţa**	moos**ta**tsa
sideboards (sideburns)	**perciunii**	per**choo**nee

Checking out *La plecare*

May I have my bill, please?	**Nota de plată, vă rog!**	**no**ta deh **pla**ter ver rog
I'm leaving early in the morning.	**Plec mâine dimineaţă.**	plec **muhy**neh deemee**na**tser
Please have my bill ready.	**Vă rog să pregătiţi nota de plată.**	ver rog ser preger**teets**^{y} **no**ta deh **pla**ter
We'll be checking out around noon	**O să părăsim hotelul în jurul orei douăsprezece.**	o ser perrer**seem** ho**te**lool uhn **zhoo**rool oray **do**-wersprezecheh
I must leave at once.	**Trebuie să plec imediat.**	**tre**booyeh ser plec eeme**dyat**
Is everything included?	**Este totul inclus?**	**yes**teh **to**tool een**cloos**
Can I pay by credit card?	**Pot plăti cu cartea de credit?**	pot pler**tee** coo **car**teh-a deh **cre**deet
I think there's a mistake in the bill.	**Cred că este o greşeală în nota de plată.**	cred cer **yes**teh o gre**sha**ler uhn **no**ta deh **pla**ter
Can you get us a taxi?	**Ne puteţi comanda un taxi?**	neh poo**tets**^{y} coman**da** oon ta**xee**
Could you have our luggage brought down?	**Puteţi să ne aduceţi bagajul în hol, vă rog?**	poo**tets**^{y} ser ne a**doo**chets^{y} baga**zhool** uhn hol ver rog
Here's the forwarding address.	**Aceasta este adresa pentru expedierea curierului.**	a**chas**ta **yes**teh a**dre**sa **pen**troo expe**dye**reh-a cooree-**e**rooloo^{y}
You have my home address.	**Aveţi adresa mea de acasă.**	a**vets**^{y} a**dre**sa meh-a deh a**ca**ser
It's been a very enjoyable stay.	**Am avut un sejur minunat.**	am a**voot** oon se**zhoor** meenoo**nat**

DAYS OF THE WEEK, see page 151

Camping *Camping*

Camping facilities of a standard acceptable to foreign visitors are almost non-existent in Romania. However, you can obtain a list of designated camp sites from Romanian National Tourist Offices.

Is there a camp site near here?	**Există un loc de campare/ un camping în apropiere?**	eg**zees**ter oon loc deh cam**pa**reh/oon **cam**-peeng uhn apropee-**e**reh
Can we camp here?	**Putem să campăm aici?**	poo**tem** ser cam**perm** a**eech**ʸ
Do you have room for a tent/caravan?	**Aveţi spaţiu pentru un cort/o rulotă?**	a**vets**ʸ **spa**tsyoo **pen**troo oon cort/o roo**lo**ter
What's the charge …?	**Cât costă?**	cuht **cos**ter
per day	**pe zi**	peh zee
per person	**de persoană**	deh pers**wa**ner
for a car	**pentru o maşină**	**pen**troo o ma**shee**ner
for a tent	**pentru un cort**	**pen**troo oon cort
for a caravan (trailer)	**pentru o rulotă**	**pen**troo oh roo**lo**ter
Is tourist tax included?	**Taxa turistică este inclusă?**	**ta**xa too**rees**teecer **yes**teh een**cloo**ser
Is there/ Are there (a) …?	**Este/Există …?**	**yes**teh/eg**zees**ter
drinking water	**apă potabilă**	**a**per pota**bee**ler
electricity	**electricitate**	electreechee**ta**teh
playground	**teren de joacă**	te**ren** de **zhwa**cer
restaurant	**restaurant**	resta°°**rant**
shopping facilities	**magazin**	maga**zeen**
swimming pool	**piscină**	pees-**chee**ner
Where are the showers/ toilets?	**Unde sunt duşurile/ toaletele?**	**oon**deh soont **doo**-shooreeleh/twa**le**teleh
Where can I get butane gas?	**De unde putem cumpăra gaz butan?**	deh **oon**deh poo**tem** coomper**ra** gaz boo**tan**
Is there a youth hostel near here?	**Ce cazare aveţi pentru tineret?**	cheh ca**za**reh a**vets**ʸ **pen**troo teene**ret**

CAMPING EQUIPMENT, see page 106

Eating out

Romania offers a variety of places where you can eat and drink, ranging from simple snack bars to luxury restaurants (*restaurant*—resta°°rant). Recently, the number of new private eating establishments has increased enormously both in and outside of Bucharest.

Most restaurants still display the category markings I, II and III; the higher the category, the higher the price you can expect to pay. Many of the larger hotels have a category I restaurant. You will also see self-service restaurants where a good range of traditional Romanian dishes is offered at reasonable prices.

Though Romania in general does not have many ethnic restaurants, in Bucharest there are now some good Chinese, Turkish, Arabian and even a few Italian restaurants. Here are some other places to look for.

Autoservire (a°°toser**vee**reh)	Inexpensive, self-service canteen.
Berărie (bere**ree**-eh)	A public house where you can drink Romanian beer as well as foreign brands. Women do not usually frequent these serious drinking dens.
Braserie (brase**ree**-eh)	A combined bar, café and restaurant usually offering a good variety of dishes at reasonable prices. Service is provided at the table.
Bufet (boo**fet**)	This is a small restaurant found in railway stations where you'll be served traditional Romanian food. The *Bufet expres* is a stand-up cafeteria for quick meals of rather limited choice.
Cafe-bar (ca**feh**-**bar**)	Serves hot beverages, soft and alcoholic drinks, and is a convenient place for a quick snack. Cafe-bars are similar to the *snack bar,* which also offers a range of light meals and drinks.
Cofetărie (cofeter**ree**-eh)	This is a cake shop that also serves coffee, ice cream and soft drinks. Tea is generally served only in large hotels.

Han (han) — A large restaurant, usually with rustic decor, serving moderately priced food and drinks. Some have Romanian folk music entertainment in the evening.

Podgorie (podgoryeh) — A wine bar serving drinks only; you won't be able to eat here.

Meal times *Mesele zilei*

Traditionally Romanians have three meals per day:

Breakfast (*micul dejun*) is normally served between 7 and 10am and is generally based on bread and cheese, or jam and butter on bread, served with tea or coffee.

Lunch (*masa de prânz* or *dejunul*) is served from 12am until 2pm, and is the main meal of the day for most people in Romania. They will generally start with borsh or soup and follow with a stew or roast. Home-made cakes such as pancakes, fritters or petits fours will end the meal. Romanians like to drink wine mixed with sparkling mineral water with their meal, and a cup of Turkish coffee to finish.

Dinner (*cina*) is taken between 7pm and 10pm. It generally comprises baked meat, pies, souffles, meat rolls, cheese rolls, *mămăligă* (polenta, or cornmeal porridge) with cheese and fried eggs, and home-made yoghurt. In the evening wine, beer or herbal teas are drunk.

Before beginning the meal people wish each other *poftă bună,* the equivalent of *bon appetit*; at the end of the meal they say *să vă fie de bine*—"I hope you enjoyed it."

Romanian cuisine *Mâncăruri româneşti*

Romanians love eating, supported by a long and notable gastronomic tradition. The country offers an intriguing culinary mixture of Latin and Slavic, a love of France with the crossing of influences from Hungary and Turkey. Traditional dishes are based on borsh, stewed vegetables (*ghiveci*), vegetable souffles, pasta, potatoes, polenta and vegetable salads. Romanian dishes are cooked using sunflower or corn oil; butter or lard is used for baking.

An à la carte menu will have a choice of starters: slices of salami or ham, feta cheese and olives, taramasalata, aubergine salad, chicken liver or meat and cheese pastries; subsequent courses will include borsh or soup, roast or grilled meat, cakes or tortes, ice cream and fruit salad. Some restaurants will also serve traditional Romanian dishes such as stewed vegetables with meat (*ghiveci cu carne*) or minced meat with vegetables. Turkish coffee is usually served at the end of the meal.

Although there are no great regional differences in Romanian cuisine, it is generally accepted the Moldavian food is more piquant and offers greater variety.

YOU MAY HEAR:

Ce doriţi?	What would you like?
Vă recomand asta.	I recommend this.
Ce doriţi să beţi?	What would you like to drink?
Nu avem …	We don't have …
Doriţi …?	Would you like …?

Hungry? *Vă este foame?*

I'm hungry.	**Mi-e foame.**	myeh **fwa**meh
I'm thirsty.	**Mi-e sete.**	myeh **se**teh
Can you recommend a good restaurant?	**Îmi puteţi recomanda un restaurant bun?**	uhm[y] poo**tets**[y] recoman**da** oon resta[oo]**rant** boon
Are there any inexpensive restaurants around here?	**Există vreun restaurant nu prea scump prin apropiere?**	eg**zees**ter vroon resta[oo]**rant** noo preh-a scoomp preen apropee-**e**reh

If you want to be sure of getting a table in a well-known restaurant, it may be better to book in advance.

I'd like to reserve a table for 4.	**Doresc să rezerv o masă pentru patru persoane.**	do**resc** ser re**zerv** o **ma**ser **pen**troo **pa**troo pers**wa**neh
We'll come at 8.	**O să venim la ora opt.**	o ser ve**neem** la **o**ra opt
Could we have a table …?	**Putem avea o masă …?**	poo**tem** **aveh-a** o **ma**ser
in the corner	**în colţ**	uhn colts
by the window	**lângă fereastră**	**luhn**ger fer**ast**rer
outside	**afară**	a**far**er
on the terrace	**pe terasă**	peh te**ra**ser
in a non-smoking area	**în zona de nefumători**	uhn **zo**na deh nefoomer**tor**^{y}

Asking and ordering *A cere şi a comanda*

Waiter/Waitress!	**Ospătar, vă rog!**	osper**tar** ver rog
I'd like something to eat/drink.	**Aş dori ceva de mâncare/băut.**	ash do**ree** che**va** deh muhn**ca**reh/ber-**oot**
The menu,please.	**Meniul, vă rog.**	me**nee**-ool ver rog
Do you have a set menu/local dishes?	**Aveţi un meniu cu preţ fix/ mâncăruri româneşti?**	a**vets**^{y} oon me**nee**^{oo} coo prets feex/ muhn**cer**roor^{y} romuh**nesht**^{y}
What do you recommend?	**Ce ne recomandaţi?**	cheh neh recoman**dats**^{y}
Do you have anything ready quickly?	**Aveţi ceva gata de servit repede?**	a**vets**^{y} che**va** **ga**ta deh ser**veet** **re**pedeh
I'm in a hurry.	**Mă grăbesc.**	mer grer**besc**
I'd like …	**Aş vrea …**	ash vreh-a
Could we have a/an …, please?	**Putem avea …, vă rog?**	poo**tem** aveh-a … ver rog
ashtray	**o scrumieră**	o scroomee-**er**er
cup	**o ceaşcă**	o **chash**cer
fork	**o furculiţă**	o foorcoo**lee**tser
glass	**un pahar**	oon pa**har**
knife	**un cuţit**	oon cu**tseet**
napkin (serviette)	**un şerveţel**	oon sherve**tsel**
plate	**o farfurie**	o farfooree-**eh**
spoon	**o lingură**	o **leen**goorer

May I have some …?	**Pot avea nişte …?**	pot a**veh-a neesh**teh
bread	**pâine**	pu**hy**neh
butter	**unt**	oont
lemon	**lămâie**	ler**muh**yeh
oil	**ulei**	oo**lay**
pepper	**piper**	pee**per**
salt	**sare**	**sa**reh
seasoning	**condimente**	condee**men**teh
sugar	**zahăr**	**za**herr
vinegar	**oţet**	ot**set**

Special diet *Regim special*

Some useful expressions for those with special requirements:

I'm on a diet.	**Ţin regim.**	tseen re**jeem**
I'm vegetarian.	**Sunt vegetarian.**	soont vejetaree-**an**
I don't drink alcohol.	**Nu beau alcool.**	noo bea^{oo} al**col**
I don't eat meat.	**Nu mănânc carne.**	noo mer**nuhnc car**neh
I mustn't eat food containing …	**Nu am voie să mănânc mâncare care conţine …**	noo am **vo**yeh ser mer**nuhnc** muhn**ca**reh **ca**reh con**tsee**neh
flour/fat	**făină/grăsime**	fer-**ee**ner/grer**see**meh
salt/sugar	**sare/zahăr**	**sa**reh/**za**herr
Do you have … for diabetics?	**Aveţi … pentru diabetici?**	a**vets**^{y} … **pen**troo dee-a**be**teech^{y}
cakes	**prăjituri**	prerzhee**toor**^{y}
fruit juice	**suc de fructe**	sooc deh **frooc**teh
a special menu	**meniu special**	me**nee**^{oo} spe**chal**
Do you have any vegetarian dishes?	**Aveţi mâncăruri pentru vegetarieni?**	a**vets**^{y} muhn**cer**roor^{y} **pen**troo vejetaree-**en**^{y}
Can I have an artificial sweetener?	**Aveţi îndulcitor artificial?**	a**vets**^{y} un**dool**chitor artificial

And …

I'd like some more.	**Mai vreau puţin.**	migh vra^{oo} poo**tseen**
Can I have more …, please?	**Mai pot avea puţin …, vă rog?**	migh pot a**veh-a** poo**tseen** … ver rog
Just a small portion.	**Numai puţin.**	**noo**migh poo**tseen**
Nothing more, thanks.	**Nimic altceva, mulţumesc.**	nee**meec** altche**va** multsoo**mesc**
Where are the toilets?	**Unde este toaleta?**	**oon**deh **yes**teh twa**le**ta

What's on the menu? *Ce aveţi în meniu?*

Under the headings below, you'll find alphabetical lists of dishes that might be offered on a Romanian menu with their English equivalent. You can simply show the book to the waiter. If you want some fruit, for instance, let *him* point to what's available on the appropriate list. Use pages 36 and 37 for ordering in general.

In addition to various à la carte dishes, restaurants usually offer one or more set menus which provide a good meal at a fair price.

Reading the menu *Răsfoind meniul*

Note that some dishes may be priced by weight (per 100 grammes, for example), and you should therefore expect a final price more expensive than that listed on the menu.

For meals without a garnish, you should specify your desired side dish or the waiter may choose this for you.

If the restaurant has run out of a dish, it may be crossed out on the menu or simply appear without a price. Establishments with a limited choice of dishes may not have a printed menu but a selection of changing daily specials.

meniu fix	set menu
meniu special	special menu
listă de vinuri	wine list
mâcăruri pentru vegetarieni	vegetarian dishes
specialităţi le zilei	specials of the day
preţ	price

antreuri	an**tre**oor^y	appetizers
băuturi	ber-oo**toor**^{y}	beverages
bere	**be**reh	beer
carne de pasăre	**car**neh deh **pa**serreh	poultry
chiftele	keef**te**leh	burgers
deserturi	de**ser**toor^y	desserts
fructe	**frooc**teh	fruit
fructe de mare	**frooc**teh deh **ma**reh	seafood
gustări	goos**terr**^{y}	snacks
îngheţată	uhnge**tsa**ter	ice cream
legume	le**goo**meh	vegetables
mâncăruri cu ouă	muhn**cer**roor^y coo **o**-wer	egg dishes
paste făinoase	**pas**teh fer-ee**nwa**seh	pasta
peşte	**pesh**teh	fish
salate	sa**la**teh	salads
supe	**soo**peh	soups
vânat	vuh**nat**	game
vin	veen	wine

Breakfast *Micul dejun*

The Romanian breakfast can be a very substantial meal consisting of bread or rolls with jam, cheese, salami, fried eggs, tomatoes and coffee or tea. Hotels serve either a continental breakfast of rolls, butter, jam, coffee or tea or a traditional breakfast with eggs, cold meats, cheese or yoghurt. Breakfast cereals are not common in Romania.

I'd like breakfast, please.	**Aş dori micul dejun, vă rog.**	ash do**ree mee**cool de**zhoon** ver rog
I'll have (a/an/some) …	**Aş dori …**	ash do**ree**
bacon and eggs	**nişte şuncă şi ouă**	**neesh**teh **shoon**cer shee **o**-wer
boiled egg	**un ou fiert**	oon o^{oo} fyert
soft/hard	**moale/tare**	**mwa**leh/**ta**reh
cereal	**nişte fulgi de cereale**	**neesh**teh foolj^{y} deh chereh**a**leh
eggs	**nişte ouă**	**neesh**teh **o**-wer
fried eggs	**nişte ouă prăjite/ochiuri**	**neesh**teh **o**-wer prer**zhee**teh/**o**kyoor^{y}
scrambled eggs	**nişte ouă jumări**	**neesh**teh **o**-wer zhoo**mer**^{y}
poached eggs	**nişte ouă ochiuri fierte în apă**	**neesh**teh **o**-wer **o**kyoor^{y} **fyer**teh uhn **a**per
fruit juice	**nişte suc de fructe**	**neesh**teh sooc deh **frooc**teh
grapefruit	**grepfrut**	**grep**froot
orange	**portocale**	porto**ca**leh
ham and eggs	**nişte şuncă şi ouă**	**neesh**teh **shoon**cer shee **o**-wer
jam	**nişte gem**	**neesh**teh jem
marmalade	**nişte marmeladă**	**neesh**teh marme**la**der
toast	**niştc pâine prăjită**	**neesh**teh **puhy**neh prer**zhee**ter
yoghurt	**un iaurt**	oon ya**oort**
May I have some …?	**Vreţi să-mi daţi nişte …?**	vrets^{y} serm^{y} dats^{y} **neesh**teh
bread	**pâine**	**puhy**neh
butter	**unt**	oont
(hot) chocolate	**ciocolată**	choco**la**ter
coffee	**cafea**	ca**feh-a**
decaffeinated	**decofeinizată**	dekofeh-ee**nee**zater
black/with milk	**neagră/cu lapte**	**na**grer/coo **lap**teh

honey	**miere**	**mye**reh
milk	**lapte**	**lap**teh
cold/hot	**cald/rece**	cald/**re**cheh
pepper	**piper**	pee**per**
rolls	**chifle**	**keef**leh
salt	**sare**	**sa**reh
tea	**ceai**	chay
with milk	**cu lapte**	coo **lap**teh
with lemon	**cu lămâie**	coo ler**muh**yeh
(hot) water	**apă (fierbinte)**	**a**per (fyer**been**teh)

Starters (Appetizers) *Antreuri*

A typical Romanian starter is a platter of feta cheese, sliced salami and black olives. In summer you may also be served traditional aubergine salad (*salată de vinete*).

I'd like an appetizer.	**Aş vrea un antreu.**	ash vreh-a oon an**tre**^{oo}
What would you recommend?	**Ce îmi recomandaţi?**	cheh uhm^{y} recoman**dats**^{y}

Cold starters *Aperitive reci*

cârnaţi	cuhr**nats**^{y}	sausages
cârnaţi cu usturoi	cuhr**nats**^{y} coo oostoo**roy**	garlic sausage
ciuperci cu maioneză	choo**perch**^{y} coo mayo**ne**zer	mushrooms in mayonnaise
covrigei	covree**jay**	savoury pretzels
măsline	mers**lee**neh	olives
mezeluri	me**ze**loor^{y}	assortment of cold meats
muşchi filet	mooshk^{y} fee**leh**	processed pork sirloin
pastramă	pas**tra**mer	smoked mutton
paté de ficat	pa**teh** deh fee**cat**	liver paté
roşii	**ro**shee	tomatoes
salam	sa**lam**	salami
salată de icre	sa**la**ter deh **ee**creh	fish roe salad (taramasalata)
salată de vinete	sa**la**ter deh **vee**neteh	aubergine salad
sardele	sar**de**leh	sardines
şuncă	**shoon**cer	ham

ouă umplute (**o**-wer oom**ploo**teh)	Hard-boiled eggs, halved, then filled with paté and topped with mayonnaise.
piftie de pui (peef**tee**yeh deh pooy)	A traditional Romanian dish of stewed chicken pieces in aspic.
salată de 'boeuf' (sa**la**ter deh boef)	A salad of diced potatoes, carrots, celery, pickled cucumbers, peas and beef or chicken meat in a mayonnaise dressing.
salată de crudităţi (sa**la**ter deh croodee**terts**y)	Coarsely grated raw celery, carrots and apples in mayonnaise.
salată orientală (sa**la**ter oryen**ta**ler)	Sliced potatoes, hard-boiled eggs, onions and olives marinated in a vinegar sauce.

Hot starters *Aperitive calde*

cabanos prăjit	caba**nos** prer**jeet**	fried pieces of sausage
chifteluţe	keefte**loot**seh	fried minced meat balls
creier pané	**cre**yer pa**neh**	brains in breadcrumbs
crenvurşti	**cren**voorshty	frankfurter
ficăţei de pasăre	feecer**tsay** deh **pa**serreh	fried or braised chicken liver
frigărui	freeger**rooy**	grilled pork kebabs

caşcaval pané (cashca**val** pa**neh**)	Cheese coated in egg and breadcrumbs and deep fried.
crochete de caşcaval (cro**ke**teh deh cashca**val**)	Grated cheese mixed with egg and flour into croquettes and fried.
drob de miel (drob deh myel)	A dish of chopped lamb's liver and kidneys, mixed with herbs and egg and baked in the oven.
mititei/mici (meetee**tay**/meechy)	A traditional Romanian dish comprising small, sausage-shaped minced meat rissoles made from a seasoned mixture of various meats, usually served with a garlic sauce.
pateuri cu carne (pa**te**oory coo **car**neh)	Puff pastry cases filled with minced meat.
ruladă de caşcaval (roo**la**der deh cashca**val**)	A sponge roll filled with grated cheese and cream.
ruladă de ciuperci (roo**la**der deh choo**perch**y)	Mushroom-filled sponge roll.

Soups and stews *Supe şi tocane*

The most popular soup in Romania is *borş*. This is a richly flavoured meat and vegetable soup soured with 'borsh' or lemon juice and dressed with sour cream. The borsh, or souring ingredient, is obtained after wheat bran, cornflour, a sprig of cherry tree, thyme and basil have been fermented in five or six litres of water. The resulting brew tastes like sour wine and is recommended in its own right as an effective hangover cure.

Soup which has been soured with lemon juice or yoghurt is called *ciorbă,* and you will frequently see this on restaurant menus instead of *borş*. Soups in the countryside are generally eaten with *mămăligă,* a yellow cornmeal porridge or polenta. Vegetarians should specify *fără carne* (**fer**rer **car**neh) when ordering vegetable soups or stews.

borş de legume	borsh deh le**goo**meh	vegetable borsh
ciorbă de legume	**ch**orber deh le**goo**meh	vegetable ciorbă
ghiveci de legume	gee**vech**ʸ deh le**goo**meh	vegetable stew, with or without meat
supă-cremă de ciuperci	**soo**per **cre**mer deh choo**perch**ʸ	cream of mushroom soup
supă-cremă de legume	**soo**per **cre**mer deh le**goo**meh	thick vegetable purée soup
supă-cremă de ţelină	**soo**per **cre**mer deh **tse**leener	cream of celery soup
supă de cartofi	**soo**per deh car**tof**ʸ	potato soup with vegetables
supă de pasăre	**soo**per deh **pa**serreh	clear chicken soup
supă de roşii	**soo**per deh **ro**shee	tomato soup
tocană	to**ca**ner	stew
tocană de legume	to**ca**ner deh le**goo**meh	vegetable stew
tocăniţă de cartofi cu carne	tocer**neet**ser deh car**tof**ʸ coo **car**neh	vegetable stew with meat, usually pork

borş cu carne de porc (borsh coo **car**neh deh porc) Pork boiled with vegetables, and seasoned with tarragon, then soured.

borş de văcuţă (borsh deh ver**coo**tser) Beef on the bone boiled with vegetables, seasoned with herbs and soured.

borş de viţel (borsh deh vee**tsel**) Veal boiled with vegetables and seasoned with herbs, then soured.

borş de perişoare (borsh deh peree**shwa**reh) Soured, seasoned vegetable soup served with rice-and-meat balls.

Main course *Felul principal*

Fish and seafood *Peşte şi fructe de mare*

Fish dishes are popular in Romania. They are often piquant, and frequently include vegetables such as carrots, tomatoes and peppers. Seafood is not common. The best fish dishes come from the Danube Delta, most notably *ciorbă pescărească* (a type of fish soup with vegetables) and *saramură de peşte* (grilled fish seasoned with hot paprika and salt). Romania also specializes in fish roe (*icre*), usually carp or pike.

I'd like some fish.	**Aş vrea o mâncare de peşte.**	ash vreh-a o muhn**ca**reh deh **pesh**teh
What kind of seafood do you have?	**Ce fructe de mare aveţi?**	cheh **froo**cteh deh **ma**reh **avets**^{y}
biban	bee**ban**	river perch
caviar	cavee**ar**	caviar
cegă	**che**ger	sterlet
cod	cod	cod
chefal	ke**fal**	grey mullet
crab	crab	crab
crap	crap	carp
creveţi	cre**vets**^{y}	shrimps
homar	ho**mar**	lobster
icre	**ee**creh	fish roe
icre negre	**ee**creh **neg**reh	caviar
macrou	ma**cro**^{oo}	mackerel
plătică	pler**tee**cer	river bream
raci	rach^{y}	freshwater crayfish
sardele	sar**de**leh	sardines
scrumbie	scroom**bee**-eh	shad
ştiucă	**shtyoo**cer	pike
sturion	stoo**ryon**	sturgeon
ţipar	tsee**par**	eel

baked	**copt**	copt
fried	**prăjit**	prer**zheet**
grilled	**la grătar**	la grer**tar**
marinated	**marinată**	maree**na**ter
poached	**fiert în apă**	fyert uhn **a**per
sautéed	**prăjiţi repede în grăsime**	prer**zheets**^{y} **re**pedeh uhn grer**see**meh
smoked	**afumat**	afoo**mat**
steamed	**în aburi**	uhn **a**boor^{y}

chifteluţe de icre (keefte**loot**seh deh **ee**creh)	Caviar or fish roe dipped in egg and breadcrumbs and fried in oil.
ghiveci de peşte (gee**vech**ʸ deh **pesh**teh)	A typical fish stew with olives, carrots, celery, cucumber and tomato purée.
marinată de peşte (maree**na**ter deh **pesh**teh)	Fish marinated in brine.
păstrăv afumat (**per**strerv afoo**mat**)	A traditional dish of trout wrapped in fir tree branches and smoked.
păstrăv cu orez (**per**strerv coo orez)	Trout cooked with onion, paprika and curry powder and served with rice.
peşte à la grecque (**pesh**teh a la grec)	Fried fish served with lemon juice and parsley.
peşte cu usturoi (**pesh**teh coo oostoo**roy**)	Fish served in a tangy garlic sauce.
peşte la cuptor (**pesh**teh la coop**tor**)	A whole fish, generally carp or pike, baked in the oven with tomatoes, carrots and green peppers.
peşte pané (**pesh**teh pa**neh**)	Fish coated in beaten egg and flour, then fried in oil and served with lemon juice.
sturion la grătar (stoo**ryon** la grer**tar**)	Grilled sturgeon.

Meat *Carne*

Romanians eat a lot of meat, particularly pork and beef. At Easter, lamb is eaten. Mutton and goat's meat is normally preferred in autumn when it is specially prepared and accompanied by *must*—new wine.

I'd like some …	**Aş vrea nişte …**	ash vreh-a **neesh**teh
beef	**carne de vacă**	**car**neh deh **va**cer
lamb	**carne de miel**	**car**neh deh myel
pork	**carne de porc**	**car**neh deh porc
veal	**viţel**	**car**neh deh vee**tsel**

caltaboş cu sînge	calta**bosh** coo **suhn**jeh	black pudding
cap de porc	cap deh porc	pig's head
chiftele	keef**tel**eh	meatballs
cârnaţi	cuhr**nats**ʸ	sausage
coadă de vacă	**cwa**der deh **va**cer	oxtail
cotlet	cot**let**	chop/cutlet
escalop	esca**lop**	escalope
filet chateaubriand	fee**leh** chateau**briand**	tenderloin
friptură la tavă	freep**too**rer la **ta**ver	pot roast
iepure	**ye**pooreh	rabbit
limbă	**leem**ber	tongue
măruntaie de porc	merroon**ta**yeh deh porc	chitterlings
muşchi de vacă	mooshkʸ deh **va**cer	sirloin
muşchi filet	mooshkʸ fee**leh**	fillet
oaie	**wa**yeh	mutton
pulpă de miel	**pool**per de myel	leg of lamb
purcel de lapte	poor**chel** deh **lap**teh	suckling pig
rinichi	ree**neek**ʸ	kidneys
slănină	sler**nee**ner	bacon
spinare	spee**na**reh	saddle
şuncă (afumată)	**shoon**cer (afoo**ma**ter)	(smoked) ham
şuncă	**shoon**cer	gammon

baked	**copt**	copt
barbecued	**la grătar**	la grer**tar**
baked in greaseproof paper	**copt în hârtie pergament**	copt uhn huhr**tee**-eh perga**ment**
boiled	**fiert**	fyert
braised	**fiert înăbuşit**	fyert uhnerboo**sheet**
fried	**prăjit**	prer**zheet**
grilled	**la grătar**	la grer**tar**
roast	**prăjit la cuptor**	prer**zheet** la coop**tor**
sautéed	**prăjit repede în grăsime**	prer**zheet re**pedeh uhn grer**see**meh
stewed	**fiert inăbuşit**	fyert uhnerboo**sheet**
very rare	**în sânge**	uhn **suhn**jeh
underdone (rare)	**cu puţin sânge**	coo poo**tseen suhn**jeh
medium	**potrivit**	potree**veet**
well-done	**bine prăjit**	**bee**neh prer**zheet**

Some meat specialities *Câteva specialităţi cu carne*

biftec à la Sinaia	beef**tec** a la see**na**ya	slices of beef steak in a thick sauce
carne de vită rasol	**car**neh deh **vee**ter ra**sol**	stewed beef
chiftele	keef**te**leh	minced meat balls
fasole verde cu carne	fasoleh **ver**deh coo **car**neh	haricot beans and meat in tomato sauce
fleică la grătar	**flay**cer la grer**tar**	grilled steak, usually with garlic sauce
frigărui de porc	freeger**rooy** deh porc	pork kebabs
friptură cu sos	freep**too**rer coo sos	roast meat with vegetable sauce
friptură de vacă la tavă	freep**too**rer deh **va**cer la **ta**ver	oven-roasted beef
mazăre cu carne	**ma**zerreh coo **car**neh	green peas and meat in tomato sauce
mâncare de limbă cu maioneză	muhn**ca**reh deh **leem**ber coo migho**ne**zer	stewed tongue in mayonnaise
şniţel de carne de viţel	**shnee**tsel deh **car**neh deh vee**tsel**	breaded veal escalope
tocană de porc	to**ca**ner deh porc	vegetable stew with pork
varză à la Cluj	**var**zer a la cloozh	shredded cabbage with minced meat and sour cream.

ardei umpluţi (ar**day** oom**ploots**ʸ) — Green peppers stuffed with minced meat and rice, topped with sour cream.

dovlecei umpluţi (dovle**chay** oom**ploots**ʸ) — Courgettes stuffed with rice and minced meat, served with sour cream.

mixed grill (´mixed grill´) — An assortment of braised chicken liver, fried sausages and *mititei,* seasoned rissoles made from pork, mutton and beef, served with a piquant garlic sauce.

sarmale în foi de varză (sar**ma**leh uhn foy deh **var**zer) — Pickled cabbage leaves stuffed with a mixture of rice, onion, minced beef and herbs, then boiled in a light tomato sauce. This typical Romanian dish is usually served with sour cream and *mămăligă.*

sarmale în foi de viţă (sar**ma**leh uhn foy deh **vee**tser)	Vine leaves stuffed with rice, onion, minced beef and herbs, cooked in tomato sauce and served with sour cream.
stufat (stoo**fat**)	Marinated beef, larded and served with a rich marinade of vegetables, garlic, tomato purée and wine.
tocană de miel (to**ca**ner deh myel)	Lamb and vegetable stew made with okra and white wine, served with slices of *mămăligă* or potatoes.
tocană de viţel (to**ca**ner deh vee**tsel**)	A rich veal stew with onions and cream or tomato sauce, served with rice or semolina dumplings.

Game and poultry *Vânat şi pasăre*

The most popular game in Romania are rabbit and pheasant, while chicken and turkey are also widely appreciated.

bibilică	beebee**lee**cer	guinea fowl
căprioară	cerpree**wa**rer	venison
clapon	cla**pon**	capon
curcan	coor**can**	turkey
fazan	fa**zan**	pheasant
gâscă	**guhs**cer	goose
iepure de câmp	**ye**pooreh deh cuhmp	hare
iepure înăbuşit	**ye**pooreh uhnerboo**sheet**	jugged hare
lişiţă	**lee**sheetser	teal
porc mistreţ	porc mees**trets**	wild boar
porumbel sălbatec	poroom**bel** serl**ba**tec	pigeon
potârniche	potuhr**nee**keh	grouse
potârniche	potuhr**nee**keh	partridge
prepeliţă	**pre**peleetser	quail
pui	pooy	chicken
piept/pulpă/aripă	pyept/**pool**per/**a**reeper	breast/leg/wing
pui la rotisor	pooy la rotee**sor**	barbecued chicken
raţă	**ra**tser	duck
raţă tânără	**ra**tser **tuh**nerrer	duckling

These are some of the poultry and game dishes you may come across:

fazan cu smântână şi ciuperci	fa**zan** coo smuhn**tuh**ner shee choo**perch**y	pheasant with cream and mushrooms
ficăţei de pasăre	feecer**tsay** deh **pa**serreh	braised or fried chicken liver
friptură de curcan	freep**too**rer deh coor**can**	roast turkey
friptură de pui	freep**too**rer deh pooy	roast chicken
găină umplută	ger**ee**ner oom**ploo**ter	whole chicken stuffed with liver, egg, breadcrumbs and herbs
ghiveci de curcan	gee**vech**y deh coor**can**	turkey with aubergines simmered in wine
iepure în vin roşu	**ye**pooreh uhn veen **ro**shoo	rabbit cooked in red wine
mâncare de iepure cu măsline	muhn**ca**reh deh **ye**pooreh coo mers**lee**neh	rabbit with olives, served cold
pateu de iepure	**pate**oo deh **ye**pooreh	rabbit pie
pilaf de pui	pee**laf** deh pooy	chicken with rice and herbs
pui cu ciuperci	pooy coo choo**perch**y	chicken in a mushroom sauce
pui cu mujdei	pooy coo moozh**day**	roasted chicken with a garlic sauce
pui la ceaun	pooy la cheh-a**oon**	chicken fried in oil
pui la grătar	pooy la grer**tar**	whole chicken roasted on a spit over an open fire
raţă pe varză	**ra**tser peh **var**zer	roast duck served with cabbage
raţă sălbatică cu varză acră	**ra**tser serl**ba**teecer coo **var**zer **a**crer	wild duck with sauerkraut

ciulama de pui (choola**ma** deh pooy) — A traditional Romanian dish consisting of pieces of chicken cooked in a white cream sauce and flavoured with herbs. It is usually eaten with *mămăligă*.

pui cu tarhon (pooy coo tar**hon**) — A popular Transylvanian dish of chicken with tarragon, sautéed with white wine, root vegetables, green peppers and sour cream

Potatoes and polenta *Cartofi şi mămăligă*

Potatoes are the Romanians' favourite vegetable. In Transylvania they are even used in bread. Cornmeal porridge (polenta) is typically eaten as an accompaniment to most meals in country areas. Dumplings made either with cornmeal and cheese or with semolina are also served with certain soups.

borş de cartofi	borsh deh car**tof**^{y}	potato borsh
cartofi prăjiţi	car**tof**^{y} prer**zheets**^{y}	chips
găluşti	ger**loosht**^{y}	semolina dumplings
găluşti cu prune	ger**loosht**^{y} coo **proo**neh	balls of mashed potatoes with plums
mămăligă	mermer**lee**ger	polenta (cornmeal mush)
musaca de cartofi	moosa**ca** deh car**tof**^{y}	potato moussaka
salată orientală	sa**la**ter oryen**ta**ler	potato salad with onions, boiled eggs and black olives

balmuş (**bal**moosh)	Butter and grated curd cheese wrapped in *mămăligă,* rolled into balls and served very hot with sour cream. They may be filled with ham, mushroom, cheese or boiled egg.
tocinei (tochee**nay**)	A Moldavian speciality of grated potato rissoles, bound with egg and fried in oil. This dish is normally served with sour cream.

Rice and pasta *Orez şi paste făinoase*

Rice is a popular staple, and is commonly used in the preparation of traditional dishes such as stuffed vine leaves and chicken pilaf. Different types of pasta are used to add substance to soups, or are served with a variety of tasty sauces. A thin porridge is also made from noodles cooked with milk and sugar.

macaroane cu brânză	macar**wa**neh coo br**uhn**zer	macaroni with cheese
macaroane cu nuci	macar**wa**neh coo **noo**ch^{y}	macaroni with nut sauce
supă de găină cu fidea/cu tăiţei	**soo**per deh ger**ee**ner coo fee**deh-a**/coo tereet**say**	chicken soup with noodles

Sauces *Sosuri*

The sauces that accompany Romanian dishes are based mainly on tomatoes and cream although wine sauces are also used. Garlic sauce is typically served with grilled meat.

aspic	as**peec**	dressing containing gelatine
ciulama	choola**ma**	white sauce
mujdei de usturoi	moozh**day** deh oostoo**roy**	garlic sauce
sos de ceapă	sos deh **cha**per	sauce made with onions, tomatoes, garlic and thyme
sos de muştar	sos deh **moosh**tar	mustard sauce
sos de piper	sos deh pee**per**	sauce made with butter, pepper and beef stock
sos de roşii	sos deh **ro**shee	tomato sauce with cream and herbs
sos de smântână	sos deh smuhn**tuh**ner	sour cream sauce

ciulama de piu (choola**ma** deh pyoo) Chicken cooked in a white sauce made with cream.

Vegetables and salads *Legume şi salate*

Romanian cuisine has a wide variety of vegetarian dishes, although there are no exclusively vegetarian restaurants. It is possible to ask for *mâncare de post,* which is food without meat, normally associated with religious fasting periods. Otherwise ask for *mâncare fără carne* if you want vegetarian options.

andive	an**dee**veh	endive (chicory)
anghinare	angee**na**reh	artichokes
ardei (gras) verde/roşu	ar**day** (gras) **ver**deh/**ro**shoo	(sweet) peppers green/red
ardei iute	ar**day yoo**teh	chilli
bame	**ba**meh	okra
brocoli	**bro**colee	broccoli
cartofi dulci	car**tof**ʸ doolchʸ	sweet potatoes
cartofi	car**tof**ʸ	potatoes
castane	cas**ta**neh	chestnuts
castravete	castra**ve**teh	cucumber
ceapă	**cha**per	onions

ciuperci	choo**perch**^{y}	mushrooms
conopidă	cono**pee**der	cauliflower
dovleac	dovl**eh-ac**	vegetable marrow
dovlecel	dovle**chel**	courgette (zucchini)
fasole (boabe)	fas**o**leh (**bwa**beh)	beans
fasole neagră	fas**o**leh n**eh-a**grer	butter beans
fasole verde	fas**o**leh **ver**deh	green beans
fasole mare	fas**o**leh **ma**reh	kidney beans
fasole de Lima	fas**o**leh deh **lee**ma	lima beans
fasole fideluţă	fas**o**leh feede**loot**ser	French beans
legume asortate	leg**oo**meh asor**ta**teh	mixed vegetables
linte	**leen**teh	lentils
mărar	mer**rar**	dill
mazăre	**ma**zerreh	peas
morcovi	**mor**cov^{y}	carrots
napi	nap^{y}	turnips
porumb	po**roomb**	sweetcorn
praz	praz	leeks
ridichi	ree**deek**^{y}	radishes
roşii	**ro**shee	tomatoes
salată verde	sa**la**ter **ver**deh	lettuce
secărică	secer**ree**cer	fennel
sfeclă	**sfec**ler	beets
sfeclă roşie	**sfec**ler **ro**shee-eh	beetroot
spanac	spa**nac**	spinach
sparanghel (vârfuri)	spa**ran**gel (**vuhr**foor^{y})	asparagus (tips)
ţelină	**tse**leener	celery
varză	**var**zer	cabbage
varză de Bruxelles	**var**zer deh broo**xel**	Brussels sprouts
vinete	**vee**neteh	aubergines (eggplant)

Vegetables may be served …

boiled	**fierte**	**fyer**teh
creamed	**pireu**	pee**re**^{oo}
diced	**tăiate în cubuleţe**	ter**ya**teh uhn coobo**olet**seh
mashed	**pireu**	pee**re**^{oo}
oven-browned	**rumenite la cuptor**	roome**nee**teh la coop**tor**
steamed	**în aburi**	uhn **a**boor^{y}
stewed	**înăbuşite**	uhnerboo**shee**teh
stuffed	**umplute**	oom**ploo**teh

Specialities *Specialităţi*

borş de legume fără carne	borsh deh le**goo**meh **fer**rer **car**neh	soured vegetable soup without meat
conopidă murată	cono**pee**der moo**ra**ter	pickled cauliflower
gogonele murate	gogo**ne**leh moo**ra**teh	pickled green tomatoes
iahnie de fasole	yah**nee**-eh deh fa**so**leh	bean purée with garlic sauce
mâncare de fasole	muhn**ca**reh deh fa**so**leh	baked beans
murături	moorer**toory**	pickles
musaca de vinete	moosa**ca** deh **vee**neteh	aubergine moussaka with meat
pilaf de post	pee**laf** deh post	rice with mushrooms or vegetables
salată de andive	sa**la**ter deh an**dee**veh	chicory in mayonnaise
salată de castraveţi	sa**la**ter deh castr**vets**[y]	sliced cucumbers in vinaigrette
salată de sfeclă roşie	sa**la**ter deh **sfe**cler **ro**shee-eh	grated beetroot salad dressed with oil and lemon
salată de varză murată	sa**la**ter deh **var**zer moo**ra**ter	pickled cabbage salad
salată de vinete	sa**la**ter deh **vee**neteh	aubergine salad
salată verde	sa**la**ter **ver**deh	green salad
tocană de legume fără carne	to**ca**ner deh le**goo**meh **fer**rer **car**neh	meatless vegetable stew

dovlecei cu mărar şi smântână (dovle**chay** coo mer**rar** shee smuhn**tuh**ner) — Courgettes cooked with dill and sour cream.

salată de ardei copţi (sa**la**ter deh ar**day** copts[y]) — Green peppers grilled over an open fire, skinned, then dressed in vinaigrette.

sarmale de post (sar**ma**leh deh post) — Rice, mushrooms and carrots wrapped in vine leaves.

vinete umplute (**vee**neteh oom**ploo**teh) — Aubergines stuffed with a seasoned mixture of rice and meat, then baked in tomato sauce or stock made with white wine.

Herbs and spices *Mirodenii şi condimente*

Although Romanian food does not contain many spices, the use of herbs is widespread. Virtually no borsh is complete without lovage (*leuştean*), while summer salads are full of dill, parsley, lovage and basil. Some dishes such as parsley stew or tarragon stew are made only using herbs.

anason	ana**son**	aniseed
ardei iute	ar**day yoo**teh	pimiento
arpagic	arpa**jeec**	chives
boia	**boy**a	paprika
busuioc	boosoo**yoc**	basil
capere	**ca**pereh	capers
castraveciori	castrave**chor**y	gherkins
ceapă de apă	**cha**per deh **a**per	shallot
chimen	**kee**men	caraway
cimbru	**cheem**broo	thyme
cuişoare	cooee**shwa**reh	clove
foi de dafin	foy deh **da**feen	bay leaf
ghimber	**geem**ber	ginger
hrean	hr**eh-an**	horseradish
măcriş	mer**creesh**	watercress
măghiran	mergee**ran**	marjoram
mărar	mer**rar**	dill
mentă	**men**ter	mint
mirodenii asortate	meero**de**nee asor**ta**teh	mixed herbs
muştar	moosh**tar**	mustard
nucşoară	nooc**shwa**rer	nutmeg
pătrunjel	pertroon**zhel**	parsley
piper	pee**per**	pepper
rozmarin	rozma**reen**	rosemary
salvie	**sal**vyeh	sage
sare	**sa**reh	salt
scorţişoară	scortsee**shwa**rer	cinnamon
sovârv	so**vuhrv**	oregano
şofran	sho**fran**	saffron
tarhon	tar**hon**	tarragon
usturoi	oostoo**roy**	garlic
vanilie	van**ee**lee-eh	vanilla

Cheese *Brânză*

Cheese is a very important constituent of Romanian cuisine, and it is eaten daily by most people. Although it is not the custom to finish meals with cheese, you'll often find it served at breakfast or as a main meal with polenta.

The most popular type of cheese is Romanian feta, although there are many other varieties.

brânză afumată	**bruhn**zer afoo**ma**ter	smoked cheese
brânză topită	**bruhn**zer to**pee**ter	processed cheese
brânză de vaci	**bruhn**zer deh vach^y	cottage cheese
caşcaval	cashca**val**	a type of cheddar
şvaiţer	**shvay**tser	a type of Swiss cheese with holes

caş (cash) — An unsalted feta cheese made from ewe's milk.

telemea (telem**eh-a**) — *Caş* that has been stored in salted brine.

urdă (**oor**der) — A soft unfermented cheese made from ewe's milk.

Fruit and nuts *Fructe şi nuci*

Do you have any fresh fruit?	**Aveţi fructe proaspete?**	a**vets**^y **froo**cteh **prwa**speteh
I'd like a (fresh) fruit cocktail.	**Aş vrea un cocteil de fructe (proaspete).**	ash vreh-a oon coc**tayl** deh **froo**cteh (**prwa**speteh)
afine	a**fee**neh	blueberries
agrişe	a**gree**sheh	gooseberries
alune de pădure	a**loo**neh deh per**doo**reh	hazelnuts
ananas	ana**nas**	pineapple
arahide	ara**hee**deh	peanuts
banane	ba**na**neh	bananas
caise	ca**ee**seh	apricots
căpşuni	cerp**shoon**^y	strawberries
castane	cas**ta**neh	chestnuts
cireşe	chee**re**sheh	cherries
coacăze negre	**cwa**cerzeh **ne**greh	blackcurrants
curmale	coor**ma**leh	dates
fructe uscate	**froo**cteh oos**ca**teh	dried fruit

grepfrut	**grep**froot	grapefruit
gutui	goo**tooy**	quinces
lămâi	ler**muh**^{y}	lemons
lămâie verde	la**muh**yeh **ver**deh	lime
mandarine	manda**ree**neh	tangerine
mere	**me**reh	apples
migdale	meeg**da**leh	almonds
nucă de cocos	**noo**cer deh **co**cos	coconut
nuci	nooch^y	walnuts
pere	**pe**reh	pears
pepene galben	**pe**peneh **gal**ben	melon
pepene roşu	**pe**peneh **ro**shoo	watermelon
piersici	**pyer**seech^y	peaches
portocale	porto**ca**leh	oranges
prune	**proo**neh	plums
prune uscate	**proo**neh oos**ca**teh	prunes
smeură	**sme**-oorer	raspberries
smochine	smo**kee**neh	figs
stafide	sta**fee**deh	raisins
struguri	**stroo**goor^y	grapes

Desserts—Pastries *Deserturi—Patiserie*

Romanian cakes or tortes are generally made from sponge moistened in light syrup and layered with various fillings including butter cream or whipped cream flavoured with vanilla, chocolate and nuts. Smaller versions of these are called *prăjituri*. At Easter and Christmas, Romanians like to eat *cozonac*, which resembles Italian panetone.

I'd like a dessert, please.	**Aş vrea un desert, vă rog.**	ash vreh-a oon de**sert** ver rog
What do you recommend?	**Ce recomandaţi?**	cheh recoman**dats**^{y}
Something light, please.	**Ceva uşor, vă rog.**	che**va** oo**shor** ver rog
Just a small portion.	**O porţie mică numai.**	o **por**tsee-eh **mee**cer **noo**migh

bezele	be**ze**leh	small meringues
budincă de brânză de vaci	boo**deen**cer deh **bruhn**zer deh vach^y	sweetened cheese souffle
chec	kec	rectangular sponge cake

clătite	cler**tee**teh	crepes
clătite cu brânză	cler**tee**teh coo **bruhn**zer	crepes filled with sweetened cheese mixed with egg
cremşnit	**crem**shneet	millefeuille (napoleon)
dulceaţa	dool**chat**ser	preserved whole fruits
fursecuri	foor**se**coor[y]	small biscuits or tea cakes
îngheţată	uhnge**tsa**ter	ice cream
pandişpan	pandeesh**pan**	sponge cake
plăcintă	pler**cheen**ter	flaky pastry pie
prăjitură	prerzhee**too**rer	an individual torte
salată de fructe	sa**la**ter deh **frooc**teh	fruit salad
spumă de fragi	**spoo**mer deh fraj[y]	wild strawberry mousse
ştrudel cu mere	**shtroo**del coo **me**reh	apple strudel
tartă cu fructe	**tar**ter coo **frooc**teh	small round fruit tart
tort	tort	large layer cake
tort de bezea	tort deh bez**eh-a**	layered cream meringue
tort de nuci	tort deh nooch[y]	walnut layer cake
tort Joffre	tort zhofr	rich chocolate cake

baclava (bacla**va**)
A flaky pastry pie from Turkey, filled with nuts and sweetened with syrup.

cozonac (cozo**nac**)
A large sweet loaf made with yeast, eggs and milk flavoured with nuts, raisins, poppy seeds or Turkish delight. This dessert is traditionally eaten at Easter and Christmas.

lapte de pasăre (**lap**teh deh **pa**serreh)
`Floating islands´: egg whites beaten with sugar until stiff and served floating on a custard sauce.

papanaşi (papa**nashy**)
A traditional dessert made from cottage cheese mixed with eggs and sugar, then formed into flattened rounds and fried or boiled. They are usually served with sweet cream or jam.

pască (**pas**cer)
An Easter treat consisting of yeast dough cases containing a variety of fillings, including chocolate cream and soft cheese mixed with egg, sugar and raisins.

savarină (sava**ree**ner)
A round sponge cake moistened in syrup and filled with whipped cream.

Drinks *Băuturi*

Beer *Bere*

The standard national measure is the *halbă,* roughly equivalent to half a litre. The name derives from the German "half litre" and describes the large glass mug in which beer is generally served.

Apart from national brands of beer, commonly sold in 1/2-litre bottles, many types of foreign beer are available in cans, but you'll find the national brands cheaper and worth a try. Look out for *Silva, Ursus, Gambrinus* or *Timisoreana,* the most popular brands.

What would you like to drink?	**Ce doriţi să beţi?**	cheh do**reets**ʸ ser betsʸ
I'd like a beer, please.	**Aş vrea o bere, vă rog.**	ash vreh-a o **be**reh ver rog
Have a beer!	**Poftiţi o bere!**	pof**teets**ʸ o **be**reh
A bottle of lager, please.	**O sticlă de bere blondă, vă rog.**	o **stee**cler deh **be**reh **blon**der, ver rog
A half litre of ale/ dark beer, please.	**O halbă de bere neagră, vă rog.**	oh **hal**ber deh **be**reh **na**grer ver rog
bere blondă	**be**reh **blon**der	pale ale/lager
bere neagră	**be**reh **na**grer	brown ale

Wine *Vin*

Romania produces many wines of worldwide renown. From the North of Moldova comes the famous wine of *Cotnari*. Further south there are other well-known vineyards—Panciu, Nicoreşti, Coteşti, Jariştea and Odobeşti—producing varieties such as Pinot Gris, Riesling and Fetească.

In Wallachia the vine cultures of Dealu Mare, Valea Călugărească, Urlaţi, Tohani and Pietroasele are equally famed, with two varieties particularly appreciated: *Tămâioasa* of *Pietroasele* and the *Busuioaca* of *Valea Călugărească.* Sweet wines come from the vineyards of Murfatlar and Babadag, and in Transylvania the wines from the Târnave vineyards are also widely enjoyed. Larger, well-stocked supermarkets and good restaurants also have a large selection of imported wines.

A refreshing drink, especially popular in summer, is wine mixed with soda/mineral water *"un şpriţ"*.

May I have the wine list?	**Puteţi să-mi daţi ? lista de vinuri**	poo**tets**ʸ sermʸ datsʸ **lee**sta deh **vee**noorʸ
I'd like a … of red wine/white wine.	**Aş vrea o … de vin roşu/vin alb.**	ash vreh-a o … deh veen **ro**shoo/veen alb
a bottle	**o sticlă**	o **stee**cler
half a bottle	**jumătate de sticlă**	joomer**ta**teh deh **stee**cler
a carafe	**o carafă**	o ca**ra**fer
a small carafe	**o carafă mică**	o ca**ra**fer **mee**cer
a glass	**un pahar**	oon pa**har**
How much is a bottle of champagne?	**Cât costă o sticlă de şampanie?**	cuht **co**ster o **stee**cler deh sham**pa**nyeh
Bring me another bottle/glass of …, please.	**Mai aduceţi-mi o sticlă/un pahar de …, vă rog.**	migh a**doo**chetseemʸ o **stee**cler/oon pa**har** deh … ver rog
Where does this wine come from?	**De unde provine acest vin?**	deh **oon**deh pro**vee**neh a**chest** veen

red	**roşu**	**ro**shoo
white	**alb**	alb
rosé	**rozé**	ro**zeh**
sweet	**dulce**	**dool**cheh
dry	**sec**	sec
medium dry	**demi-sec**	**de**mee-sec
sparkling	**spumos**	spoo**mos**
chilled	**rece**	**re**cheh
at room temperature	**la temperatura camerei**	la tempera**too**ra **ca**meray

Other alcoholic drinks *Alte băuturi alcoolice*

Other national drinks include *ţuică,* a plum brandy, *vişinată,* a liquor made from cherry syrup and white spirit, and vodka. A refreshing drink, often sold by itinerant street-sellers from barrels, is *braga,* a sweet, low alcohol, bread beer.

I'd like a/an …	**Aş vrea …**	ashy vreh-a
aperitif	**un aperitiv**	oon apereet**eev**
cognac	**un coniac**	oon conee-**ac**
liqueur	**un lichior**	oon lee**kyor**
rum	**un rom**	oon rom
vermouth	**un vermut**	oon **ver**moot
vodka	**o vodcă**	o **vod**cer
whisky	**un whisky**	oon **wee**sky
neat (straight)	**simplu**	**seem**ploo
on the rocks	**cu cuburi de ghiaţă**	coo **coo**boor^y deh **gya**tser
with a little water	**cu puţină apă**	coo poot**see**ner **a**per
Give me a large gin and tonic, please.	**Daţi-mi o măsură mare de gin şi apă tonică, vă rog.**	**da**tseem^y o mer**soo**rer **ma**reh deh jeen shee aper **to**neecer ver rog
Just a dash of soda, please.	**Puţin sifon, vă rog.**	poot**seen** see**fon** ver rog

Nonalcoholic drinks *Băuturi nealcoolice*

Fruit juices and well-known brands of canned soft drinks are available everywhere. Mineral water, carbonated or still (*apă minerala cu sau fără gaz*), bottled, at one of over 100 Romanian spas, is widely drunk, even though it is safe to drink tap water.

apple juice	**suc de mere**	sooc deh **me**reh
fruit juice	**suc de fructe**	sooc deh **frooc**tch
grapefruit juice	**suc de grepfrut**	sooc deh **grep**froot
herb tea	**ceai de plante medicinale**	chay deh **plan**teh medeechee**na**leh
lemon juice	**suc de lămâie**	sooc deh ler**muh**yeh
lemonade	**limonadă**	leemo**na**der
milk	**lapte**	**lap**teh
mineral water	**apă minerală**	**a**per meene**ra**ler
fizzy (carbonated)	**apă gazoasă**	**a**per gaz**wa**ser
still	**apă simplă**	**a**per **seem**pler
orange juice	**suc de portocale**	sooc deh porto**ca**leh
orangeade	**oranjadă**	oran**zha**der
tomato juice	**suc de roşii**	sooc deh **ro**shee
tonic water	**apă tonică**	**a**per **to**neecer

cvas/socată	cvas/so**ca**ter	elderflower cordial
lapte acru/bătut	**lap**teh acroo/ber**toot**	drinking yoghurt

sirop (see**rop**) Home-made syrup made from various fruits, for example raspberries or cherries, and drunk diluted with water.

Hot beverages *Băuturi calde*

Romanians drink Turkish coffee, although the trend is changing to instant coffee or freshly ground filtered coffee. Tea is generally not consumed in public – but can be ordered without a problem. Many people drink lemon or herbal teas at home.

I'd like a/an …	**Aş vrea …**	ash vreh-a o/oon
(hot) chocolate	**un lapte cald cu cacao**	oon **lap**teh cald coo ca**cao**
coffee	**o cafea**	o caf**eh-a**
with cream	**cu frişcă**	coo **freesh**cer
with milk	**cu lapte**	coo **lap**teh
back	**neagră**	**neh-a**grer
decaffeinated	**decofeinizată**	decofeh-eene**ee**zater
Turkish coffee	**turcească**	toor**chash**cer
espresso coffee	**espresso**	es**pre**sso
mokka	**moca**	**mo**ca
tea	**un ceai**	oon chay
cup of tea	**o cana de ceai**	o **ca**ner deh chay
with milk/lemon	**cu lapte/cu lămâie**	coo **lap**teh/ coo ler**muh**yeh
iced tea	**ceai cu ghiaţă**	chay coo **gya**tser

Complaints *Reclamaţii*

There's a plate/. glass missing	**Lipseşte o farfurie/ un pahar.**	leep**sesh**teh o farfoo**ree**-eh/oon pa**har**
I don't have a knife/ fork/spoon.	**Nu am cuţit/ furculiţă/lingură.**	noo am coo**tseet**/foorcoo**lee**tser/**leen**goorer
That's not what I ordered.	**Aceasta nu este ce am comandat.**	a**chas**ta noo **yes**teh cheh am coman**dat**
I asked for …	**Am comandat …**	am coman**dat**
There must be some mistake.	**Cred că este o greşeală.**	cred cer **yes**teh o gresh**a**ler
I asked for a small portion (for the child).	**Am comandat o porţie mică (pentru copil).**	am coman**dat** o **por**tsee-eh **mee**cer (**pen**troo co**peel**)

The meat is …	**Carnea este …**	carn**eh-a yes**teh
overdone	**prea prăjită**	preh-a prer**zhee**ter
underdone	**nu este prăjită bine**	noo **yes**teh prer**zhee**ter **bee**neh
too rare	**prea crudă**	preh-a **croo**der
too tough	**prea tare**	preh-a **ta**reh
This is too …	**Asta este prea …**	**as**ta **yes**teh preh-a
bitter/salty/sweet	**amară/sărată/dulce**	a**ma**rer/ser**ra**ter/ **dool**cheh
I don't like this.	**Asta nu-mi place.**	**as**ta noom^y **pla**cheh
The food is cold.	**Mâncarea este rece.**	muhn**ca**reh-a **yes**teh **re**cheh
This isn't fresh.	**Asta nu este proaspăt.**	**as**ta noo **yes**teh **prwa**spert
What's taking you so long?	**De ce durează aşa de mult?**	de cheh doo**ra**zer asha deh moolt
Have you forgotten our drinks?	**Aţi uitat de băuturile noastre?**	ats^y ooy**tat** de beroo**too**-reeleh **nwas**treh
The wine doesn't taste right.	**Nu e bun vinul.**	noo yeh boon **vee**nool
This isn't clean.	**Acesta nu este curat.**	a**ches**ta noo **yes**teh coo**rat**
Would you ask the head waiter to come over?	**Vreţi să chemaţi pe ospătarul şef ?**	vrets^y ser ke**mats**^{y} peh osper**ta**rool shef

The bill (check) *Nota de plată*

It is customary to leave a tip if the service has been good. Most restaurants expect payment in cash but some large hotels have restaurants that will accept credit cards.

I'd like to pay.	**Aş vrea să plătesc.**	ash vreh-a ser pler**tesc**
We'd like to pay separately.	**Vrem să plătim separat.**	vrem ser pler**teem** sepa**rat**
I think there's a mistake in this bill.	**Cred că este o greşeală în nota de plată.**	cred cer **yes**teh o gre**sha**ler uhn **no**ta deh **pla**ter
What's this amount for?	**Ce reprezintă suma aceasta?**	cheh repre**zeen**ter **soo**ma a **chas**ta
Is service included?	**Serviciul este inclus?**	ser**vee**chyool **yes**teh een**cloos**

Is everything included?	**Totul este inclus?**	**to**tool **yes**teh een**cloos**
Do you accept traveller's cheques?	**Acceptaţi cecuri de voiaj?**	acchep**tats**y **che**coory deh vo-**yazh**
Can I pay with this credit card?	**Pot plăti cu această carte de credit?**	pot pler**tee** coo a**chas**ter **car**teh deh **cre**deet
Please round it up to …	**Rotunjiţi suma la …**	rotoon**zheets**y **soo**ma la
Keep the change.	**Păstraţi restul.**	per**strats**y **res**tool
That was delicious.	**Mâncarea a fost delicioasă.**	muhn**ca**reh-a a fost delee**chywa**ser
We enjoyed it, thank you.	**Ne-a plăcut foarte mult, mulţumesc.**	na pler**coot fwar**teh moolt mooltsoo**mesc**

SERVICIUL ESTE INCLUS
SERVICE INCLUDED

Snacks—Picnic *Gustări—Picnic*

Give me two of these and one of those.	**Dati-mi, va rog, două de acestea şi una de aceea.**	**dat**seemy ver rog **do**-wer deh a**ches**teh-a shee oona deh a**che**-a
to the left/right	**din stânga/ din dreapta**	deen **stuhn**ga/ deen **drap**ta
above/below	**de deasupra/ de dedesubt**	deh da**soo**pra/ deh dede**soobt**
It's to take away.	**De luat acasă.**	deh lw**at** a**ca**ser
I'd like a piece of cake.	**Aş vrea o prăjitură.**	ash vreh-a o prerzhee**too**rer
fried sausage	**cârnat prăjit**	cuhr**nat** prer**zheet**
omelette	**omletă**	om**le**ter
open sandwich	**sendvici/sandviş**	**send**veechy/**sand**veesh
with ham	**cu şuncă**	coo **shoon**cer
with cheese	**cu brânză**	coo **bruhn**zer
potato salad	**salată de cartofi**	sa**la**ter deh car**tof**y
sandwich	**sendvici/sandviş**	**send**veechy/**sand**veesh

Here's a basic list of food and drink that might come in useful when shopping for a picnic.

apples	**mere**	**me**reh
bananas	**banane**	ba**na**neh
biscuits (Br.)	**biscuiţi**	bees**cooeets**y

beer	**bere**	**be**reh
bread	**pâine**	**puhy**neh
butter	**unt**	oont
cheese	**brânză**	**bruhn**zer
chips (Am.)	**cartofi prăjiţi**	car**tof**^{y} prer**zheets**^{y}
chocolate bar	**ciocolată**	choco**la**ter
coffee	**cafea**	caf**eh-a**
cold cuts	**salamuri**	sa**la**moor^{y}
cookies	**fursecuri**	foor**se**coor^{y}
crisps	**cartofi prăjiţi**	car**tof**^{y} prer**zheets**^{y}
eggs	**ouă**	**o**-wer
gherkins (pickles)	**castraveciori muraţi**	castrave**chor**^{y} moo**rats**^{y}
grapes	**struguri**	**stroo**goor^{y}
ice cream	**îngheţată**	uhnge**tsa**ter
milk	**lapte**	**lap**teh
mustard	**muştar**	moosh**tar**
oranges	**portocale**	porto**ca**leh
pepper	**piper**	pee**per**
roll	**chiflă**	**cheef**ler
salt	**sare**	**sa**reh
sausage	**cârnat**	cuhr**nat**
soft drink	**băuturi răcoritoare**	ber-oo**toor**^{y} rercoree**twa**reh
sugar	**zahăr**	**za**herr
tea bags	**pliculeţe de ceai**	pleecoo**le**tseh deh chay
yoghurt	**iaurt**	ya**oort**

You may find also these a tasty addition to your picnic:

covrigi	cov**reej**^{y}	pretzels
crenvurşti	**cren**voorsht^{y}	hot dog sausage
croissant	crwa**sant**	French croissant
gogoşi	go**gosh**^{y}	doughnuts
napolitane	napoleet**a**neh	wafers with filling
pateuri cu brânză	pat**e**oor^{y} coo **bruhn**zer	puff pastries filled with cheese
pateuri cu carne	pat**e**oor^{y} coo **car**neh	puff pastries filled with meat
pizza	**pee**tsa	pizza

Travelling around

Plane *Avion*

The national airline that provides a direct daily service to Romania is TAROM, although there are now other Romanian airlines. International airlines such as Lufthansa, Swiss Air, Alitalia and Austrian Airlines operate flights to Bucharest.

Almost all major towns have an airport. The Timişoara airport operates international flights to Austria and Germany. However, the national airports are small and become very busy during peak season. Every town has a TAROM booking agency and you should have no difficulty purchasing a flight ticket.

Is there a flight to Constanţa?	**Există un zbor pentru Constanţa?**	eg**zees**ter oon zbor **pen**troo con**stan**tsa
Is it a direct flight?	**Este direct?**	**yes**teh dee**rect**
When's the next flight to Cluj?	**La ce oră este urmatorul zbor pentru Cluj?**	la cheh **o**rer **yes**teh oormer**to**rool zbor **pen**troo cloozh
Is there a connection to Timişoara?	**Există o legătură cu Timişoara?**	eg**zees**ter o leger**too**rer coo teeme**shwa**ra
I'd like to book a ticket to Oradea.	**Aş vrea să rezerv un bilet pentru Oradea.**	ash vreh-a ser re**zerv** oon bee**let pen**troo o**ra**deh-a
single (one-way)	**numai dus**	**noo**migh doos
return (round trip)	**dus-întors**	doos-uhn**tors**
business class	**business class**	business class
aisle seat	**un loc spre culoar**	oon loc spreh cool**war**
window seat	**un loc la fereastră**	oon loc la fe**ras**trer
What time do we take off?	**La ce oră decolează avionul?**	la cheh **o**rer deco**la**zer avee-**o**nool
What time should I check in?	**La ce ora trebuie să înregistrez bagajele?**	la cheh **o**rer **tre**booyeh ser uhnrejees**trez** ba**ga**zheleh
Is there a bus to the airport?	**Există un autobuz care merge la aeroport?**	eg**zees**ter oon aooto-**booz ca**reh **mer**jeh la a-ero**port**
What's the flight number?	**Care este numărul de zbor?**	**ca**reh **yes**teh **noo**merrool deh zbor

What time do we arrive?	**La ce oră ajungem?**	la cheh **o**rer a**zhoon**jem
I'd like to … my reservation.	**Aş vrea să … rezervarea.**	ash vreh-a ser … rezer**va**reh-a
cancel	**anulez**	anoo**lez**
change	**schimb**	skeemb
confirm	**confirm**	con**feerm**

SOSIRI
ARRIVAL

PLECĂRI
DEPARTURE

Train *Tren*

Romanian National Railways (SNCFR) have a well-developed rail network and provide a good service at a reasonable price. However, Romanian trains are slow by Western European standards.

The three main types of train service are as follows.

rapid (ra**peed**)	These express trains offer the fastest service. They stop only at major towns and seats must be reserved in advance.
accelerat (acchele**rat**)	Direct trains; you should reserve your seat as these trains are very popular.
tren de persoane (tren deh pers**wa**neh/ tren perso**nal**)	These are normally local trains, which provide the slowest method of rail travel. They are not advisable for long journeys, but can be ideal for enjoying some picturesque scenery in the Carpathian mountains.

Intercity trains, which meet the Western European standard, are in service on all important routes.

First and second class tickets are available on all trains. It is advisable to book your seat in advance; reservations (*loc rezervat*) are obligatory on *rapide* trains. Sleeping berths and couchettes on *rapide* trains should also be booked in advance. Besides on the Intercity trains, facilities are rather basic: there is no running water, soap or toilet paper in the WC, and dining cars frequently run out of supplies.

However, trains do run on time and connections are good. The main train station in Bucharest is *Gara de Nord,* and there are generally between four and five trains per day for any major destination.

Tickets can be purchased from railway stations and travel agencies. Enquire about reductions for students, children, disabled travellers, or pensioners when buying tickets. Romanian trains are not equipped for wheelchairs.

To the railway station *Spre gară*

Where's the railway station?	**Unde este gara?**	**oon**deh **yes**teh **ga**ra
Taxi!	**Taxi!**	ta**xee**
Take me to the …	**Vreau să merg la …**	vra^oo ser merg la
main railway station	**gară**	**ga**rer
What's the fare?	**Cât costă?**	cuht **cos**ter

INTRARE	ENTRANCE
IEȘIRE	EXIT
SPRE PEROANE	TO THE PLATFORMS
BIROU DE INFORMAȚII	INFORMATION

Where's the …? *Unde este …?*

Where is/are (the) …?	**Unde se află …?**	**oon**deh seh **a**fler
bar	**barul**	**ba**rool
booking office	**agenţia de voiaj**	ajen**tsee**a deh vo**yazh**
currency exchange office	**biroul de schimb valutar**	bee**ro**-ool deh skeemb valoo**tar**
left-luggage office (baggage check)	**biroul de bagaje**	bee**ro**-ool deh ba**ga**zheh
lost property (lost and found) office	**biroul de obiecte pierdute**	bee**ro**-ool deh o**byec**teh pyer**doo**teh
newsstand	**chioşcul de ziare**	kyoshcool deh zee-**a**reh
platform 7	**linia şapte**	**lee**nya **shap**teh
reservations office	**biroul de rezervări**	bee**ro**-ool deh rezer**verr**^y
restaurant	**restaurantul**	resta^oo**rant**ool
snack bar	**chioşcul cu gustări**	kyoshcool coo goos**terr**^y
ticket office	**casa de bilete**	**ca**sa deh bee**le**teh
waiting room	**sala de aşteptare**	**sa**la deh ashtep**ta**reh
Where are the toilets?	**Unde sunt toaletele?**	**oon**deh soont twa**le**teleh

TAXI, see page 21

Inquiries *Biroul de informaţii*

When is the … train to Suceava?	**La ce ora pleacă … tren spre Suceava?**	la cheh **o**rer **pla**cer … tren spreh soo**cha**va
first/last/next	**primul/ultimul/ urmatorul**	**pree**mool/**ool**teemool/ oormer**to**rool
What time does the train to Bacău leave?	**La ce oră pleacă trenul de Bacău?**	la cheh **o**rer **pla**cer **tre**nool deh ba**coh**
What's the fare to Bucharest?	**Cât costă biletul până la Bucureşti?**	cuht **co**ster bee**le**tool **puh**ner la boocoo**resht**ʸ
Is it a through train?	**Este un tren direct?**	**yes**teh oon tren dee**rect**
Is there a connection to …?	**Este o legatură cu …?**	**yes**teh o leger**too**rer coo …
Do I have to change trains?	**Trebuie să schimb trenul?**	**tre**boo-yeh ser skeemb **tre**nool
Is there enough time to change?	**Am destul timp să schimb trenul?**	am des**tool** teemp ser skeemb **tre**nool
Is the train running on time?	**Trenul are vreo întârziere?**	**tre**nool **a**reh vro uhntuhrzee-**e**reh
What time does the train arrive in Ploieşti?	**La ce oră ajunge trenul în Ploieşti?**	la cheh **o**rer a**zhoon**jeh **tre**nool uhn plo**yesht**ʸ
Is there a dining car/ sleeping car on the train?	**Trenul acesta are vagon restaurant/ vagon de dormit?**	**tre**nool a**ches**ta **a**reh va**gon** restaᵒᵒ**rant**/ va**gon** deh dor**meet**
Does the train stop in Sinaia?	**Trenul acesta opreşte în Sinaia?**	**tre**nool a**ches**ta o**presh**teh uhn see**na**ya
Which platform does the train to Cluj leave from?	**De la ce peron pleacă trenul de Cluj?**	deh la cheh pe**ron** **pla**cer **tre**nool deh cloozh
Which platform does the train from Iaşi arrive at?	**La ce peron vine trenul de Iaşi?**	la cheh pe**ron** **vee**neh **tre**nool deh yashʸ
I'd like a time-table.	**Aş vrea un mers al trenurilor.**	ash vreh-a oon mers al **tre**nooreelor

YOU MAY HEAR:

Trebuie să schimbaţi la …	You have to change at …
Schimbaţi la … şi luaţi un tren local.	Change at … and get a local train.
Peronul şapte este …	Platform 7 is …
acolo/la etaj	over there/upstairs
la stânga/la dreapta	on the left/on the right
Aveţi un tren spre … la …	There's a train to … at …
Trenul dumneavoastră o să plece de la linia opt.	Your train will leave from platform 8.
Trenul are o întârziere de … minute.	There will be a delay of … minutes.
Clasa întâi la capul trenului/la mijlocul trenului/la coada trenului.	First class at the front/in the middle/at the rear.

Tickets *Bilete*

I'd like a ticket to Bucharest.	**Aş dori un bilet pentru Bucureşti.**	ash d**oree** oon bee**let** **pen**troo boocoo**resht**ʸ
single (one-way)	**dus**	doos
return (round trip)	**dus-întors**	doos-uhn**tors**
first/second class	**clasa întâi/ clasa a doua**	**cla**sa uhn**tuhy**/ **cla**sa a **do**wa
half price	**jumătate de preţ**	zhoomer**ta**teh deh prets

Reservation *Rezervări*

I'd like to reserve a …	**Aş vrea să rezerv un …**	ash vreh-a ser re**zerv** oon
seat (by the window)	**loc (lângă fereastră)**	loc (**luhn**ger fe**ras**trer)
berth	**cuşetă**	coo**she**ter
upper	**patul de sus**	**pa**tool deh soos
middle	**patul de la mijloc**	**pa**tool deh la **meezh**loc
lower	**patul de jos**	**pa**tool deh zhos
berth in the sleeping car	**cuşeta la vagonul de dormit**	coo**she**ter la va**go**nool deh dor**meet**

All aboard *În vagoane*

Is this the right platform for the train to Sibiu?	**Acesta este peronul pentru trenul de Sibiu?**	a**ches**ta **yes**teh pe**ro**nool **pen**troo **tre**nool deh see**bee**^{oo}
Is this the right train to Predeal?	**Trenul acesta merge la Predeal?**	**tre**nool a**ches**ta **mer**jeh la pre**dal**
Excuse me. Could I get past?	**Pardon, vă rog. Vreţi să-mi faceţi loc?**	par**don** ver rog. vrets^{y} serm^{y} **fa**chets^{y} loc
Is this seat taken?	**Este liber locul acesta?**	**yes**teh **lee**ber **lo**cool a**ches**ta?

FUMĂTORI
SMOKER

NEFUMĂTORI
NONSMOKER

I think that's my seat.	**Cred că acesta este locul meu.**	cred cer a**ches**ta **yes**teh **lo**cool me^{oo}
What station is this?	**Ce staţie este aici?**	cheh **stat**see-eh **yes**teh a-**eech**^{y}
How long does the train stop here?	**Cât timp stă trenul în gara aceasta?**	cuht teemp ster **tre**nool uhn **ga**ra a**chas**ta
When do we arrive in Bucharest?	**Când ajungem la Bucureşti?**	cuhnd a**zhoon**jem la boocoo**resht**^{y}

Sleeping car *Vagon de dormit*

Couchettes and sleepers need to be booked well in advance and Western standards should not be expected. Rates vary according to distance.

Are there any free compartments in the sleeping car?	**Sunt locuri libere la vagonul de dormit?**	soont **lo**coor^{y} **lee**bereh la va**go**nool deh dor**meet**
Where's the sleeping car?	**Unde este vagonul de dormit?**	**oon**deh **yes**teh va**go**nool deh dor**meet**
Where's my berth?	**Unde este cuşetă mea?**	**oon**deh **yes**teh coo**she**ter meh-a
I'd like a lower berth.	**Aş vrea o cuşetă mai jos.**	ash vreh-a o coo**she**ter migh zhos
Would you make up our berths?	**Vreţi să ne faceţi patul, vă rog?**	vrets^{y} ser neh **fa**chets^{y} **pa**tool ver rog

Eating *La masă*

All *rapide* and *accelerate* trains have dining cars (*vagon restaurant*). However, the food is not always of the highest quality and Romanians tend to use the restaurant for drinking.

Where's the dining car?	**Unde este vagonul restaurant?**	**oon**deh **yes**teh va**go**nool resta^{oo}**rant**

Baggage—Porters *Bagaje—Hamali*

Porter!	**Alo! Hamal!**	alo ha**mal**
Can you help me with my luggage?	**Vreţi să mă ajutaţi şi pe mine cu bagajele, vă rog?**	vrets[y] ser mer azhoo**tats**[y] shee peh **mee**neh coo baga**zh**eleh ver rog
Where are the luggage trolleys (carts)?	**Unde sunt cărucioarele de bagaje?**	**oon**deh soont cerroo**chwa**releh deh baga**zh**eh
Where are the luggage lockers?	**Unde sunt cabinele de bagaje?**	**oon**deh soont ca**bee**neleh deh ba**ga**zheh
Where's the left luggage office (baggage check)?	**Unde este biroul de bagaje?**	**oon**deh **yes**teh bee**ro**-ool deh ba**ga**zheh
I'd like to leave my luggage, please.	**Aş vrea să las bagajele, vă rog.**	ash vreh-a ser las ba**ga**zheleh ver rog
I'd like to register (check) my luggage.	**Aş vrea să fac înregistrarea bagajelor.**	ash vreh-a ser fac uhnrejees**tra**reh-a ba**ga**zhelor

ÎNREGISTRAREA BAGAJELOR
REGISTERING (CHECKING) BAGGAGE

Underground (subway) *Metrou*

Bucharest is the only city in Romania with an underground network. There are three main lines and trains run very frequently. Fares are inexpensive, and the monthly ticket provides an economical way of travelling around. Apart from this, single tickets, or magnet tickets for multiple journeys, can be purchased at all underground kiosks and should be validated in the punch machine at the entrance.

Where's the nearest underground station?	**Este vreo staţie de metrou prin apropiere?**	**yes**teh vro **sta**tsee-eh deh met**ro**^{oo} preen apropee-**e**reh
Does this train go to …?	**Acest tren merge la …?**	a**chest** tren **mer**jeh la
Where do I change for …?	**Unde trebuie să schimb pentru …?**	**oon**deh **tre**booyeh ser skeemb **pen**troo
Is the next station …?	**Prima staţie este …?**	**pree**ma **sta**tsee-eh **yes**teh
Which line should I take to …?	**Ce tren trebuie să iau pentru …?**	cheh tren **tre**booyeh ser ya^{oo} **pen**troo

Coach (long-distance bus) *Autocar*

Travelling long-distance by coach has developed enormously over the last few years and offers a welcome alternative to the train. Every town has a main coach station (*autogară*) and in Bucharest and the larger cities there are now numerous small, private coach stations. Tickets can be purchased from the coach driver, or in advance from the coach station kiosks.

When's the next coach to …?	**La ce oră pleacă următorul autocar spre …?**	la cheh **o**rer **pla**cer oormer**to**rool a^{oo}to**car** spreh
Does this coach stop at …?	**Autocarul acesta se opreşte la …?**	a^{oo}to**ca**rool a**ches**ta seh o**presh**teh la
How long does the journey (trip) take?	**Cât durează călătoria?**	cuht doo**ra**zer cerlerto**reea**

Bus—Tram (streetcar) *Autobuz—Tramvai*

Buses, trolleybuses and trams do not have conductors. You must buy your ticket before your journey from a kiosk belonging to RATB or ITB, the local transport institutions. On entering the bus, tram or trolleybus, you should validate your ticket in the punch machine. The penalty for travelling without a ticket is a heavy on-the-spot fine. Since a flat fare is charged regardless of distance, it is advisable to purchase a book of tickets (*carnet de bilete*).

I'd like a booklet of tickets.	**Aş vrea un carnet de bilete.**	ash vreh-a oon car**net** deh bee**le**teh

Which tram (streetcar) goes to the town centre?	**Ce tramvai merge în centru?**	cheh tram**vigh mer**jeh uhn **chen**troo
Where can I get a bus to the opera?	**De unde pot lua un autobuz pentru operă?**	deh **oon**deh pot lwa oon a^{oo}to**booz pen**troo **o**perer
Which bus do I take to Palatul Cotroceni?	**Ce autobuz merge la Palatul Cotroceni?**	cheh a^{oo}to**booz mer**jeh la pa**la**tool cotro**chen**^{y}
Where's the bus stop?	**Unde este staţia de autobuz?**	**oon**deh **yes**teh **sta**tsee-a deh a^{oo}to**booz**
When is the … bus to Palatul Cotroceni?	**La ce oră vine … autobuzul care merge la Palatul Cotroceni?**	la cheh **o**rer **vee**neh … a^{oo}to**boo**zool **ca**reh **mer**jeh la pa**la**tool cotro**chen**^{y}
first/last/ next	**primul/ultimul/ următorul**	**pree**mool/**ool**teemool/ oormer**to**rool
How much is the fare to …?	**Cât costă pâna la …?**	cuht **cos**ter **puh**ner la
Do I have to change buses?	**Trebuie să schimb autobuzul?**	**tre**booyeh ser skeemb a^{oo}to**boo**zool
How many bus stops are there to …?	**Câte staţii sunt până la …?**	**cuh**teh **sta**tsee soont **puh**ner la
Will you tell me when to get off?	**Puteţi să-mi spuneţi când să cobor?**	poo**tets**^{y} serm^{y} **spoo**nets^{y} cuhnd ser co**bor**
I want to get off at Piaţa Unirii.	**Aş vrea să cobor la Piaţa Unirii.**	ash vreh-a ser co**bor** la **pya**tsa u**nee**ree

STAȚIE DE AUTOBUZ	BUS STOP
STAŢIE FACULTATIVA	REQUEST STOP

Boat service *Debarcader*

Cruises on the Danube (*Dunărea*) and boat trips in the Danube Delta (*Delta Dunării*) can be booked through the National Tourist Office (ONT), or directly at one of the numerous private travel agencies offering such trips.

When does the next boat for … leave?	**La ce oră pleacă următoarea barcă …?**	la cheh **o**rer **pla**cer oormer**twa**reh-a **bar**cer

Where's the embarkation point?	**Unde se face îmbarcarea?**	**oon**deh seh **fa**cheh uhmbar**ca**reh-a
How long does the crossing take?	**Cât timp durează traversarea?**	cuht teemp doo**ra**zer traver**sa**reh-a
Which port(s) do we stop at?	**La ce port(uri) vă opriţi?**	la cheh **port**(oory) ver o**preets**y
I'd like to take a cruise/ tour of the harbour.	**Aş vrea să fac o croazieră în jurul portului.**	ash vreh-a ser fac o crwa-zee-**erer** uhn **zhoo**rool **por**toolooy
boat	**barcă**	**bar**cer
cabin	**cabină**	ca**bee**ner
single/ double	**de o persoană/ de două persoane**	deh o pers**wa**ner/ deh **do**-wer pers**wa**neh
deck	**punte**	**poon**teh
ferry	**bac**	bac
hydrofoil	**navă cu aripi portante**	**na**ver coo a**reep**y por**tan**teh
life belt/ boat	**colac de salvare/ barcă de salvare**	**co**lac deh sal**va**reh/ **bar**cer deh sal**va**reh
port	**port**	port
reclining seat	**scaun rabatabil**	**sca**-oon raba**ta**beel
river cruise	**croazieră pe fluviu**	crwazee-**e**rer peh **floo**vyoo
ship	**vapor**	va**por**
steamer	**vapor cu abur**	va**por** coo **a**boor

Other means of transport *Alte mijloace de transport*

Although people occasionally hitchhike in Romania, bear in mind that compared to the West the cars are smaller and there are less of them on the road. It is not advisable for women to hitchhike alone.

to hitchhike	**a face autostopul**	a **fa**cheh aootos**to**pool
to walk	**a merge pe jos**	a **mer**jeh peh zhos
cable car	**teleferic**	tele**fe**reec
helicopter	**elicopter**	eleecop**ter**
moped	**motoretă**	moto**re**ter
motorbike/scooter	**motocicletă/scuter**	motochee**cle**ter/**scoo**ter

Bicycle hire *Închirieri de biciclete*

I'd like to hire a bicycle.	**Aş vrea să închiriez o bicicletă.**	ash vreh-a ser uhnkeeree-**ez** o beechee**cle**ter

Car *Autoturismul*

Most roads are not very wide but the major routes are reasonably well maintained. There are no motorways except for a short toll motorway between Bucharest and Pitesti. Traffic regulations are similar to any Western European country, with priority given to vehicles coming from the right at main junctions. It is customary to give a short signal on your horn when overtaking.

Driving at night is not advised as roads are poorly lit and cyclists and horse carts frequently travel without adequate lights. The wearing of seatbelts is compulsory, and driving with any alcohol in the bloodstream is prohibited.

There is a very good network of petrol stations across the whole country, and all types of petrol are available. Aside from the motorway roads do not have phone facilities in case of accident.

Where's the nearest (self-service) filling station?	**Unde este cea mai apropiată staţie de benzină (cu autoservire) prin apropiere?**	**oon**deh **yes**teh cha migh apropee-**a**ter **stat**see-eh deh ben**zee**ner (coo a[oo]toser**vee**reh) preen apropee-**ereh**
Fill it up, please.	**Faceţi plinul, vă rog.**	**fa**chets[y] **plee**nool ver rog
Give me … litres of petrol (gasoline).	**Puneţi … litri de benzină.**	**poo**nets[y] … **lee**tree deh ben**zee**ner
super (premium)/ regular/unleaded/ diesel	**super/normală/ fără plumb/ motorină**	**soo**per/nor**ma**ler/ **fer**rer ploomb/ moto**ree**ner
Please check the …	**Vă rog să verificaţi …**	ver rog ser vereefee**cats**[y]
battery	**bateria**	bate**reea**
brake fluid	**lichidul de frână**	lee**kee**dool deh **fruh**ner
oil/water	**uleiul/apa**	oo**le**yool/**a**pa
Would you check the tyre pressure?	**Vă rog să verificaţi presiunea roţilor.**	ver rog ser vereefee**cats**[y] presee-**oo**neh-a **ro**tseelor
1.6 front, 1.8 rear.	**1,6 în faţă, 1,8 în spate.**	1,6 uhn **fa**tser 1,8 uhn **spa**teh
Please check the spare tyre, too.	**Vă rog, verificaţi şi roata de rezervă.**	ver rog vereefee**cats**[y] shee **rwa**ta deh re**ser**ver

CAR HIRE, see page 20

Can you mend this puncture (fix this flat)?	**Puteţi vulcaniza roata aceasta?**	poo**tets**^{y} voolcanee**za** **rwa**ta a**chas**ta
Would you change the … please?	**Vreţi să schimbaţi … vă rog?**	vrets^{y} ser skeem**bats**^{y} ver rog
bulb	**becul**	**be**cool
tyre	**roata**	**rwa**ta
wipers	**ştergătoarele de parbriz**	shterger**twa**releh deh par**breez**
Would you clean the windscreen (windshield)?	**Vreţi să spălaţi parbrizul, vă rog?**	vrets^{y} ser sper**lats**^{y} par**bree**zool ver rog

Asking the way—Street directions *Cum să găsim drumul*

Can you tell me the way to …?	**Puteţi să-mi spuneţi care este drumul spre …?**	poo**tets**^{y} serm^{y} **spoo**nets^{y}**ca**reh **yes**teh **droo**mool spreh
In which direction is …?	**In ce direcţie se află …?**	uhn cheh dee**rec**tsee-eh seh **a**fler
How do I get to …?	**Cum ajung la …?**	coom a**zhoong** la
Are we on the right road for …?	**Suntem pe drumul bun pentru …?**	**soon**tem peh **droo**mool boon **pen**troo
How far is the next village?	**Cât de departe este satul următor?**	cuht deh de**par**teh **yes**teh **sa**tool oormer**tor**
How far is it to … from here?	**Ce distanţă este până la … de aici?**	cheh dees**tan**tser **yes**teh **puh**ner la… deh a-**eech**^{y}
Is there a motorway (expressway)?	**Există autostradă?**	eg**zee**ster a^{oo}to**stra**der
How long does it take by car/on foot?	**Cât timp ne ia cu maşina/pe jos?**	cuht teemp neh ya coo ma**shee**na/peh zhos
Can you tell me where … is?	**Puteţi să-mi spuneţi unde este …?**	poo**tets**^{y} serm^{y} **spoo**nets^{y} **oon**deh **yes**teh
How can I find this place/address?	**Unde este acest loc/Unde este această adresă?**	**oon**deh **yes**teh a**chest** loc/ **oon**deh **yes**teh a**chas**ter a**dre**ser
Where's this?	**Unde este aceasta?**	**oon**deh **yes**teh a**chas**ta
Can you show me on the map where I am?	**Puteţi să-mi arătaţi pe hartă unde sunt?**	poo**tets**^{y} serm^{y} arer**tats**^{y} peh **har**ter **oon**deh soont
Where are the nearest public toilets?	**Unde este o toaletă publică prin apropiere?**	**oon**deh **yes**teh oh twa**le**ter **poo**bleecer preen apropee-**ereh**

YOU MAY HEAR:

Sunteţi pe un drum greşit.	You're on the wrong road.
Mergeţi drept înainte.	Go straight ahead.
E mai departe pe stânga/pe dreapta.	It's down there on the left/right.
vis-a-vis/în spate ...	opposite/behind ...
lângă/după ...	next to/after ...
nord/sud	north/south
est/vest	east/west
Mergeţi până la prima/ a doua intersecţie.	Go to the first/second crossroads (intersection).
Luaţi-o la stânga la semafor.	Turn left at the traffic lights.
Luaţi-o la dreapta la colţul . următor	Turn right at the next corner.
Mergeţi pe strada ...	Take the ... road.
Este o stradă cu sens unic.	It's a one-way street.
Trebuie să vă întoarceţi la ...	You have to go back to ...
Urmaţi indicatoarele pentru Constanţa.	Follow signs for Constanţa.

Parking *Parcare*

An attendant usually collects the fee at parking lots, in Bucharest or larger cities parking meters have been introduced. In Bucharest your vehicle may be clamped if parked in a no-parking zone.

Where can I park?	**Unde se poate parca?**	**oon**deh seh **pwa**teh par**ca**
Is there a car park nearby?	**Există o parcare prin apropiere?**	eg**zees**ter o par**care** preen apropee-**ereh**
May I park here?	**Pot să parchez aici?**	pot ser par**kez** a-**eech**ʸ
How long can I park here?	**Cât timp pot să parchez aici?**	cuht teemp pot ser par**kez** a-**eech**ʸ
What's the charge per hour?	**Cât costă pe oră?**	cuht **co**ster peh **o**rer
Do you have some change?	**Aveţi nişte mărunt?**	a**vets**ʸ **neesh**teh mer**roont**

Road assistance *Asistenţă rutieră*

If your car needs to be towed, dial 927 for the Romanian Automobile Club (ACR—*Automobil Club Român*).

Where's the nearest garage?	**Este vreun Servis prin apropiere?**	**yes**teh vroon **ser**vees preen apropee-**e**reh
My car has broken down.	**Maşina mea are o pană de motor.**	ma**shee**na meh-a **a**reh o **pa**ner deh mo**tor**
Where can I make a phone call?	**De unde pot da un telefon?**	deh **oon**deh pot da oon tele**fon**
I've had a break-down at …	**Sunt în pană la …**	soont uhn **pa**ner la
Can you send a mechanic?	**Puteţi să trimiteţi un mecanic?**	poo**tets**ʸ ser tree**mee**tetsʸ oon me**ca**neec
My car won't start.	**Motorul nu porneşte.**	mo**to**rool noo por**nesh**teh
The battery is dead.	**Bateria este consumată.**	bate**ree-a yes**teh consoo**ma**ter
I've run out of petrol (gasoline).	**Am rămas în pană de benzină.**	am rer**mas** uhn **pa**ner deh ben**zee**ner
I have a flat tyre.	**Am o roată dezumflată.**	am o **rwa**ter dezoom**fla**ter
The engine is overheating.	**Motorul se încălzeşte prea tare.**	mo**to**rool seh uhncerl**zesh**teh preh-a **ta**reh
There's something wrong with the …	**E o defecţiune la …**	yeh o defectsee-**oo**neh la
brakes	**frâne**	**fruh**neh
carburettor	**carburator**	carboora**tor**
exhaust pipe	**ţeava de eşapament**	**tsa**va deh eshapa**ment**
radiator	**radiator**	radee-a**tor**
wheel	**roată**	**rwa**ter
Can you send a break-down van (tow truck)?	**Puteţi trimite o maşină de depanare?**	poo**tets**ʸ tree**mee**teh o ma**shee**ner deh depa**na**reh
How long will you be?	**Cât o să dureze?**	cuht o ser doo**re**zeh
Can you give me an estimate?	**Puteţi să-mi spuneţi cât costă cu aproximaţie?**	poo**tets**ʸ sermʸ **spoo**netsʸ cuht **co**ster coo aproxee**ma**tsee-eh

Accident—Police *Accident—Poliţie*

Please call the police.	**Vă rog chemaţi poliţia.**	ver rog ke**mats**^{y} pol**ee**tsee-a
Where's there a telephone?	**Unde se găseşte un telefon?**	**oon**deh seh gerse**sh**teh oon tele**fon**
Call a doctor/ an ambulance quickly.	**Chemaţi un doctor/ o salvare imediat.**	ke**mats**^{y} oon **doc**tor/ o sal**va**reh eemedee-**at**
There are people injured.	**Sunt răniţi.**	soont rer**neets**^{y}
Here's my driving licence.	**Poftiţi carnetul meu de conducere.**	pof**teets**^{y} car**ne**tool me^{oo} deh con**doo**chereh
What's your name and address?	**Numele şi adresa dumneavoastră!**	**noo**mele shee a**dre**sa doomna**wa**strer
What's your insurance company?	**Care este compania dumneavoastră de asigurări?**	**ca**reh **yes**teh compa**nee**a doomna**wa**strer deh aseegoo**rerr**^{y}

Road signs *Semne de circulaţie*

ANIMALE	Animals
ATENȚIE	Caution
ATENȚIE ȘCOALĂ	Caution school
CĂDERI DE PIETRE	Falling rocks
CEDEAZĂ TRECEREA	Give way
COBORÂRE PERICULOASĂ	Dangerous descent
CURBĂ DEOSEBIT DE PERICULOASĂ	Dangerous bend
DEPĂȘIREA INTERZISĂ	No overtaking
DEVIERE	Diversion
DRUM CU DENIVELĂRI	Uneven road surface
ÎNTOARCEREA INTERZISĂ	No turning
LIMITĂ DE VITEZĂ	Speed limit
PARCAREA INTERZISĂ	No parking
POLEI	Icy road
REDUCEȚI VITEZA	Slow down
ȘANTIER ÎN LUCRU	Road works ahead
SENS GIRATORIU	Roundabout
SENS UNIC	One way
ȚINETI DREAPTA	Keep right
TRAFIC INTERZIS	No traffic allowed
TRECERE PIETONI	Pedestrian crossing

NUMBERS, see page 147

Sightseeing

Where's the tourist office?	**Unde se află oficiul de turism?**	**oon**deh seh **a**fler **ofee-**chee-ool deh too**reesm**
What are the main points of interest?	**Care sunt obiectivele turistice importante?**	**ca**reh soont obyec**tee-**veleh too**rees**teecheh eempor**tan**teh
We're here for …	**Suntem aici numai pentru …**	**soon**tem a-**eech**^{y} **noo**migh **pen**troo
only a few hours	**câteva ore**	**cuh**teva **o**reh
a day	**o zi**	o zee
a week	**o săptămână**	o serpter**muh**ner
Can you recommend a sightseeing tour/ an excursion?	**Ne puteţi recomanda un traseu prin împrejurimi/ o excursie?**	neh poo**tets**^{y} recoman**da** oon tra**se**^{oo} **preen** uhmprezhoo**reem**^{y}/ o ex**coor**see-eh
Where do we leave from?	**De unde se pleacă?**	deh **oon**deh seh **pla**cer
Will the bus pick us up at the hotel?	**Vine autobuzul să ne ia de la hotel?**	**vee**neh a^{oo}to**boo**zool ser neh ya deh la ho**tel**
How much does the tour cost?	**Cât costă această excursie?**	cuht **co**ster a**chas**ter ex**coor**see-eh
What time does the tour start?	**La ce oră începe excursia?**	la cheh **o**rer uhn**che**peh ex**coor**see-a
Is lunch included?	**Masa de prânz este inclusă în biletul de excursie?**	**ma**sa deh pruhnz **yes**teh een**cloo**ser uhn bee**le**tool deh ex**coor**see-eh
What time do we get back?	**La ce oră ne întoarcem?**	la cheh **o**rer neh uhn**twar**chem
Do we have free time in …?	**Avem timp liber în …?**	a**vem** teemp **lee**ber uhn
Is there an English-speaking guide?	**Aveţi un ghid care vorbeşte englezeşte?**	a**vets**^{y} oon geed **ca**reh vor**besh**teh engle**zesh**teh
I'd like to hire a private guide for …	**Aş vrea să angajez un ghid particular pentru …**	ash vreh-a ser anga**zhez** oon geed parteecoo**lar** **pen**troo
half a day	**jumătate de zi**	zhoomer**ta**teh deh zee
a day	**o zi**	o zee

Where is/are the …?	**Unde este/sunt …?**	**oon**deh **yes**teh/soont
art gallery	**galeria de artă**	gale**ree-**a deh **ar**ter
birth place	**casa memorială**	**ca**sa memoree-**a**ler
botanical gardens	**grădina botanică**	grer**dee**na bo**ta**neecer
building	**clădirea**	cler**dee**reh-a
business district	**zona băncilor**	zona **bern**cheelor
castle	**castelul**	cas**te**lool
cathedral	**catedrala**	cate**dra**la
cave	**peştera**	**pesh**tera
cemetery	**cimitirul**	cheemee**tee**rool
citadel	**cetatea**	che**ta**teh-a
city centre	**centrul oraşului**	**chen**trool o**ra**shooloo^y
chapel	**capela**	ca**pe**la
church	**biserica**	bee**se**reeca
concert hall	**sala de concert**	**sa**la deh con**cher**t
convent	**mănăstirea**	merner**stee**reh-a
court house	**tribunalul**	treeboo**na**lool
embankment	**cheiul**	**ke-**yool
exhibition	**expoziţia**	expo**zee**tsee-a
factory	**uzina**	oo**zee**na
fair	**târgul**	**tuhr**gool
flea market	**talciocul**	tal**cho**cool
fortress	**cetatea**	che**ta**teh-a
fountain	**fântâna**	fuhn**tuh**na
gardens	**grădina (publică)**	grer**dee**na **poo**bleecer
harbour	**portul**	**por**tool
lake	**lacul**	**la**cool
library	**biblioteca**	beeblee-o**te**ca
market	**piaţa**	**pya**tsa
memorial	**monumentul comemorativ**	monoo**men**tool comemora**teev**
monastery	**mănăstirea**	merner**stee**reh-a
monument	**monumentul**	monoo**men**tool
museum	**muzeul**	moo**ze-**ool
old town	**oraşul vechi**	**ora**shool vek^y
opera house	**opera**	**o**pera
palace	**palatul**	pa**la**tool
park	**parcul**	**par**cool
parliament building	**clădirea parlamentului**	cler**dee**reh-a parla**men**toolooy
planetarium	**planetarul**	plane**ta**rool
royal palace	**palatul regal**	pa**la**tool re**gal**

ruins	**ruinele**	roo-**ee**neleh
shopping area	**centrul comercial**	**chen**trool comerchee-**al**
square	**piaţa**	**pya**tsa
stadium	**stadionul**	stadee-**o**nool
statue	**statuia**	sta**too**-ya
theatre	**teatrul**	**ta**trool
tomb	**mormântul**	mor**muh**ntool
tower	**turnul**	**toor**nool
town hall	**primărie**	preemer**ree**-a
university	**universitatea**	ooneeverseet**a**teh-a
zoo	**grădina zoologică**	grer**dee**na zo-o**lo**jeecer

Admission *Intrare*

Is … open on Sundays?	**Este … deschis duminica?**	**yes**teh … des**kees** doo**mee**neeca
What are the opening hours?	**La ce oră deschideţi?**	la cheh **o**rer des**kee**dets^{y}
When does it close?	**La ce ora închideţi?**	la cheh **o**rer uhn**kee**dets^{y}
How much is the entrance fee?	**Cât costă intrarea?**	cuht **cos**ter een**tra**reh-a
Is there any reduction for (the) …?	**Faceţi reduceri pentru …?**	**fa**chets^{y} re**doo**cher^{y} **pen**troo
children	**copii**	co**pee**
disabled	**persoane invalide**	pers**wa**neh eenva**lee**deh
pensioners	**pensionari**	pensyo**nar**^{y}
students	**studenţi**	stoo**dents**^{y}
Do you have a guide-book (in English)?	**Aveţi un ghid în englezeşte?**	a**vets**^{y} oon geed uhn engle**zesh**teh
Can I buy a catalogue?	**Pot cumpăra un catalog?**	pot coomper**ra** oon cata**log**
Is it all right to take pictures?	**Este permis să fac poze?**	**yes**teh per**mees** ser fac **po**zeh
Is there easy access for the disabled?	**Există acces pentru persoane invalide?**	eg**zees**ter ac**ches** **pen**troo pers**wa**neh eenva**lee**deh
Are there facilities/ activities for children?	**Există amenajări/ jocuri pentru copii?**	eg**zees**ter amena**zheer**^{y}/ **zho**coor^{y} **pen**troo co**pee**

INTRAREA GRATUITĂ	ADMISSION FREE
FOTOGRAFIEREA INTERZISĂ	NO CAMERAS ALLOWED

Who—What—When? *Cine—Ce—Când?*

What's that building?	**Ce clădire este aceea?**	cheh clerdeereh yesteh achea
Who was the …?	**Cine a fost …?**	**chee**neh a fost
architect	**arhitectul**	arhee**tec**tool
artist	**artistul**	ar**tees**tool
painter	**pictorul**	**peec**torool
sculptor	**sculptorul**	**scoolp**torool
Who built it?	**Cine a construit-o?**	**chee**neh a constroo-**ee**to
Who painted that picture?	**Cine a pictat acel tablou?**	**chee**neh a peec**tat** a**chel** ta**blo**[oo]
When did he live?	**Când a trăit?**	cuhnd a trer-**eet**
When was it built?	**Când a fost construit?**	cuhnd a fost constroo-**eet**
Where's the house where … lived?	**Unde este casa în care a locuit …?**	**oon**deh **yes**teh **ca**sa uhn **ca**reh a locoo-**eet**
We're interested in …	**Ne interesează …**	neh eenteres**a**zer
antiques	**antichităţile**	anteekee**ter**tseeleh
archaeology	**arheologia**	arheolo**jee**a
art	**arta**	**ar**ta
botany	**botanica**	bo**ta**neeca
ceramics	**ceramica**	che**ra**meeca
coins	**numismatica**	noomees**ma**teeca
fine arts	**arte frumoase**	**ar**te froom**wa**seh
furniture	**mobila stil**	**mo**beela steel
geology	**geologia**	jeolo**jee**a
handicrafts	**artizanatul**	arteeza**na**tool
history	**istoria**	ees**to**rya
medicine	**medicina**	medee**chee**na
music	**muzica**	**moo**zeeca
natural history	**ştiinţele naturale**	shtee-**een**tseleh natoo**ra**leh
ornithology	**ornitologia**	orneetolo**jee**a
painting	**pictura**	peec**too**ra
pottery	**olăritul**	oler**ree**tool
religion	**religia**	re**lee**jee-a
sculpture	**sculptura**	scoolp**too**ra
zoology	**zoologia**	zoolo**jee**-a
Where's the … department?	**Unde se află departamentul de …?**	**oon**deh seh **a**fler departa**men**tool deh

It's …	**Este …**	**yes**teh
amazing	**uluitor**	ooloo-ee**tor**
awful	**groaznic**	**grwaz**neec
beautiful	**frumos**	froo**mos**
gloomy	**sumbru**	**soom**broo
impressive	**impresionant**	eempresyo**nant**
interesting	**interesant**	eenteres**sant**
magnificent	**magnific**	mag**nee**feec
pretty	**drăguţ**	drer**goots**
strange	**straniu**	**stran**yoo
superb	**superb**	soo**perb**
terrifying	**îngrozitor**	uhngrozee**tor**
tremendous	**nemaipomenit**	neh-mighpome**neet**
ugly	**urât**	oo**ruht**

Churches—Religious services *Biserici—Slujbe religioase*

The Orthodox religion is the national religion in Romania, though others are also practised.

Is there a … near here?	**Există o … prin apropiere?**	eg**zees**ter o … preen apropee-**e**reh
Catholic church	**biserică catolică**	bee**se**reecer ca**to**leecer
Orthodox church	**biserică ortodoxă**	bee**se**reecer orto**dox**er
Protestant church	**biserică protestantă**	bee**se**reecer protes**tan**ter
mosque	**moschee**	mos**ke**-yeh
synagogue	**sinagogă**	seena**go**ger
What time is …?	**La ce ora este …?**	la cheh **o**rer **yes**teh
mass/the service	**slujba**	**sloozh**ba
Where can I find a … who speaks English?	**Unde pot găsi un … care vorbeşte englezeşte?**	**oon**deh pot ger**see** oon … **ca**reh vor**besh**teh engle**zesh**teh
priest/minister/rabbi	**preot/pastor/rabin**	**pre**-ot/**pas**tor/**ra**been
I'd like to visit the church.	**Aş vrea să vizitez biserica.**	ash vreh-a ser veezee**tez** bee**se**reeca
I'd like to go to confession.	**Aş vrea să merg să mă spovedesc.**	ash vreh-a ser merg ser mer spove**desc**

In the countryside *La ţară*

Is there a scenic route to …?	**Este vreun traseu turistic spre …?**	**yes**teh vroon tra**se**^{oo} **tooreest**eec spreh
How far is it to …?	**Este departe până la …?**	**yes**teh de**par**teh **puh**ner la
Can we walk there?	**Putem merge pe jos până acolo?**	poo**tem mer**jeh peh zhos **puh**ner a**co**lo
What kind of … is that?	**Ce fel de … este acesta/aceasta?**	cheh fel deh … **yes**teh a**ches**ta/a**chas**ta
animal	**animal**	anee**mal**
bird	**pasăre**	**pa**serreh
flower	**floare**	**flwa**reh
tree	**copac**	co**pac**

Landmarks *Puncte de reper*

bridge	**pod**	pod
cliff	**stâncă**	**stuhn**cer
farm	**fermă**	**fer**mer
field	**câmp**	cuhmp
footpath	**potecă**	po**te**cer
forest	**pădure**	per**doo**reh
garden	**grădină**	grer**dee**ner
hill	**deal**	dal
house	**casă**	**ca**ser
lake	**lac**	lac
meadow	**pajişte**	**pa**zheeshteh
mountain	**munte**	**moon**teh
(mountain) pass	**trecătoare**	trecer**twa**reh
path	**potecă**	po**te**cer
peak	**vârf**	vuhrf
pond	**iaz**	yaz
river	**râu**	ruh^{oo}
road	**drum**	droom
sea	**mare**	**ma**reh
spring	**izvor**	eez**vor**
valley	**vale**	**va**leh
village	**sat**	sat
vineyard	**vie**	**vee**-eh
wall	**zid**	zeed
waterfall	**cascadă**	cas**ca**der
wood	**pădure**	per**doo**reh

ASKING THE WAY, see page 76

Relaxing

Cinema (movies)—Theatre *Cinema—Teatru*

Going to the cinema is a popular pastime in Romania. Both national films and subtitled foreign films are regularly screened. You can find out what's on from the local newspapers.

What's on at the cinema tonight?	**Ce film rulează la cinema diseară?**	cheh feelm roo**la**zer la cheene**ma** de**sa**rer
What's playing at the … Theatre?	**Ce piesă se joacă la Teatrul …**	cheh **pye**ser seh **zhwa**cer la **ta**trool
What sort of play is it?	**Ce fel de piesă este?**	cheh fel deh **pye**ser **yes**teh
Who's it by?	**De cine este?**	deh **chee**neh **yes**teh
Can you recommend (a) …?	**Puteţi recomanda …?**	poo**tets**^{y} recoman**da**
good film	**un film bun**	oon feelm boon
comedy	**o comedie**	o come**dee**-eh
musical	**o comedie muzicală**	o come**dee**-eh moozee**ca**ler
Where's that new film directed by … being shown?	**Unde rulează acel nou film regizat**	**oon**deh roo**la**zer a**chel** no^{OO} **fee**lm rejee**zat**
	de …	deh
Who's in it?	**Cine joacă?**	**chee**neh **zhwa**cer
Who's playing the lead?	**Cine joacă rolul principal?**	**chee**neh **zhwa**cer **ro**lool preenchee**pal**
Who's the director?	**Cine a regizat filmul?**	**chee**neh a rejee**zat** **feel**mool
At which theatre is that new play by … being performed?	**La ce teatru se joacă noua piesă a lui …?**	la cheh **ta**troo seh **zhwa**cer **no**wa **pye**ser a loo^{y}
What time does it begin?	**La ce oră începe?**	la cheh **o**rer uhn**che**peh
Are there any seats for tonight?	**Sunt locuri pentru diseară?**	soont **lo**coor^{y} **pen**troo de**sa**rer
How much are the seats?	**Cât costă un bilet?**	cuht **cos**ter oon bee**let**

I'd like to reserve 2 seats for the show on Friday evening.	**Aş vrea să rezerv 2 locuri pentru spectacolul de vineri seara.**	ash vreh-a ser re**zerv** 2 lo**coor**ʸ **pen**troo spec**ta**colool deh **vee**nerʸ **sa**ra
Can I have a ticket for the matinée on Tuesday?	**Aveţi un bilet pentru marţi la matineu?**	a**vets**ʸ oon bee**let** **pen**troo martsʸ la mateene**oo**
I'd like a seat in the stalls (orchestra).	**Aş vrea un loc în stal.**	ash vreh-a oon loc uhn stal
Not too far back.	**Nu prea în spate.**	noo preh-a uhn **spa**teh
Somewhere in the middle.	**Undeva pe la mijloc.**	oonde**va** peh la **meezh**loc
How much are the seats in the circle (mezzanine)?	**Cât costă biletele la balcon?**	cuht **cos**ter bee**le**teleh la bal**con**
May I have a programme, please?	**Pot avea un program,vă rog?**	pot **aveh-a** oon pro**gram** ver rog
Where's the cloakroom?	**Unde este garderoba?**	**oon**deh **yes**teh garde**ro**ba

YOU MAY HEAR:

Regret, nu mai sunt bilete.	I'm sorry, we're sold out.
Mai sunt doar câteva bilete la balcon.	There are only a few seats left in the circle (mezzanine).
Biletul, vă rog!	May I see your ticket?
Acesta este locul dumneavoastră.	This is your seat.

Opera—Ballet—Concert *Operă—Balet—Concert*

Can you recommend a(n) …?	**Puteţi recomanda …?**	poo**tets**ʸ recoman**da**
ballet	**un balet**	oon ba**let**
concert	**un concert**	oon con**chert**
opera	**o operă**	o **o**perer
operetta	**o operetă**	o ope**re**ter

DAYS OF THE WEEK, see page 151

Where's the opera house/the concert hall?	**Unde este Opera/ sala de concert?**	**oon**deh **yes**teh **o**pera/ **sa**la deh con**chert**
What's on at the opera tonight?	**Ce se joacă la operă deseară?**	cheh seh **zhwa**car la **o**perer de**sa**rer
Who's singing/ dancing?	**Cine cântă/ dansează?**	**chee**neh **cuhn**ter/ dan**sa**zer
Which orchestra is playing?	**Ce orchestră cântă?**	cheh or**kes**trer **cuhn**ter
What are they playing?	**Ce cântă?**	cheh **cuhn**ter
Who's the conductor/ soloist?	**Cine dirijează/ Cine este solist?**	**chee**neh deeree**zha**zer/ **chee**neh **yes**teh so**leest**

Nightclubs *Cluburi de noapte*

Can you recommend a good nightclub?	**Puteţi să recomandaţi un club de noapte bun?**	poo**tets**ʸ ser recoman-**dats**ʸ oon cloob deh **nwap**teh boon
Is there a floor show?	**Este un spectacol în mijlocul publicului?**	**yes**teh oon spec**ta**col uhn **meezh**locool **poo**bleecooloo ʸ
What time does the show start?	**La ce oră începe spectacolul?**	la cheh **o**rer uhn**che**peh spec**ta**colool
Is evening dress required?	**Ţinuta este obligatorie?**	tsee**noo**ta **yes**teh obleega**to**ree-e

Discos *Discoteci*

Where can we go dancing?	**Unde putem merge să dansăm?**	**oon**deh poo**tem mer**jeh ser dan**serm**
Is there a discotheque in town?	**Exista o discotecă în oraş?**	eg**zees**ter o deesco**te**cer uhn o**rash**
Would you like to dance?	**Vreţi să dansati?**	vretsʸ ser dan**sats**ʸ

Sports *Sport*

Romanians love both outdoor and indoor sports. Football is the most popular and every city has its own team. Handball, basketball, tennis and rugby also have a good following. Winter sports are widely enjoyed, and there are well-equipped ski resorts at Sinaia, Predeal, Poiana and Braşov.

For information about sporting events, contact the National Tourist Office or buy the local sports paper *Sportul*.

Is there a football (soccer) match anywhere this Saturday?	**Este vreun meci de fotbal pe undeva sâmbăta asta?**	**yes**teh vroon mech^y deh **fot**bal peh oon**deva** **suhm**berta **asta**
Which teams are playing?	**Ce echipe joacă?**	cheh e**kee**peh **zhwa**cer
Can you get me a ticket?	**Puteţi să-mi luaţi şi mie un bilet?**	poo**tets**^y serm^y lwats^y shee **mee**-eh oon bee**let**

basketball	**baschet**	**bas**ket
boxing	**box**	box
car racing	**raliu**	ra**lee**^oo
cycling	**ciclism**	chee**cleesm**
football (soccer)	**fotbal**	**fot**bal
horse racing	**curse de cai**	**coor**seh deh cay
(horse-back) riding	**călărie**	cerler**ree**-eh
mountaineering	**alpinism**	alpee**neesm**
skiing	**schi**	skee
swimming	**înot**	uh**not**
tennis	**tenis**	**te**nees
volleyball	**voleibal**	**vo**leybal

I'd like to see a boxing match.	**Aş vrea să văd un meci de box.**	ash vreh-a ser verd oon mech^y deh box
What's the admission charge?	**Cât costă biletul de intrare?**	cuht **cos**ter bee**le**tool deh een**tra**reh
Where's the nearest golf course?	**Unde este terenul de golf cel mai apropiat?**	**oon**deh **yes**teh te**re**nool deh golf chel migh apropee-**at**
Where are the tennis courts?	**Unde se află terenurile de tenis?**	**oon**deh seh **a**fler te**re**nooreeleh deh **te**nees
What's the charge per …?	**Cât costă pe …?**	cuht **cos**ter peh
day/round/hour	**zi/meci/oră**	zee/mech^y/**o**rer
Can I hire (rent) rackets?	**Pot să închiriez rachete de tenis?**	pot ser uhnkeeree-**ez** ra**ke**teh deh **te**nees
Where's the race course (track)?	**Unde este hipodromul?**	**oon**deh **yes**teh heepo**dro**mool

Is there any good fishing/hunting around here?	**Există un loc bun de pescuit/vânat prin împrejurimi?**	eg**zee**ster oon loc boon deh pescoo**eet**/vuh**nat** preen uhmprezhoo**reem**^{y}
Do I need a permit?	**Am nevoie de permis?**	am ne**vo**-yeh deh per**mees**
Where can I get one?	**De unde pot obţine un permis?**	deh **oon**deh pot ob**tsee**neh oon per**mees**
Can one swim in the lake/river?	**E permis înotul în lac/râu?**	yeh per**mees** uh**no**tool uhn lac/ruh^{oo}
Is there a swimming pool here?	**Există o piscină aici?**	eg**zee**ster o pees**chee**ner a-**eech**^{y}
Is it open-air or indoor?	**Este piscină în aer liber sau bazin acoperit?**	**yes**teh pees**chee**ner uhn aer **lee**ber sa^{oo} ba**zeen** acope**reet**
Is it heated?	**Apa bazinului este încalzită?**	**a**pa ba**zee**noolooʸ **yes**teh uhncerl**zee**ter

On the beach La plajă

The Black Sea resorts are very popular for their smooth sandy beaches and beautiful hot weather during summer months. Mamaia, the 'pearl' of the Black Sea, offers the sandiest beach.

Is there a sandy beach?	**Există o plajă cu nisip?**	eg**zee**ste o **pla**zher coo nee**seep**
Is it dangerous to swim here?	**Înotul aici este periculos?**	**uhno**tool a-**eech**^{y} **yes**teh pereecoo**los**
Is there a lifeguard?	**Există salvamar?**	eg**zee**ster salva**mar**
Is it safe for children?	**Nu este periculos pentru copii?**	noo **yes**teh pereecoo**los** **pen**troo co**pee**
The sea is very calm.	**Marea este foarte liniştită.**	**ma**reh-a **yes**teh **fwar**teh leenee**shtee**ter
There are some big waves.	**Sunt nişte valuri mari.**	soont **neesh**teh **va**loor^{y} mar^{y}
Are there any dangerous currents?	**Sunt curenţi periculoşi?**	soont coo**rents**^{y} pereecoo**losh**^{y}
I want to hire (rent) a/an/ some…	**Vreau să închiriez…**	vra^{oo} ser uhnkeeree-**ez**
bathing hut (cabana)	**o cabină**	o ca**bee**ner
deck chair	**un şezlong**	oon shez**long**
motorboat	**o barcă cu motor**	o **bar**cer coo mo**tor**
rowing-boat	**o barcă cu rame**	o **bar**cer coo **ra**meh

sailing boat	**o barcă cu pânze**	o barcer coo **puhn**zeh
skin-diving equipment	**un echipament de plonjat**	oon ekeepa**ment** deh plon**zhat**
sunshade (umbrella)	**o umbrelă de soare**	o oom**bre**ler deh **swa**reh
surfboard	**un acuaplan/ o planşă de surf**	oon acwa**plan/** o **plan**sher deh surf
water-skis	**nişte schiuri nautice**	**neesh**teh **skee**oor^{y} na**oo**teecheh
windsurfer	**o planşă de windsurf**	o **plan**sher deh **weend**surf

PLAJĂ PARTICULARĂ	PRIVATE BEACH
ÎNOTUL INTERZIS	NO SWIMMING

Winter sports *Sporturi de iarnă*

Is there a skating rink near here?	**Există un patinoar prin apropiere?**	eg**zees**ter oon patee**nwar** preen apropee-**e**reh
I'd like to ski.	**Aş vrea să schiez.**	ash vreh-a ser skee-**ez**
Are there any ski runs for …?	**Sunt piste de schi pentru…?**	soont **pees**teh deh skee **pen**troo
beginners	**începători**	uhncheper**tor**^{y}
average skiers	**schiori de nivel mediu**	skee**or**^{y} deh nee**vel** **me**dyoo
good skiers	**schiori buni**	skee**or**^{y} boon^{y}
Can I take skiing lessons?	**Pot să iau lecţii de schiat?**	pot ser ya^{oo} **lec**tsee deh skee**at**
Are there any ski lifts?	**Există teleschi?**	eg**zees**ter tele**skee**
I want to hire…	**Vreau să închiriez…**	vra^{oo} ser uhnkeeree-**ez**
poles	**o prăjină**	o prer**zhee**ner
skates	**nişte patine**	**neesh**teh pa**tee**neh
ski boots	**nişte ghete de schi**	**neesh**teh **ge**teh deh skee
skiing equipment	**un echipament de schi**	oon ekeepa**ment** deh skee
skis	**nişte schiuri**	**neesh**teh **skee**oor^{y}

Making friends

Introductions *Prezentări*

Romanians have a reputation for being outgoing and friendly, and you should have no problem making friends. However, it is regarded as impolite if you address someone you don't know very well using the informal *tu*. This privilege is reserved for relatives, close friends and young people of a similar age and professional standing. You should use the formal *dumneavoastră* until your acquaintance makes it clear that he or she wants you to use the more familiar form of address.

May I introduce...?	**Daţi-mi voie să vă prezint pe...?**	**dat**seem^y **vo**yeh ser ver pre**zeent** peh
Mihai, this is ...	**Mihai, ţi-l prezint pe...**	mee**hay** tseel pre**zeent** peh
My name is...	**Mă numesc...**	mer noo**mesc**
Pleased to meet you!	**Încântat de cunoştinţă!**	uhncuhn**tat** deh coonosh**teen**tser
What's your name?	**Cum vă numiţi?**	coom ver noo**meets**^{y}
How are you?	**Ce mai faceţi?**	cheh migh **fa**chets^y
Fine, thanks. And you?	**Bine, mulţumesc. Şi dumneavoastră?**	**bee**neh mooltsoo**mesc.** shee doomna**vwas**trer

Follow up *Pentru a sparge gheaţa*

How long have you been here?	**De câtă vreme sunteţi aici?**	deh c**uh**ter **vre**meh **soon**tets^y a-**eech**^{y}
We've been here a week.	**Suntem aici de o săptămână.**	**soon**tem a-**eech**^{y} deh o serpter**muh**ner
Is this your first visit?	**Aceasta este prima vizită?**	**ach**as**ta yes**teh **pree**ma **vee**zeeter
No, we came here last year.	**Nu, am fost aici şi anul trecut.**	noo am fost a-**eech**^{y} shee **a**nool tre**coot**
Are you enjoying your stay?	**Vă place aici?**	ver **pla**cheh a-**eech**^{y}
Yes, I like it very much.	**Da, îmi place foarte mult.**	da uhm^y **pla**cheh **fwar**teh moolt
I like the scenery a lot.	**Îmi place peisajul foarte mult.**	uhm^y **pla**cheh pay**sa**-zhool **fwar**teh moolt

What do you think of the country/people?	**Ce părere aveţi despre ţară/oameni?**	cheh per**re**reh a**vets**^{y} **des**preh **tsa**rer/**wa**men^{y}
Where do you come from?	**De unde veniţi?**	deh **oon**deh ve**neets**^{y}
I'm from…	**Vin din…**	veen deen
What nationality are you?	**Ce naţionalitate aveţi?**	cheh natsyonalee**ta**teh a**vets**^{y}
I'm…	**Sunt…**	soont
American	**american**	ameree**can**
British	**britanic**	bree**ta**neec
Canadian	**canadian**	canadee-**an**
English	**englez**	eng**lez**
Irish	**irlandez**	eerlan**dez**
Where are you staying?	**Unde locuiţi?**	**oon**deh locoo**eets**^{y}
Are you on your own?	**Sunteţi singur?**	**soon**tets^{y} **seen**goor
I'm with my…	**Sunt cu…**	soont coo
wife	**soţia mea**	so**tsee**a meh-a
husband	**soţul meu**	**so**tsool me^{oo}
family	**familia mea**	fa**mee**lee-a meh-a
children	**copiii mei**	co**pee**-ee may
parents	**părinţii mei**	per**reen**tsee may
boyfriend/girlfriend	**prietenul meu/ prietena mea**	pree-**e**tenool me^{oo}/ pree-**e**tena meh-a

father/mother	**tata/mama**	**ta**ta/**ma**ma
son/daughter	**băiat/fată**	ber**yat**/**fa**ter
brother/sister	**frate/soră**	**fra**teh/**so**rer
uncle/aunt	**unchi/mătuşă**	oonk^{y}/mer**too**sher
nephew/niece	**nepot/nepoată**	ne**pot**/nep**wa**ter
cousin	**văr**	verr

Are you married/ single?	**Sunteţi căsătorit/ necăsătorit?**	**soon**tets^{y} cerserto**reet**/ necerserto**reet**
Do you have children?	**Aveţi copii?**	a**vets**^{y} co**pee**
What do you do?	**Cu ce vă ocupaţi?**	coo cheh ver ocoo**pats**^{y}
I'm a student.	**Sunt student.**	soont stoo**dent**

COUNTRIES, see page 146

What are you studying?	**Ce studiaţi?**	cheh stoodee-**ats**^{y}
I'm here on a business trip/ on holiday.	**Sunt aici în interes de serviciu/ în vacanţă.**	soont a-**eech**^{y} uhn eente**res** deh ser**vee**choo/ uhn va**can**tser
Do you travel a lot?	**Călătoriţi mult?**	cerlerto**reets**^{y} moolt
Do you play cards/ chess?	**Jucaţi cărţi/şah?**	zhoo**cats**^{y} certs^{y}/shah

The weather *Vremea*

What a lovely day!	**Ce zi frumoasă!**	cheh zee froo**mwa**ser
What awful weather!	**Ce vreme urâtă!**	cheh **vre**meh oo**ruh**ter
Isn't it cold/ hot today?	**Nu-i aşa că e frig/ cald afară?**	noo^{y} a**sha** cer yeh freeg/ cald a**fa**rer
Is it usually as warm as this?	**E de obicei aşa de cald?**	yeh deh obee**chay** **a**sha deh cald
Do you think it's going to… tomorrow?	**Credeţi că va fi … mâine?**	**cre**dets^{y} cer va fee … **muh**yneh
be a nice day	**frumos**	froo**mos**
rain	**ploaie**	**plwa**-yeh
snow	**zăpadă**	zer**pa**der
What's the weather forecast?	**Ce vreme se prevede?**	cheh **vre**meh seh pre**ve**deh

cloud	**nori**	nor^{y}
fog	**ceaţă**	**cha**tser
frost	**ger**	jer
ice	**gheaţă**	**ga**tser
lightning	**fulgere**	**fool**jereh
moon	**lună**	**loo**ner
rain	**ploaie**	**plwa**-yeh
sky	**cer**	cher
snow	**zăpadă**	zer**pa**der
star	**stea**	steh-a
sun	**soare**	**swa**reh
thunder	**tunet**	**too**net
thunderstorm	**furtună**	foor**too**ner
wind	**vânt**	vuhnt

Invitations *Invitaţii*

Would you like to have dinner with us on…?	**Vreţi să veniţi să luăm masa de seară împreună…?**	vrets^y^ ser ve**neets**^y^ ser lwerm **ma**sa deh sarer uhmpre-**oo**ner
May I invite you to lunch?	**Vreţi să luaţi masa de prânz cu mine?**	vrets^y^ ser lwats^y^ **ma**sa deh pruhnz coo **mee**neh
Can you come round for a drink this evening?	**Pot să vă invit la o băutură deseară?**	pot ser ver een**veet** la o beroo**too**rer de**sa**rer
There's a party. Are you coming?	**Dau o petrecere. Veniţi?**	da^oo^ oh pe**tre**chereh. ve**neets**^y^
That's very kind of you.	**Sunteţi foarte amabil.**	**soon**tets^y^ **fwar**teh a**ma**beel
Great. I'd love to come.	**Da, cu multă plăcere.**	da coo **mool**ter pler**che**reh
What time shall we come?	**La ce oră să venim?**	la cheh **o**rer ser ve**neem**
May I bring a friend?	**Pot să aduc un prieten?**	pot ser a**dooc** oon pree-**e**ten
I'm afraid we have to leave now.	**Regret, trebuie să plecăm.**	re**gret tre**booyeh ser **ple**cerm
Next time you must come to visit us.	**E rândul dumneavoastră să ne vizitaţi.**	yeh **ruh**ndool doomna**vwas**trer ser neh veezee**tats**^y^
Thanks for the evening. It was great.	**Mulţumim pentru invitaţie. Ne-am simţit foarte bine.**	mooltsoo**meem pen**troo eenvee**ta**tsee-eh. neh-**am** seem**tseet fwar**teh **bee**neh

Dating *Întâlniri*

Do you mind if I smoke?	**Vă deranjează dacă fumez?**	ver deran**zha**zer **da**cer foo**mez**
Would you like a cigarette?	**Doriţi o ţigară?**	do**reets**^y^ o tsee**ga**rer
Do you have a light, please?	**Aveţi un foc, vă rog?**	a**vets**^y^ oon foc ver rog
Why are you laughing?	**De ce râdeţi?**	de cheh **ruh**dets^y^
Is my Romanian that bad?	**Vorbesc aşa de rău româneşte?**	vor**besc asha** deh roh romuh**nesh**teh
Do you mind if I sit here?	**Pot sta aici?**	pot sta a-**eech**^y^

Can I get you a drink?	**Ce doriţi să beţi?**	cheh do**reets**^{y} ser bets^{y}
Are you waiting for someone?	**Aşteptaţi pe cineva?**	ashtep**tats**^{y} peh cheene**va**
Are you free this evening?	**Sunteţi liber/ liberă deseară?**	**soon**tets^{y} **lee**ber/ **lee**berer des**a**rer
Would you like to go out with me tonight?	**Putem ieşi împreună deseară?**	poo**tem** ye**shee** uhmpre-**oo**ner des**a**rer
Would you like to go dancing?	**Aţi vrea să mergem să dansăm?**	ats^{y} vreh-a ser **mer**jem ser dan**serm**
I know a good discotheque.	**Ştiu o discotecă bună.**	shtee^{oo} o deesco**te**cer **boo**ner
Shall we go to the cinema (movies)?	**Vreţi să mergem la cinema?**	vrets^{y} ser **mer**jem la cheene**ma**
Would you like to go for a drive?	**Vreţi să ne plimbăm cu maşina?**	vrets^{y} ser neh pleem**berm** coo ma**shee**na
Where shall we meet?	**Unde ne întâlnim?**	**oon**deh neh uhntuhl**neem**
I'll pick you up at your hotel.	**O să vin să vă iau de la hotel**	o ser veen ser ver ya^{oo} deh la ho**tel**
I'll call for you at 8.	**O să vin la ora 8.**	o ser veen la **o**ra opt.
May I take you home?	**Vă pot conduce acasă?**	ver pot con**doo**cheh a**ca**ser
Can I see you again tomorrow?	**Ne putem întâlni din nou mâine?**	**neh** poo**tem** uhntuhl**nee** deen no^{oo} m**uhy**neh
I hope we'll meet again.	**Sper să ne întâlnim din nou.**	sper ser neh uhntuhl**neem** deen no^{oo}

… and you might answer:

I'd love to, thank you.	**Mulţumesc, cu plăcere.**	mooltsoo**mesc** coo pler**che**reh
Thank you, but . I'm busy	**Mulţumesc, sunt ocupat/ ocupată.**	mooltsoo**mesc** soont oco**opat**/ocoo**pa**ter
No, I'm not interested, thank you.	**Mulţumesc, nu mă interesează.**	mooltsoo**mesc** noo mer eenteres**a**zer
Leave me alone, please!	**Lasaţi-mă în pace, vă rog!**	las**at**see-mer uhn **pa**cheh ver rog
Thank you, it's been a wonderful evening.	**Mulţumesc, a fost o seară minunată.**	mooltsoo**mesc** a fost o seh-**a**rer meenoo**na**ter
I've enjoyed myself.	**M-am distrat foarte bine.**	mam dees**trat fwar**teh **bee**neh

Shopping Guide

This shopping guide is designed to help you find what you want with ease, accuracy and speed. It features:

1. A list of all major shops, stores and services (p. 98).
2. Some general expressions required when shopping to allow you to be specific and selective (p. 100).
3. Full details of the shops and services most likely to concern you. Here you'll find advice, alphabetical lists of items and conversion charts listed under the headings below.

Shops, stores and services *Magazine şi servicii*

Opening hours vary. As a general rule, state-owned shops are open from 8am until 8pm, although some privately owned shops stay open around the clock. Department stores are open from 9am until 8pm or 9pm. All shops stay open on Saturdays and quite a few open on Sundays too, so one can buy food at practically any time.

Romanians usually buy fresh fruit, vegetables and herbs from open-air markets, *piaţa,* which can be found all over Bucharest and other cities.

Where's the nearest ...?	**Unde este prin apropiere ...?**	**oon**deh **yes**teh preen apropee-**e**reh
antique shop	**un magazin de antichităţi**	oon maga**zeen** deh anteekee**terts**ʸ
art gallery	**o galerie de artă**	o galer**ee**-eh deh **ar**ter
baker's	**o brutărie**	o brooter**ree-**eh
bank	**o bancă**	o **ban**cer
barber's	**o frizerie**	o freezeh**ree**-eh
beauty salon	**un salon de cosmetică**	oon sa**lon** deh cos**me**teecer
bookshop	**o librărie**	o leebrer**ree-**eh
butcher's	**o măcelărie**	o merchelerr**ee-**eh
camera shop	**un magazin foto**	oon maga**zeen** foto
chemist's	**o farmacie**	o farma**chee**-eh
delicatessen	**un magazin de delicatese**	oon maga**zeen** deh deleeca**te**seh
dentist	**un cabinet dentar**	oon cabee**net** den**tar**
department store	**un magazin universal**	oon maga**zeen** ooneever**sal**
drugstore	**o farmacie**	o farma**chee**-eh
dry cleaner's	**o curăţătorie**	o coorertsertor**ee**-eh
electrical goods shop	**un magazin de aparatură electrică**	oon maga**zeen** deh apara**too**rer ele**c**treecer
fishmonger's	**o pescărie**	o pescer-**ree**-eh
florist's	**o florărie**	o florer-**ree**-eh
greengrocer's	**un aprozar**	oon apro**zar**
grocer's	**o băcănie**	o bercer**nee**-eh
hospital	**un spital**	oon spee**tal**

LAUNDRY, see page 29/HAIRDRESSER'S see page 30

ironmonger's	**o fierărie**	o fyerer**ree**-eh
jeweller's	**un magazin de bijuterii**	oon maga**zeen** deh beezhooter**ee**
launderette	**o spălătorie/ curăţătorie Nufărul**	o sperlerto**ree**-eh/ coorertserto**ree**-eh **noo**ferrool
laundry	**o spălătorie**	o sperlerto-**ree**-eh
library	**o bibliotecă**	o beeblee-o**te**cer
market	**o piaţă**	o **pya**tser
newsstand	**un chioşc de ziare**	oon kyoshc deh zee-**a**reh
optician	**un optician**	oon opteechee-**an**
pastry shop	**o plăcintărie**	o plercheenter**ree**-eh
photographer	**un atelier de fotografiat**	oon atelee-**er** deh fotografee**at**
police station	**un post de poliţie**	oon post deh po**lee**tsee-eh
post office	**o poştă**	o **posh**ter
second-hand bookshop	**un anticariat**	oon anteecaree-**at**
shoemaker's (repairs)	**o cizmărie**	o cheezmer**ree**-eh
shoe shop	**un magazin de încălţăminte**	oon maga**zeen** deh uhncerltser**meen**teh
shopping centre	**un centru comercial**	oon **chen**troo comerchee-**al**
souvenir shop	**un magazin de suveniruri**	oon maga**zeen** deh sooveneeroor[y]
stationer's	**o papetărie**	o papeter**ree**-eh
supermarket	**un magazin alimentar**	oon maga**zeen** aleemen**tar**
tailor's	**o croitorie**	o croeeto**ree**-eh
tobacconist's	**o tutungerie**	o tootoonjeh**ree**-eh
toy shop	**un magazin de jucării**	oon maga**zeen** deh zhoocer-**ree**
travel agency	**o agenţie de voiaj**	o ajen**tsee**-eh deh vo**yazh**
veterinarian	**un veterinar**	oon veteree**nar**
watchmaker's	**o ceasornicărie**	o chasorneecer**ree**-eh

General expressions *Expresii de uz general*

Where? *Unde?*

Where's there a good …?	**Unde este un/o … de bună calitate?**	**oon**deh **yes**teh oon/o … deh **boo**ner calee**ta**teh
Where can I find a …?	**Unde se găseşte un/o …?**	**oon**deh seh ger**sesh**teh oon/o
Where's the main shopping area?	**Unde este centrul comercial principal?**	**oon**deh **yes**teh **chen**trool comerchee-**al** preenchee**pal**
Is it far from here?	**Este departe de aici?**	**yes**teh de**par**teh deh a-**eech**ʸ
How do I get there?	**Cum se ajunge acolo?**	coom seh a**zhoon**jeh a**co**lo

SOLDURI	SALE

Service *Servicii*

Can you help me?	**Puteţi să mă ajutaţi?**	poo**tets**ʸ ser mer azhoo**tats**ʸ
I'm just looking.	**Mă uit doar.**	mer ooyt dwar
Do you sell …?	**Vindeţi …?**	**veen**detsʸ
I'd like to buy …	**Aş vrea să cumpăr …**	ash vreh-a ser **coom**perr
I'd like …	**Aş vrea …**	ash vreh-a
Can you show me some …?	**Puteţi să-mi arătaţi nişte …?**	poo**tets**ʸ sermʸ arer**tats**ʸ **neesh**teh
Do you have any …?	**Aveţi …?**	a**vets**ʸ
Where's the … department?	**Unde este raionul de …**	**oon**deh **yes**teh ray**o**nool deh…
Where is the lift (elevator)/escalator?	**Unde este liftul/ escalatorul?**	**oon**deh **yes**teh **leef**tool/ escala**to**rool

INTRARE	ENTRANCE
IEȘIRE	EXIT
IEȘIRE DE INCENDIU	EMERGENCY EXIT
INVENTAR	CLOSED FOR STOCKTAKING

That one *Acela*

Can you show me …?	**Puteţi să-mi arătaţi …**	poo**tets**ʸ serm**ʸ** arer**tats**ʸ
this/that	**acesta/acela**	a**ches**ta/a**che**la
the one in the window	**pe cel din vitrină**	peh chel deen vee**tree**ner

Defining the article *Descrierea obiectului*

I'd like a … one.	**Aş vrea una …**	ash vreh-a **oo**na
big	**mare**	**ma**reh
cheap	**ieftină**	**yef**teener
dark	**închisă la culoare**	uhn**kee**ser la cool**wa**reh
good	**bună**	**boo**ner
heavy	**grea**	greh-a
large	**largă**	**lar**ger
light (weight)	**uşoară**	oo**shwa**rer
light (colour)	**deschisă la culoare**	des**kee**ser la cool**wa**reh
oval	**ovală**	o**va**ler
rectangular	**rectangulară**	rectangoo**la**rer
round	**rotundă**	ro**toon**der
small	**mică**	**mee**cer
square	**pătrată**	per**tra**ter
sturdy	**durabilă**	doo**ra**beeler
I don't want anything too expensive.	**Nu vreau nimic prea scump.**	noo vra°° nee**meec** preh-a scoomp

Preference *Preferinţe*

Can you show me some others?	**Puteţi să-mi arătaţi şi altele?**	poo**tets**ʸ serm**ʸ** arer**tats**ʸ shee **al**teleh
Don't you have anything …?	**Nu aveţi ceva …?**	noo a**vets**ʸ che**va**
cheaper/better	**mai ieftin/mai bun**	migh **yef**teen/ migh boon
larger/smaller	**mai mare/mai mic**	migh **ma**reh/ migh meec

How much *Cât costă*

How much is this?	**Cât costă aceasta?**	cuht **co**ster a**chas**ta
How much are they?	**Cât costă acestea?**	cuht **co**ster a**ches**teh-a
I don't understand.	**Nu înţeleg.**	noo uhntse**leg**
Please write it down.	**Vă rog scrieţi asta.**	ver rog **scree**-etsʸ **as**ta

COLOURS see page 112

I don't want to spend more than … lei.	**Nu vreau să cheltuiesc mai mult de … lei.**	noo vra^{oo} ser keltoo**yesc** migh moolt deh … lay

Decision *Decizii*

It's not quite what I want.	**Nu este chiar ce vreau eu.**	noo **yes**teh kyar cheh vra^{oo} ye^{oo}
No, I don't like it.	**Nu-mi place.**	noom^{y} **pla**cheh
I'll take it.	**Îl cumpăr.**	uhl **coom**perr

Ordering *A face o comandă*

Can you order it for me?	**Îl puteţi comanda?**	uhl poo**tets^{y}** coman**da**
How long will it take?	**Cât timp va dura?**	cuht teemp va doo**ra**

Delivery *Livrarea*

I'll take it with me.	**Îl iau cu mine.**	uhl ya^{oo} coo **mee**neh
Deliver it to the … Hotel.	**Livraţi-l la Hotelul …**	lee**vra**tseel la ho**te**lool
Please send it to this address.	**Vă rog să-l livraţi la această adresă.**	ver rog serl lee**vrats^{y}** la a**cha**ster a**dre**ser
Will I have any difficulty with the customs?	**Credeţi că pot avea dificultaţi la vamă?**	**cre**dets^{y} cer pot a**veh-a** deefeecool**terts^{y}** la **va**mer

Paying *Plata*

How much is it?	**Cât costă?**	cuht **cos**ter
Can I pay by traveller's cheque?	**Pot plăti cu cec de călătorie?**	pot pler**tee** coo chec deh cerlerto**ree**-eh
Do you accept dollars/pounds?	**Primiţi dolari/ lire sterline?**	pree**meets^{y}** do**lar^{y}**/ **lee**reh ster**lee**neh
Do you accept credit cards?	**Acceptaţi cărţi de credit?**	acchep**tats^{y}** certs^{y} deh **cre**deet
Do I have to pay the VAT (sales tax)?	**Trebuie să plătesc TVA?**	**tre**booyeh ser pler**tesc** teh-veh-a
I think there's a mistake in the bill.	**Cred că este o greşeală în nota de plată.**	cred cer **yes**teh o gre**sha**ler uhn **no**ta deh **pla**ter

Anything else? *Mai doriţi ceva?*

No, thanks, that's all.	**Nu, mulţumesc, asta-i tot.**	noo mooltsoo**mesc** **as**tay tot
Yes, I'd like …	**Da, aş vrea …**	da ash vreh-a
Can you show me …?	**Puteţi să-mi arătaţi … ?**	poo**tets**^{y} serm^{y} arer**tats**^{y}
May I have a bag, please?	**Puteţi să-mi daţi o pungă, vă rog?**	poo**tets**^{y} serm^{y} dats^{y} o **poon**ger ver rog
Could you wrap it up for me, please?	**Vreţi să-l împache taţi,vă rog?**	vrets^{y} serl uhmpake**tats**^{y} ver rog
May I have a receipt?	**Puteţi să-mi daţi, vă rog, o chitanţă?**	poo**tets**^{y} serm^{y} dats^{y} ver rog o kee**tan**tser

Dissatisfied? *Nemulţumit?*

Can you exchange this, please?	**Puteţi să-mi schimbaţi aceasta, vă rog?**	poo**tets**^{y} serm^{y} skeem**bats**^{y} a**chas**ta ver rog
I want to return this.	**Vreau să înapoiez aceasta.**	vra^{oo} ser uhnapo**yez** a**chas**ta
I'd like a refund. Here's the receipt.	**Aş vrea banii înapoi. Poftiţi chitanţa.**	ash vreh-a **ba**nee uhna**poy.** pof**teets**^{y} kee**tan**tsa

YOU MAY HEAR:

Cu ce vă pot ajuta?	Can I help you?
Ce doriţi?	What would you like?
Ce … doriţi?	What … would you like?
culoare/măsură/calitate	colour/shape/quality
Regret, dar nu mai avem.	I'm sorry, we don't have any.
S-a terminat stocul.	We're out of stock.
Vreţi să vi-l comandăm?	Shall we order it for you?
Îl luaţi cu dumneavoastră sau vreţi să vi-l expediem noi?	Will you take it with you or shall we send it?
Mai doriţi ceva?	Anything else?
Aceasta face … lei, vă rog.	That's … lei, please.
Casa este acolo.	The cash desk is over there.

Bookshop—Stationer's *Librărie—Papetărie*

There are plenty of kiosks selling national newspapers, and some offer foreign newspapers too. In big hotels in Bucharest and in other larger cities, one can get foreign newspapers without a problem.

Where's the nearest …?	**Există prin apropiere …?**	egzeester preen apropee-ereh
bookshop	**o librărie**	o leebrerree-eh
stationer's	**o papetărie**	o papeterree-eh
newsstand	**un chioşc de ziare**	oon kyoshc deh zee-areh
Where can I buy an English-language newspaper?	**Unde pot cumpăra un ziar în limba engleză?**	oondeh pot coomperra oon zee-ar uhn leemba englezer
Where's the guidebook section?	**Unde este raionul de ghiduri?**	oondeh yesteh rayonool deh geedoor^y
Where do you keep the English books?	**Unde ţineţi cărţile englezeşti?**	oondeh tseenets^y cerrtseeleh engleezesht^y
Do you have secondhand books?	**Aveţi cărţi la mâna a doua?**	avets^y certs^y la muhna a do-wa
I want to buy a/an/ some …	**Vreau să cumpăr …**	vra^oo ser coomperr
address book	**o agendă de adrese**	o ajender deh adreseh
adhesive tape	**nişte scoci**	neeshteh scoch^y
ball-point pen	**un pix cu pastă**	oon peex coo paster
book	**o carte**	o carteh
calendar	**un calendar**	oon calendar
crayons	**nişte creioane**	neeshteh creywaneh
dictionary	**un dicţionar**	oon deectsee-onar
Romanian-English	**Român-Englez**	romuhn-englez
pocket	**de buzunar**	deh boozoonar
drawing pins	**nişte pioneze**	neeshteh pee-onezeh
envelopes	**nişte plicuri**	neeshteh pleecoor^y
eraser	**o gumă**	o goomer
exercise book	**un caiet**	oon cayet
felt-tip pen	**o cariocă**	o caree-ocer
glue	**nişte lipici**	neeshteh leepeech^y
grammar book	**o carte de gramatică**	o carteh deh gramateecer
guidebook	**un ghid**	oon geed

ink black/red/blue	**nişte cerneală neagră/roşie/ albastră**	**neesh**teh cher**na**ler **na**grer/**ro**shee-eh/ al**ba**strer
(adhesive) labels	**nişte etichete (colante)**	**neesh**teh etee**ke**teh (co**lan**teh)
magazine	**o revistă**	o re**vees**ter
map	**o hartă**	o **har**ter
street map	**o hartă a străzilor**	o **har**ter a **strer**zeelor
road map of …	**o hartă a drumurilor naţionale**	o **har**ta a **droo**mooreelor natsee-o**na**leh
mechanical pencil	**un creion mecanic**	oon cre**yon** me**ca**neec
newspaper American/ English	**un ziar american/ englezesc**	oon zee-**ar** ameree**can**/ engle**zesc**
notebook	**un carnet**	oon car**net**
note paper	**nişte hârtie de scris**	**neesh**teh huhr**tee**-eh deh screes
paintbox	**o cutie de culori**	o coo**tee**-eh deh coo**lor**^{y}
paper	**nişte hârtie**	neeshteh huhr**tee**-eh
paperclips	**nişte agrafe pentru hârtie**	**neesh**teh **agra**feh **pen**troo huhr**tee**-eh
paper napkins	**nişte şerveţele de hârtie**	**neesh**teh sherve**tse**leh deh huhr**tee**-eh
paste	**nişte clei**	**neesh**teh clay
pen	**un stilou**	oon stee**lo**^{oo}
pencil	**un creion**	oon cre**yon**
pencil sharpener	**o ascuţitoare**	o ascootsee**twa**reh
playing cards	**nişte carţi de joc**	**neesh**teh cerrts^{y} deh zhoc
pocket calculator	**un calculator de buzunar**	un calcoola**tor** deh boozoo**nar**
postcard	**o vedere**	o ve**de**reh
refill (for a pen)	**o rezervă de stilou**	o re**zer**ver deh stee**lo**^{oo}
ruler	**o linie**	o **lee**nee-eh
stapler	**un capsator**	oon capsa**tor**
staples	**nişte capse pentru capsator**	**neesh**teh **cap**seh **pen**troo capsa**tor**
string	**nişte sfoară**	**neesh**teh **sfwa**rer
thumbtacks	**nişte pioneze**	**neesh**teh pee-o**ne**zeh
travel guide	**un ghid turistic**	oon geed too**rees**teec
writing pad	**un bloc notes**	oon bloc **no**tes

Camping and sports equipment *Camping şi echipament de sport*

I'd like (to hire) a(n)/some …	**Aş vrea … (să închiriez)**	ash vreh-a (ser uhnkeeree-**ez**)
air bed (mattress)	**o saltea pneumatică**	o sal**teh-a** pneoo**ma**teecer
backpack	**un rucsac**	oon **rooc**sac
beach towel	**un prosop de plajă**	oon pros**op** deh **pla**zher
butane gas	**o butelie de gaz**	o boo**te**lee-eh deh gaz
campbed	**un pat de camping**	oon pat deh **kem**peeng
(folding) chair	**un scaun (pliant)**	oon sca-oon (plee-**ant**)
charcoal	**cărbune pentru grătar**	cerr**boo**neh **pen**troo grer**tar**
compass	**o busolă**	o boo**so**ler
cool box	**o geantă frigorifică**	o **jan**ter freego**ree**feecer
deck chair	**un şezlong**	oon shez**long**
fishing tackle	**nişte unelte de pescuit**	**neesh**teh oon**el**teh deh pescoo**eet**
groundsheet	**o folie de muşama pentru cort**	o **fol**ee-eh deh mu**sha**ma **pen**troo cort
insect spray (killer)	**un insecticid**	oon eensectee**cheed**
kerosene	**gaz**	gaz
lamp	**o lampă**	o **lam**per
mallet	**un ciocan**	oon cho**can**
matches	**nişte chibrituri**	**neesh**teh kee**bree**tooryh
(foam rubber) mattress	**o saltea (de burete/ de cauciuc)**	o sal**teh-a** (deh boo**re**teh/ deh caoo**chooc**)
mosquito net	**o plasă contra ţânţarilor**	o **pla**ser **con**tra tsuhnts**areelor**
paraffin	**parafină**	para**fee**ner
picnic basket	**un coş pentru picnic**	oon cosh **pen**troo **peec**neec
pump	**o pompă**	o **pom**per
rope	**o frânghie**	o fruhn**gee-eh**
rucksack	**un rucsac**	oon **rooc**sac
skin-diving equipment	**echipament de plonjat**	ekeepa**ment** deh plon**zhat**
sleeping bag	**un sac de dormit**	oon sac deh dor**meet**
(folding) table	**o masă pliantă**	o **ma**ser plee-**an**ter
tent	**un cort**	oon cort
tent pegs	**nişte cârlige de cort**	**neesh**teh cuhr**lee**jeh deh cort
tent pole	**un stâlp de cort**	oon stuhlp deh cort
torch/flashlight	**o lanternă**	o lan**ter**ner
water flask	**un termos**	oon **ter**mos

CAMPING see page 32

Chemist's (drugstore) *Farmacie*

Cosmetics and toiletries can be purchased at a *drogherie* or in the cosmetic department of large stores, while medicine and cotton wool can be bought at a *farmacie*. All privately owned pharmacies also stock a good range of imported medicine and personal care products.

General expressions *Expresii de uz general*

Where's the nearest (all-night) chemist's?	**Unde se află o farmacie (non stop) prin apropiere?**	**oon**deh seh **a**fler o farma**chee-**eh (non stop) preen apropee-**e**reh
What time does the chemist's open/close?	**La ce oră se deschide/închide farmacia?**	la cheh **o**rer seh des**kee**deh/ uhn**kee**deh farma**chee-**a

1—Pharmaceutical *Expresii pentru uz farmaceutic*

I'd like something for …	**Aş vrea ceva pentru …**	ash vreh-a che**va** **pen**troo
a cold/a cough	**răceală/tuse**	rer**cha**ler/**too**seh
hay fever	**alergie la polen**	aler**jee-**eh la pol**en**
insect bites	**înţepături de insecte**	uhntseper**toor**^{y} deh een**sec**teh
sunburn	**arsuri de soare**	ars**oor**^{y} deh **swa**reh
travel/altitude sickness	**rău de călătorie/ rău de înălţime**	roh deh cerlerto**ree-**eh/ roh deh uhnerl**tsee**meh
an upset stomach	**stomac deranjat**	sto**mac** deran**zhat**
Can you prepare this prescription for me?	**Puteţi să-mi preparaţi această reţetă?**	poo**tets**^{y} serm^{y} prepar**ats**^{y} **a**cha**s**ter ret**se**ter
Can I get it without a prescription?	**Pot cumpăra asta fără reţetă?**	pot coomper**ra** **a**sta **fer**rer ret**se**ter
Shall I wait?	**Pot să aştept?**	pot ser ash**tept**
Can I have a/an/ some …?	**Puteţi să-mi daţi …?**	poo**tets**^{y} serm^{y} dats^{y}
adhesive plaster	**nişte leucoplast**	**neesh**teh le-ooco**plast**
analgesic	**un calmant**	oon cal**mant**
antiseptic cream	**o cremă antiseptică**	o **cre**mer antee**sep**teecer
aspirin	**nişte aspirină**	**neesh**teh aspee**ree**ner
bandage	**un bandaj**	oon ban**dazh**
elastic bandage	**un bandaj elastic**	oon ban**dazh** elas**teec**
Band-Aids®	**nişte pansamente**	**neesh**teh pansa**men**teh

DOCTOR see page 137

condoms	**nişte prezervative**	**neesh**teh prezerva**teeveh**
contraceptives	**nişte anti-concepţionale**	**neesh**teh antee-concheptsee-**ona**leh
cotton wool (absorbent cotton)	**nişte vată**	**neesh**teh **va**ter
cough drops	**nişte picături de tuse**	**neesh**teh peecer**toor**^{y} deh **too**seh
disinfectant	**un desinfectant**	oon dezeenfec**tant**
ear drops	**nişte picături pentru urechi**	**neesh**teh peecer**toor**^{y} **pen**troo oo**rek**^{y}
eye drops	**nişte picături pentru ochi**	**neesh**teh peecer**toor**^{y} **pen**troo ok^{y}
first-aid kit	**o trusă de prim ajutor**	o **troo**ser deh preem azhoo**tor**
gauze	**nişte tifon**	**neesh**teh tee**fon**
insect repellent/spray	**un spray contra insectelor**	oon spray **con**tra een**sec**telor
iodine	**nişte iod**	**neesh**teh yod
laxative	**nişte laxative**	**neesh**teh laxa**tee**veh
mouthwash	**o apă de gură**	o **a**per deh **goo**rer
nose drops	**nişte picături de nas**	**neeh**teh peecer**toor**^{y} deh nas
sanitary towels (napkins)	**nişte tampoane externe**	**neesh**teh tam**pwa**neh ex**ter**neh
sleeping pills	**nişte somnifere**	**neesh**teh somnee**feh**-reh
suppositories	**nişte supozitoare**	**neesh**teh soopozee**twa**reh
… tablets	**nişte pastile …**	**neesh**teh pas**tee**leh
tampons	**nişte tampoane interne**	**neesh**teh tam**pwa**neh een**ter**neh
thermometer	**un termometru**	oon termo**me**troo
throat lozenges	**nişte pastile pentru dureri de gât**	**neesh**teh pas**tee**leh **pen**troo doo**rer**^{y} deh guht
tranquillizers	**nişte tranchilizante**	**neesh**teh trankeeleez**an**teh
vitamin pills	**nişte vitamine (tablete)**	**neesh**teh veeta**mee**neh (ta**ble**teh)

OTRAVĂ	POISON
NUMAI PENTRU UZ EXTERN	FOR EXTERNAL USE ONLY

DOCTOR see page 137

2—Toiletry *Parfumerie*

I'd like a/an/some …	**Aş vrea …**	ash vreh-**a**
after-shave lotion	**o loţiune după ras**	o lotsee-**oo**neh **doo**per ras
bath salts	**nişte săruri de baie**	**neesh**teh ser**roor**y deh **ba**yeh
blusher (rouge)	**un ruj de obraz**	oon roozh deh o**braz**
bubble bath	**o spumă de baie**	o **spoo**mer deh **ba**yeh
cream	**o cremă**	o **cre**mer
cleansing cream	**un lapte demachiant**	oon **lap**teh demakee-**ant**
foundation cream	**un fond de ten**	oon fond deh ten
moisturizing cream	**o cremă hidratantă**	o **cre**mer heedra**tan**ter
deodorant	**un deodorant**	oon deodo**rant**
eyeliner	**un creion de pleoape**	oon cre**yon** deh **plewa**peh
eye shadow	**un fard de pleoape**	oon fard deh **plewa**peh
face powder	**o pudră de obraz**	o **poo**drer deh o**braz**
lipsalve	**un strugurel de buze**	oon stroogoo**rel** deh **boo**zeh
lipstick	**un ruj de buze**	oon roozh deh **boo**zeh
make-up remover pads	**nişte tampoane pentru demachiat**	**neesh**teh tam**pwa**neh **pen**troo demakee-**at**
mascara	**un rimel**	oon ree**mel**
nail brush	**o periuţă de unghii**	o peree-**oo**tser deh **oon**gee
nail file	**o pilă de unghii**	o **pee**ler deh **oon**gee
nail polish	**o ojă de unghii**	o **o**zher deh **oon**gee
nail polish remover	**acetonă**	ache**to**ner
nail scissors	**o forfecuţă de unghii**	o forfe**coot**ser deh **oon**gee
perfume	**un parfum**	oon par**foom**
powder	**pudră**	**poo**drer
powder puff	**un puf de pudră**	oon poof deh **poo**drer
razor	**un aparat de ras**	oon apa**rat** deh ras
razor blades	**nişte lame**	**neesh**teh **la**meh
rouge	**un ruj de obraz**	oon roozh deh o**braz**
safety pins	**nişte ace de siguranţă**	**neesh**teh **a**cheh deh seegoo**ran**tser
shaving brush	**un pămătuf de ras**	oon permer**toof** deh ras
shaving cream	**o cremă de ras**	o **cre**mer deh ras
soap	**un săpun**	oon ser**poon**

sponge	**un burete**	oon boo**re**teh
sun-tan cream	**o cremă de bronzat**	o **cre**mer deh bron**zat**
sun-tan oil	**un ulei de bronzat**	oon oo**lay** deh bron**zat**
talcum powder	**o pudră de talc**	o **poo**drer deh talc
tissues	**nişte batiste de hârtie**	**neesh**teh ba**tees**teh deh huhr**tee-**eh
toilet paper	**nişte hârtie igienică**	**neesh**teh huhr**tee-**eh eejee-**e**neecer
toilet water	**o apă de toaletă**	o **a**per deh twa**le**ter
toothbursh	**o perie de dinţi**	o **per**ee-eh deh deents^{y}
toothpaste	**o pastă de dinţi**	o **pas**ter deh deents^{y}
towel	**un prosop**	oon pro**sop**
tweezers	**o pensetă**	o pen**se**ter

For your hair *Articole pentru păr*

bobby pins	**agrafe**	a**gra**feh
comb	**un pieptene**	oon **pyep**terneh
curlers	**bigudiuri**	beegoo**dee-**oor^{y}
dye	**o vopsea**	o vop**seh-a**
hairbrush	**o perie de păr**	o **pe**ree-eh deh perr
hair gel	**un gel de păr**	oon jel deh perr
hairgrips	**clame**	**cla**meh
hair lotion	**o loţiune de păr**	o lotsee-**oo**neh deh perr
hairpins	**ace da păr**	**a**cheh deh perr
hair spray	**un fixativ de par**	oon feexa**teev** deh perr
setting lotion	**o loţiune de fixat**	o lotsee-**oo**neh deh fee**xat**
shampoo	**un şampon**	oon sham**pon**
for dry/ greasy (oily) hair	**pentru păr uscat/ gras**	**pen**troo perr oos**cat/** gras
tint	**o vopsea**	o vop**seh-a**
wig	**o perucă**	o pe**roo**cer

For the baby *Articole pentru sugaci*

baby food	**alimente pentru sugaci/sugari**	alee**men**teh **pen**troo soo**gach**^{y}/soo**gar**^{y}
dummy (pacifier)	**o suzetă**	o soo**ze**ter
feeding bottle	**un biberon**	oon beebe**ron**
nappies (diapers)	**scutece de unică folosinţă**	scoote**cheh** deh **oo**neecer folo**seen**tser

Clothing *Îmbrăcăminte*

If you want to buy something specific, prepare yourself in advance. Look at the list of clothing on page 115. Get some idea of the colour, material and size you want. They're all listed on the next few pages.

General *Fraze de uz general*

I'd like …	**Aş vrea …**	ash vreh-a
I' like … for a tenyear-old boy/girl.	**Aş vrea … pentru un băiat/o fată de zece ani.**	ash vreh-a … **pen**troo oon ber**yat**/oh **fa**ter deh **ze**cheh an^y
I'd like something like this.	**Aş vrea ceva ca aceasta.**	ash vreh-a che**va** ca a**chas**ta
I like the one in the window.	**Îmi place cel din vitrină.**	uhm^y **pla**cheh chel deen vee**tree**ner
How much is that per metre?	**Cât costă un metru din aceasta?**	cuht **cos**ter oon **me**troo deen a**chas**ta

1 centimetre (cm) = 0.39 in.	1 inch = **2.54 cm**
1 metre (m) = 39.37 in.	1 foot = **30.5 cm**
10 metres = 32.81 ft.	1 yard = **0.91 m.**

Colour *Culoarea*

I'd like something in …	**Aş vrea ceva în …**	ash vreh-a che**va** uhn
I'd like a darker/ lighter shade.	**Aş vrea o culoare mai închisă/ mai deschisă.**	ash vreh-a o cool**wa**reh migh uhn**kee**ser/ migh des**kee**ser
I'd like something to match this.	**Aş vrea ceva să se potrivească cu aceasta.**	ash vreh-a che**va** ser se potree**va**scer coo a**chas**ta
I don't like the colour.	**Nu-mi place culoarea.**	noom^y **pla**cheh cool**wa**reh-a

beige	**bej**	bezh
black	**negru**	**ne**groo
blue	**albastru**	al**bas**troo
brown	**maro**	ma**ro**
fawn	**gălbui**	gerl**boo**^{y}
golden	**auriu**	a-oo**ree**^{oo}
green	**verde**	**ver**deh
grey	**gri**	gree
orange	**portocaliu**	portoca**lee**^{oo}
pink	**roz**	roz
purple	**roşu-închis (purpuriu)**	**ro**shu-uhn**kees** (poorpoo**ree**^{oo})
red	**roşu**	**ro**shoo
scarlet	**roşu-aprins (stacojiu)**	**ro**shu-a**preens** (staco**zhe**^{oo})
silver	**argintiu**	argeen**tee**^{oo}
turquoise	**turcoaz**	toor**cwaz**
white	**alb**	alb
yellow	**galben**	**gal**ben
light …	**deschis**	des**kees**
dark …	**închis**	uhn**kees**

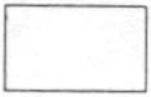

simplă (**seem**pler)

cu dungi (coo doonj^{y})

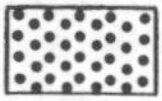

cu buline (coo boo**lee**neh)

în carouri (uhn ca**ro**-oor^{y})

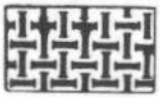

cu imprimeu (coo eempree**me**^{oo})

Fabric *Pânzeturi*

Do you have anything in …?	**Aveţi ceva din …?**	a**vets**^{y} che**va** deen
Is that …?	**Asta este …?**	**asta yes**teh
handmade	**lucrat de mână**	loo**crat** deh **muh**ner
made here	**făcut aici**	fer**coot** a**eech**^{y}
I'd like something thinner.	**Aş vrea ceva mai subţire.**	ash vreh-a che**va** migh soob**tsee**reh
Do you have anything of better quality?	**Aveţi ceva de calitate mai bună?**	a**vets**^{y} che**va** deh calee**ta**teh migh **boo**ner
What's it made of?	**Din ce este facut?**	deen cheh **yes**teh fer**coo**

camel-hair	**păr de cămilă**	perr deh cer**mee**ler
chiffon	**şifon**	shee**fon**
corduroy	**velur**	ve**loor**
cotton	**bumbac**	boom**bac**
crepe	**crep**	crep
denim	**doc**	doc
felt	**fetru**	**fe**troo
flannel	**flanelă**	fla**ne**ler
gabardine	**gabardină**	gabar**dee**ner
lace	**dantelă**	dan**te**ler
leather	**piele**	**pye**leh
linen	**in**	een
satin	**satin**	sa**teen**
silk	**mătase**	mer**ta**seh
suede	**piele de căprioară**	**pye**leh deh cerpree**wa**rer
towelling	**bumbac flauşat**	boom**bac** fla-oo**shat**
velvet	**catifea**	cateefeh-**a**
velveteen	**bumbac pluşat**	boom**bac** ploo**shat**
wool	**lână**	**luh**ner

Is it …?	**Este …?**	**yes**teh
pure cotton/wool	**de bumbac/lână pură**	deh boom**bac/luh**ner **poo**rer
synthetic	**material sintetic**	materee-**al** seen**te**teec
colourfast	**nu iese la spălat**	noo **ye**seh la sper**lat**
crease (wrinkle) resistant	**nu se şifonează**	noo seh sheefo**na**zer
Is it hand washable/ machine washable?	**Se spală de mână/ la maşină?**	seh **spa**ler deh **muh**ner/ la ma**shee**ner
Will it shrink?	**Intră la apă?**	een**trer** la **a**per

Size *Măsura*

I take size 38.	**Port măsura 38.**	port mer**soo**ra 38
Could you measure me?	**Puteţi să-mi luaţi măsura?**	poo**tets**ʸ serm**ʸ** loo-**ats**ʸ mer**soo**ra
I don't know the Romanian sizes.	**Nu cunosc măsurile româneşti.**	noo coo**nosc** mer**soo**reeleh romuh**nesht**ʸ

Sizes can vary somewhat from one manufacturer to another, so be sure to try on shoes and clothing before you buy.

NUMBERS see page 147

Women *Femei*

	Dresses/Suits					
American	8	10	12	14	16	18
British	10	12	14	16	18	20
Continental	36	38	40	42	44	46

	Stockings					
American / British	8½	9	9½	10	10½	
Continental	0	1	2	3	4	5

	Shoes			
American	6	7	8	9
British	4½	5½	6½	7½
Continental	37	38	40	41

Men *Bărbaţi*

	Suits/overcoats					
American / British	36	38	40	42	44	46
Continental	46	48	50	52	54	56

	Shirts			
American / British	15	16	17	18
Continental	38	40	42	44

	Shoes								
American / British	5	6	7	8	8½	9	9½	10	11
Continental	38	39	40	41	42	43	44	44	45

small (S)	**mic**	meec
medium (M)	**mediu**	**me**dyoo
large (L)	**mare**	**ma**reh
extra large (XL)	**extralarg**	**ex**tralarg
larger/smaller	**mai mare/mai mic**	migh **ma**reh/migh meec

A good fit? *O măsură potrivită?*

Can I try it on?	**Pot să probez?**	pot ser pro**bez**
Where's the fitting room?	**Unde este cabina de probă?**	**oon**deh **yes**teh ca**bee**na deh **pro**ber
Is there a mirror?	**Aveţi o oglindă?**	a**vets**ʸ o og**leen**der
It fits very well.	**Îmi vine foarte bine.**	uhmʸ **vee**neh **fwar**teh **bee**neh
It doesn't fit.	**Nu-mi vine bine.**	noomʸ **vee**neh **bee**neh
It's too …	**Este prea …**	**yes**teh preh-a
short/long	**scurt/lung**	scoort/loong
tight/loose	**strâmt/larg**	struhmt/larg

NUMBERS see page 147

Clothes and accessories *Haine şi accesorii*

I would like a/ an/some …	**Aş vrea …**	ash vreh-a
bathing cap	**o cască de înot**	o **cas**cer deh uh**not**
bathing suit	**un costum de baie**	oon cos**toom** deh **ba**yeh
bathrobe	**un halat de baie**	oon ha**lat** deh **ba**yeh
blouse	**o bluză**	o **bloo**zer
boxer shorts	**chiloţi bărbăteşti**	kee**lots**^{y} berber**tesht**^{y}
bow tie	**un papion**	oon papee-**on**
bra	**un sutien**	oon sootee-**en**
cap	**o şapcă**	o **shap**cer
coat	**o haină**	o **hay**ner
dress	**o rochie**	o **ro**kee-eh
with long sleeves	**cu mâneci lungi**	coo **muh**nech^{y} loonj^{y}
with short sleeves	**cu mâneci scurte**	coo **muh**nech^{y} **scoor**teh
sleeveless	**fară mâneci**	**fer**rer **muh**nech^{y}
dressing gown	**un capot**	oon ca**pot**
evening dress (woman's)	**o rochie de seară**	o **ro**kee-eh deh **sa**rer
girdle	**o centură**	o chen**too**rer
gloves	**nişte mănuşi**	**neesh**teh mer**noosh**^{y}
handbag	**o geantă**	o **jan**ter
handkerchief	**o batistă**	o ba**tees**ter
hat	**o pălărie**	o perler**ree**-eh
jacket	**o jachetă**	o zha**ke**ter
jeans	**nişte blugi**	**neesh**teh blooj^{y}
jersey	**un jerseu**	oon zher**se**^{oo}
nightdress	**o pijama**	o peezha**ma**
overalls	**o salopetă**	o salo**pe**ter
pair of …	**o pereche de …**	o pe**re**keh deh
panties	**chiloţi**	kee**lots**^{y}
pants (Am.)	**pantaloni**	panta**lon**^{y}
panty girdle	**o burtieră**	o boortee-**e**rer
panty hose	**ciorapi cu chilot**	cho**rap**^{y} coo kee**lot**
pullover	**un pulovăr**	oon poo**lo**verr
polo (turtle)-neck	**cu guler pe gât**	coo **goo**ler peh guht
round-neck	**cu guler în jurul gâtului**	coo **goo**ler uhn **zhoo**rool **guh**tooloo^{y}
V-neck	**cu guler în formă de V**	coo **goo**ler uhn **for**mer deh veh
with long/ short sleeves	**cu mâneci lungi/ scurte**	coo **muh**nech^{y} loonj^{y}/ **scoor**teh
without sleeves	**fără mâneci**	**fer**rer **muh**nech^{y}

pyjamas	**o pijama**	o peezha**ma**
raincoat	**o haină de ploaie**	o **hay**ner deh **plwa**yeh
scarf	**un fular**	oon foo**lar**
shirt	**o cămaşă**	o cer**ma**sher
shorts	**şort**	short
skirt	**o fustă**	o **foos**ter
slip	**un jupon**	oon zhoo**pon**
socks	**nişte şosete**	**neesh**teh sho**se**teh
stockings	**nişte ciorapi lungi**	**neesh**teh cho**rap**^{y} loonj^{y}
suit (man's)	**un costum bărbătesc**	oon cos**toom** berrber**tesc**
suit (woman's)	**un costum de damă**	oon cos**toom** deh **da**mer
suspenders (Am.)	**nişte bretele**	**neesh**teh bre**te**leh
sweater	**un pulover**	oon poo**lo**ver
sweatshirt	**o bluză de trening din bumbac**	o **bloo**zer deh **tre**neeng deen boom**bac**
swimming trunks	**un costum de baie/ un slip**	oon cos**toom** deh **ba**yeh/ oon sleep
swimsuit	**un costum de înot**	oon cos**toom** deh uh**not**
T-shirt	**o cămaşă**	o cer**ma**sher
tie	**o cravată**	o cra**va**ter
tights	**nişte dresuri**	**neesh**teh **dre**soor^{y}
tracksuit	**un trening**	oon **tre**neeng
trousers	**nişte pantaloni**	**neesh**teh panta**lon**^{y}
umbrella	**o umbrelă**	o oom**bre**ler
underpants	**nişte chiloţi**	**neesh**teh kee**lots**^{y}
undershirt	**un maiou/tricou**	oon ma**yo**^{oo}/tree**co**^{oo}
vest (Am.)	**o vestă**	o **ves**ter
vest (Br.)	**un maiou**	oon ma**yo**^{oo}
waistcoat	**o vestă**	o **ves**ter

belt	**curea**	coo**reh-a**
buckle	**cataramă**	cata**ra**mer
button	**nasture**	**nas**tooreh
collar	**guler**	**goo**ler
cuff links	**butoni de manşetă**	boo**ton**^{y} deh man**she**ter
pocket	**buzunar**	boozoo**nar**
press stud (snap fastener)	**capsă**	**cap**ser
zip (zipper)	**fermoar**	fer**mwar**

Shoes *Încălţăminte*

I'd like a pair of …	**Aş vrea o pereche de …**	ash vreh-**a** o pe**re**keh deh
boots	**cizme**	**cheez**meh
plimsolls (sneakers)	**tenişi**	**te**neesh^{y}
sandals	**sandale**	san**da**leh
shoes	**pantofi**	pan**tof**^{y}
flat	**plaţi**	plats^{y}
with a heel	**cu tocuri**	coo **to**coor^{y}
with leather soles	**cu talpă de piele**	coo **tal**per deh **pye**leh
with rubber soles	**cu talpă de cauciuc**	coo **tal**per deh caoo**chooc**
slippers	**papuci**	pa**pooch**^{y}
These are too …	**Aceştia sunt …**	**achesh**tya soont
narrow/wide	**strâmţi/largi**	struhmts^{y}/larj^{y}
big/small	**mari/mici**	mar^{y}/meech^{y}
Do you have a larger/smaller size?	**Aveţi un număr mai mare/mic?**	a**vets**^{y} oon **noo**mer migh **mareh**/**mee**c
Do you have the same in black?	**Aveţi acelaşi model pe negru?**	a**vets**^{y} **ache**lash^{y} mo**del** peh **ne**groo
leather	**piele**	**pye**leh
rubber	**cauciuc**	caoo**chooc**
suede	**piele de căprioară**	**pye**leh deh cerpree**wa**rer
Is it real leather?	**Este piele veritabilă?**	**yes**teh **pye**leh veree**ta**beeler
I need some shoe polish/shoelaces.	**Am nevoie de nişte cremă de pantofi/ şireturi.**	am ne**vo**yeh deh **neesh**-teh **cre**mer deh pan**tof**^{y}/ shee**re**toor^{y}

Shoes worn out? Here's the key to getting them fixed again:

Can you repair these shoes?	**Puteţi repara aceşti pantofi?**	poo**tets**^{y} repa**ra** a**chesht**^{y} pan**tof**^{y}
Can you stitch this?	**Puteţi coasc asta?**	poo**tets**^{y} **cwa**sch **a**sta
I want new soles and heels.	**Vreau pingele şi călcâie noi.**	vra^{oo} peen**je**leh shee cerl**cuh**yeh no^{y}
When will they be ready?	**Când vor fi gata?**	cuhnd vor fee **ga**ta

NUMBERS see page 147/COLOURS see page 112

Electrical appliances *Aparatură electrică*

Voltage in Romania is 220 AC. Plugs are the common European two-pin type. It is advisable to bring an adaptor with you.

What's the voltage?	**Ce voltaj este pe reţea?**	cheh vol**tazh yes**teh peh ret**seh-a**
Do you have a battery for this?	**Aveţi o baterie pentru asta?**	a**vets**y o bate**ree**-eh **pen**troo **as**ta
This is broken.	**(Asta) este defect.**	(**as**ta) **yes**teh de**fect**.
Can you repair it?	**Puteţi repara asta?**	poo**tets**y repa**ra as**ta
Can you show me how it works?	**Puteţi să-mi arătaţi cum funcţionează?**	poo**tets**y sermy arer**tats**y coom foonctsee-o**na**zer
I'd like a/an/ some …	**Aş vrea …**	ash vreh-a
adaptor	**un adaptor**	oon adap**tor**
amplifier	**un amplificator**	oon ampleefeeca**tor**
bulb	**un bec**	oon bec
CD player	**un 'compact disc player'**	oon **com**pact deesc **pla**yer
clock-radio	**un radio-ceas**	oon **ra**dee-o-chas
electric toothbrush	**o perie de dinţi electrică**	o **pe**ree-eh deh deentsy **elec**treecer
extension lead (cord)	**un prelungitor**	oon preloonjee**tor**
hair dryer	**un uscător de păr**	oon ooscer**tor** deh perr
headphones	**nişte căşti audio**	**neesh**teh cershty a**oo**dee-o
(travelling) iron	**un fier de călcat (de voiaj)**	oon fyer deh cer**lcat** (deh vo**yazh**)
lamp	**o lampă**	o **lam**per
plug	**un ştecher**	oon **shte**ker
portable …	**… portabil**	por**ta**beel
radio	**un radio**	oon **ra**dee-o
car radio	**un radio de maşină**	oon **ra**dee-o deh ma**shee**ner
(cassette) recorder	**un casetofon**	oon caseto**fon**
shaver	**un aparat de ras**	oon apa**rat** deh ras
speakers	**nişte difuzoare**	**neesh**teh deefoo**zwa**reh
(colour) television	**un televizor (color)**	oon televee**zor** (co**lor**)
transformer	**un transformator**	oon transforma**tor**
video-recorder	**un aparat video**	oon apa**rat vee**de-o

Grocery *Băcănie*

I'd like some bread, please.	**Aş vrea nişte pâine, vă rog.**	ash vreh-a **neesh**teh **puhy**neh ver rog
What sort of cheese do you have?	**Ce fel de brânză aveţi?**	cheh fel deh **bruhn**zer a**vets**ʸ
A piece of …	**O bucată de …**	o boo**ca**ter deh
that one	**aceea**	**ache-**a
the one on the shelf	**cea de pe raft**	cheh-a deh peh raft
I'll have one of those, please.	**Vreau una dintre acelea, vă rog.**	vraᵒᵒ **oo**na **deen**treh a**che**leh-a ver rog
I'd like …	**Aş vrea …**	ash vreh-a
a kilo of apples	**un kilogram de mere**	oon keelo**gram** deh **me**reh
half a kilo of tomatoes	**o jumătate de kilogram de roşii**	o zhoomer**ta**teh deh keelo**gram** deh **ro**shee
100 grams of butter	**o sută de grame de unt**	o **su**ter deh **gra**meh deh oont
a litre of milk	**un litru de lapte**	oon **lee**troo deh **lap**teh
half a dozen eggs	**şase ouă**	**sha**seh **o-**wer
4 slices of ham	**patru felii de şuncă**	**pa**troo fe**lee** deh **shoon**cer
a packet of tea	**un pachet de ceai**	oon pa**ket** de chay
a jar of jam	**un borcan de gem**	oon bor**can** deh jem
a tin (can) of peaches	**o cutie de piersici**	o coo**tee-**eh deh **pyer**seechʸ
a tube of mustard	**un tub de muştar**	oon toob deh moosh**tar**
a box of chocolates	**o cutie de bomboane de ciocolată**	o coo**tee-**eh deh bom**bwa**neh deh chocol**a**ter

1 kilogram or kilo (kg.) = 1000 grams (g.)

100 g. = 3.5 oz.	1/2 kg. = 1.1 lb.
200 g. = 7.0 oz.	1 kg. = 2.2 lb.

1 oz. = 28.35 g.

1 lb. = 453.60 g.

1 litre (l.) = 0.88 imp. quarts = 1.06 U.S. quarts

1 imp. quart = 1.14 l.	1 U.S. quart = 0.95 l.
1 imp. gallon = 4.55 l.	1 U.S. gallon = 3.8 l.

FOOD see also page 63

Household articles *Articole de menaj*

aluminiumfoil	**folie de aluminiu**	**fo**lee-eh deh aloo**mee**nyoo
bottle opener	**deschizător de sticle**	deskeezer**tor** deh **stee**cleh
bucket	**găleată**	ger**la**ter
can/tin opener	**deschizător de conserve**	deskeezer**tor** deh con**ser**veh
candles	**lumânări**	loomuh**nerr**y
clothes pegs (pins)	**cârlige de rufe**	cuhr**lee**jeh deh **roo**feh
corkscrew	**tirbuşon**	teerboo**shon**
frying pan	**tigaie**	tee**ga-**yeh
matches	**chibrituri**	kee**bree**toory
paper napkins	**şerveţele de hârtie**	sherve**tse**leh deh huhr**tee-**eh
plastic bags	**pungi de plastic**	poonjy deh **plas**teec
saucepan	**cratiţă**	**cra**teetser
washing powder	**detergent de rufe**	deter**jent** deh **roo**feh
washing-up liquid	**detergent de vase**	deter**jent** deh **va**seh

Tools *Scule*

hammer	**ciocan**	cho**can**
nails	**cuie**	**coo-**yeh
penknife	**briceag**	bree**chag**
pliers	**cleşte**	**clesh**teh
scissors	**foarfece/foarfecă**	**fwar**fecheh **fwar**fecer
screws	**şuruburi**	shoo**roo**boory
screwdriver	**şurubelniţă**	shooroo**bel**neetser
spanner/wrench	**cheie de piuliţe**	**ke-**yeh deh pee-oo**leet**seh

Crockery *Veselă*

cups	**ceşti**	cheshty
mugs	**căni**	cerny
plates	**farfurii**	farfoo**ree**
saucers	**farfurioare**	farfoo**reewa**reh
tumblers	**pahare**	pa**ha**reh

Cutlery (flatware) *Tacâmuri*

forks	**furculiţe**	foorcoo**lee**tseh
knives	**cuţite**	coo**tsee**teh
spoons	**linguri**	**leen**goory
teaspoons	**linguriţe**	leegoo**ree**tseh

Jeweller's—Watchmaker's *Bijuterie—Ceasornicărie*

Could I see that, please?	**Puteţi să-mi arătaţi acela, vă rog?**	poo**tets**^{y} sermi arer**tats**^{y} **ache**la ver rog
Do you have anything in gold?	**Aveţi ceva din aur?**	a**vets**^{y} che**va** deen **a**-oor
How many carats is this?	**Câte carate are acesta?**	**cuh**teh ca**ra**teh **a**reh a**ches**ta
Is this real silver?	**Este argint veritabil?**	**yes**teh ar**jeent** vereeta**beel**
Can you repair this watch?	**Puteţi repara acest ceas?**	poo**tets**^{y} repa**ra** a**chest** chas
I'd like a/an/some …	**Aş vrea …**	ash vreh-a
alarm clock	**un ceas deşteptător**	oon chas deshtepter**tor**
battery	**o baterie**	o bate**ree**-eh
bracelet	**o brăţară**	o brer**tsa**rer
chain bracelet	**o brăţară lănţişor**	o brer**tsa**rer lerntsee**shor**
charm bracelet	**o brăţară cu talismanuri**	o brer**tsa**rer coo talees**man**oor^y
brooch	**o broşă**	o **bro**sher
chain	**un lanţ**	oon lants
charm	**talisman**	talees**man**
cigarette case	**o tabacheră**	o taba**ke**rer
cigarette lighter	**o brichetă**	o bree**ke**ter
clip	**o clamă**	o **cla**mer
clock	**un ceas**	oon chas
cross	**o cruce**	o **croo**cheh
cuff links	**butoni de manşetă**	boo**ton**^{y} deh man**she**ter
cutlery	**nişte tacâmuri**	**neesh**teh ta**cuh**moor^y
earrings	**nişte cercei**	**neesh**teh cher**chay**
gem	**o piatră preţioasă**	o **pya**trer pretsee-**wa**ser
jewel box	**cutie pentru bijuterii**	coo**tee**-eh **pen**troo beejoote**ree**
mechanical pencil	**un creion mecanic**	oon cre**yon** me**ca**neec
music box	**o cutie muzicală**	o coo**tee**-eh moozee**ca**ler
necklace	**un colier**	oon colee-**er**
pendant	**un pandantiv**	oon pandan**teev**
pin	**un ac**	oon ac
pocket watch	**un ceas de buzunar**	oon chas deh boozoo**nar**
ring	**un inel**	oon ee**nel**
engagement ring	**un inel de logodnă**	oon ee**nel** deh lo**god**ner
wedding ring	**o verighetă**	o veree**ge**ter

rosary	**un rozariu**	oon roz**ar**yoo
silverware	**obiecte de argint**	o**byec**teh deh ar**jeent**
tie clip	**o clamă de cravată**	o **cla**mer deh cra**va**ter
tie pin	**un ac de cravată**	oon ac deh cra**va**ter
watch	**un ceas**	oon chas
automatic	**automat**	a-ooto**mat**
digital	**digital**	deejee**tal**
quartz	**cu cuarţ**	coo cwarts
waterproof	**antiacvatic**	**an**tee-acvateec
watchstrap	**o curea de ceas**	o coo**reh-a** de chas
wristwatch	**un ceas de mână**	oon chas deh **muh**ner

amber	**chihlimbar**	keehleem**bar**
amethyst	**ametist**	ame**teest**
chromium	**crom**	crom
copper	**cupru**	**coo**proo
coral	**coral**	co**ral**
crystal	**cristal**	cree**stal**
cut glass	**sticlă şlefuită**	**stee**cler shlefoo**ee**ter
diamond	**diamant**	dee**amant**
emerald	**smarald**	sma**rald**
enamel	**email/smalţ**	e**maighl**/smalts
gold	**aur**	**a**-oor
gold plate	**aurit**	a-oo**reet**
ivory	**fildeş**	**feel**desh
jade	**jad**	zhad
onyx	**onix**	o**neex**
pearl	**perlă**	**per**ler
pewter	**aliaj pe bază de cositor**	alee-**azh** peh **ba**zer deh cosee**tor**
platinum	**platină**	**pla**teener
ruby	**rubin**	roo**been**
sapphire	**safir**	sa**feer**
silver	**argint**	ar**jeent**
silver plate	**argintat**	arjeen**tat**
stainless steel	**inox**	ee**nox**
topaz	**topaz**	to**paz**
turquoise	**turcoaz**	toor**cwaz**

Optician *Optician*

I've broken my glasses.	**Mi-am spart ochelarii.**	myam spart oke**la**ree
Can you repair them for me?	**Puteţi să mi-i reparaţi?**	poo**tets**^{y} ser mee repa**rats**^{y}
When will they be ready?	**Când vor fi gata?**	cuhnd vor fee **ga**ta
Can you change the lenses?	**Puteţi schimba lentilele?**	poo**tets**^{y} skeem**ba** len**tee**leleh
I'd like tinted lenses.	**Aş vrea lentile fumurii.**	ash vreh-a len**tee**leh foomoo**ree**
The frame is broken.	**Rama este ruptă.**	**ra**ma **yes**teh **roop**ter
I'd like a spectacle case.	**Aş vrea un portochelari.**	ash vreh-a oon port-oke**lar**^{y}
I'd like to have my eyesight checked.	**Aş dori un control al vederii.**	ash do**ree** oon con**trol** al ve**de**ree
I'm short-sighted/ long-sighted.	**Sunt miop/ prezbit.**	soont mee-**op**/ prez**beet**
I'd like some contact lenses.	**Aş vrea lentile de contact.**	ash vreh-a len**tee**leh deh con**tact**
I've lost one of my contact lenses.	**Am pierdut o lentilă de contact.**	am pyer**doot** o len**tee**ler deh con**tact**
Could you give me another one?	**Puteţi să-mi daţi alta?**	poo**tets**^{y} serm^y dats^y **al**ta
I have hard/ soft lenses.	**Am lentile dure/ flexibile.**	am len**tee**leh **doo**reh/ fle**xee**beeleh
Do you have any contact-lens fluid?	**Aveţi lichid pentru lentile de contact?**	a**vets**^{y} lee**keed pen**troo len**tee**leh deh con**tact**
I'd like to buy a pair of sunglasses.	**Aş vrea să cumpăr o pereche de ochelari de soare.**	ash vreh-a ser **coom**-perr o pe**re**keh deh oke**lar**^{y} deh **swa**reh
May I look in a mirror?	**Pot să mă uit într-o oglindă?**	pot ser mer ooyt **uhn**tro o**gleen**der
I'd like to buy a pair of binoculars.	**Aş vrea să cumpăr un binoclu.**	ash vreh-a ser **coom**-perr oon bee**no**cloo

Photography *La fotograf*

I'd like a(n) … camera.	**Aş vrea un aparat de fotografiat …**	ash vreh-a oon apa**rat** deh fotografee**at**
automatic	**automat**	a-ooto**mat**
digital	**digital**	deejee**tal**
inexpensive	**nu prea scump**	noo preh-a scoomp
simple	**simplu**	**seem**ploo
Can you show me some …, please?	**Puteţi să-mi arătaţi, vă rog, nişte …?**	poo**tets**ʸ sermʸ arer**tats**ʸ ver rog **neesh**teh
cine (movie) cameras	**aparate de filmat**	apa**ra**teh deh feel**mat**
video cameras	**camere video**	**ca**mereh **vee**de-o
I'd like to have some passport photos taken.	**Aş vrea să fac nişte poze de paşaport.**	ash vreh-a ser fac **neesh**teh **p**ozeh deh pasha**port**

Film *Film*

I'd like a memory card for this camera.	**Aş dori un card de memorie pentru aparatul acesta.**	ash do**ree** oon card de me**mo**ree-e **pen**troo apa**ra**tool a**ches**ta
I'd like a film for this camera.	**Aş vrea un film pentru aparatul acesta.**	ash vreh-a oon feelm **pen**troo apa**ra**tool a**ches**ta
black and white	**alb-negru**	alb-**ne**groo
colour	**color**	co**lor**
colour negative	**negativ color**	nega**teev** co**lor**
colour slide	**diapozitiv color**	deeapozee**teev** co**lor**
cartridge	**încărcător de film**	uhncercer**tor** deh feelm
disc film	**disc de film**	deesc deh feelm
roll film	**bobină de film**	bo**bee**ner deh feelm
video cassette	**casetă video**	ca**se**ter **vee**de-o
24/36 exposures	**24/36 expuneri**	24/36 ex**poo**nerʸ
this size	**mărimea aceasta**	mer**ree**meh-a a**chas**ta
this ASA/DIN number	**numărul acesta de ASA/DIN**	**noo**merrool a**ches**ta deh ASA/DIN
artificial light type	**pentru lumină artificială**	**pen**troo loo**mee**ner arteefeechee-**a**ler
daylight type	**pentru lumină de zi**	**pen**troo loo**mee**ner deh zee
fast (high-speed)	**de viteză ultrarapidă**	deh vee**te**zer ooltrara**pee**der
fine grain	**film cu sensibilitate mare**	feelm coo senseebeelee-**ta**teh **ma**reh

Processing *Developat*

How much do you charge for processing?	**Cât costă developatul?**	cuht **cos**ter develo**pa**tool
I' like … prints of each negative.	**Aş vrea … poze pentru fiecare negativ.**	ash vreh-a … **po**zeh **pen**troo fee-e**ca**reh nega**teev**
with a matt finish	**cu faţă mată**	coo **fa**tser **ma**ter
with a glossy finish	**cu faţă lucioasă**	coo **fa**tser loo**chwa**ser
When will the photos be ready?	**Când vor fi gata pozele?**	cuhnd vor fee **ga**ta **po**zeleh

Accessories and repairs *Accesorii şi reparaţii*

I'd like a/an/some …	**Aş vrea …**	ash vreh-a
batteries	**nişte baterii**	**neesh**teh bate**ree**
camera case	**un port-aparat**	oon port-apa**rat**
(electronic) flash	**un blitz (electronic)**	oon bleets (elec**tro**neec)
filter	**un filtru**	oon **feel**troo
for black and white	**pentru film alb-negru**	**pen**troo feelm alb**ne**groo
for colour	**pentru film color**	**pen**troo feelm co**lor**
lens	**un obiectiv**	oon obyec**teev**
telephoto lens	**un teleobiectiv**	oon tele-obyec**teev**
wide-angle lens	**un obiectiv superangular**	oon obyec**teev** sooperangoo**lar**
lens cap	**capacul obiectivului**	ca**pa**cool obyec**tee**vooloo^y
Can you repair this camera?	**Puteţi repara acest aparat de fotografiat?**	poo**tets**^{y} repa**ra** a**chest** apa**rat** deh fotografee**at**
The film is jammed.	**Filmul este blocat.**	**feel**mool **yes**teh blo**cat**
There's something wrong with the …	**Ceva este în neregulă cu …**	che**va yes**teh uhn ne**re**gooler coo
exposure counter	**dispozitivul de numărătoare**	deespozee**tee**vool deh noomerer**twa**reh
film winder	**maneta de rulat filmul**	ma**ne**ta deh roo**lat** **feel**mool
flash attachment	**legăturile de blitz**	leger**too**reeleh deh bleets
lens	**obiectiv**	obyec**teev**
light meter	**celula fotoelectrică**	che**loo**la fotoe**lec**treecer
shutter	**obturator**	obtoora**tor**

NUMBERS see page 147

Tobacconist's *Tutungerie*

All shops, kiosks and minimarkets sell Romanian and imported cigarettes.

A packet of cigarettes, please.	**Un pachet de ţigări, vă rog.**	oon pa**ket** deh tsee**gerr**^{y} ver rog.
Do you have any American/English cigarettes?	**Aveţi ţigări americane/ englezeşti?**	a**vets**^{y} tsee**gerr**^{y} ameree**ca**neh/ engle**zesht**^{y}
I'd like a carton.	**Aş vrea un cartuş.**	ash vreh-a oon car**toosh**
Give me a/some …, please.	**Daţi-mi …, vă rog.**	**dat**seem^{y} … ver rog
candy	**nişte dropsuri**	**neesh**teh **drop**soor^{y}
chewing gum	**nişte gumă de mestecat**	**neesh**teh **goo**mer deh meste**cat**
chewing tobacco	**nişte tutun de mestecat**	**neesh**teh too**toon** deh meste**cat**
cigarette case	**o tabacheră**	o taba**ke**rer
cigarette holder	**un port-ţigaret**	oon port-tseega**ret**
cigarettes	**nişte ţigări**	**neesh**teh tsee**gerr**^{y}
filter-tipped/ without filter	**cu filtru/ fără filtru**	coo **feel**troo/ **fer**rer **feel**troo
light/dark tobacco	**blonde/brune**	**blon**deh/**broo**neh
mild/strong	**slabe/tari**	**sla**beh/tar^{y}
menthol	**mentolate**	mento**la**teh
king-size	**superlungi**	**soo**per-**loonj**^{y}
cigars	**trabuc**	tra**booc**
lighter	**o brichetă**	o bree**ke**ter
lighter fluid/gas	**nişte gaz de brichetă**	**neesh**teh gaz de bree**ke**ter
matches	**nişte chibrituri**	**neesh**teh kee**bree**toor^{y}
pipe	**o pipă**	o **pee**per
pipe cleaners	**nişte instrumente pentru curăţat pipa**	**neesh**teh eenstroo**men**teh **pen**troo coorer**tsat pee**pa
pipe tobacco	**nişte tutun de pipă**	**neesh**teh too**toon** deh **pee**per
pipe tool	**un dispozitiv de curăţat pipa**	oon deespozee**teev** deh coorer**tsat pee**pa
postcard	**o vedere**	o ve**de**reh
snuff	**nişte tutun de prizat**	**neesh**teh too**toon** deh pree**zat**
stamps	**nişte timbre**	**neesh**teh **teem**breh
sweets	**nişte dulciuri**	**neesh**teh **dool**choor^{y}

Miscellaneous *Diverse*

Souvenirs *Suveniruri*

Shops called *artizanat* sell typical Romanian souvenirs including finely embroidered tunics, blouses, napkins, tablecloths and headscarves. You'll also find traditional woollen carpets handwoven with intricate geometric patterns, hand-painted Easter eggs, decorative pottery and beautifully carved wooden utensils.

If you are interested in *objets d' art,* including icons on wood or glass, look for the shops belonging to the Artists' Union called *Fondul plastic*. There are many good contemporary art shops in Bucharest, notably Dominus (at the National Theatre)

Catalogues of medieval art make excellent souvenirs of Romania, as do records or CDs of Romanian folk and classical music. And don't forget to take home a bottle or two of Romanian plum brandy (*ţuică*).

art book	**album de artă**	al**boom** deh **ar**ter
carpet	**carpetă/covor**	car**pe**ter/**co**vor
ceramics	**ceramică**	che**ra**meeker
embroidered headscarf	**maramă**	ma**ra**mer
embroidered tablecloth	**faţă de masă brodată**	**fa**tser der **ma**ser bro**da**ter
folk music	**muzică populară**	**moo**ziker popoo**lar**er
icon	**icoană**	ee**kwa**ner
painting	**tablou/pictură**	ta**blo**oo/pic**too**rer
pottery	**olărit**	olerr**eet**
tapestry	**tapiserie**	tapeese**ree-**eh
wooden utensil	**unelte de lemn**	oo**nel**teh deh lemn

Music *Muzică*

I'd like a …	**Aş vrea …**	ash vreh-a
cassette	**o casetă**	ca**se**ter
video cassette	**o video casetă**	**vee**de-o ca**se**ter
compact disc	**un compact disc**	oon **com**pact deesc
DVD	**un DVD**	oon deevee**dee**

NUMBERS see page 147

Do you have any records by …?	**Aveţi discuri de …**	a**vets**^{y} **dees**coor^{y} deh
Can I listen to this album?	**Pot asculta discul acesta?**	pot ascool**ta dees**cool a**ches**ta
chamber music	**muzică de cameră**	**moo**zeecer deh **ca**merer
classical music	**muzică clasică**	**moo**zeecer **cla**seecer
folk music	**muzică populară**	**moo**zeecer popoo**la**rer
folk song	**cântec popular**	**cuhn**tec popoo**lar**
instrumental music	**muzică instrumentală**	**moo**zeecer eenstroomen**ta**ler
jazz	**jazz**	jazz
light music	**muzică uşoară**	**moo**zeecer oo**shwa**rer
orchestral music	**muzică simfonică**	**moo**zeecer seem**fo**nicer
pop music	**muzică pop**	**moo**zeecer pop

Toys *Jucării*

I'd like a toy/game …	**As vrea o jucărie/ un joc …**	ash vreh-a o zhoocer**ree**eh/oon zhoc
for a boy	**pentru un băiat**	**pen**troo oon ber**yat**
for a 5-year-old girl	**pentru o fetiţă de 5 ani**	**pen**troo o fe**tee**tser deh cheench^{y} an^{y}
(beach) ball	**o minge (de plajă)**	o **meen**jeh (deh **pla**zher)
bucket and spade (pail and shovel)	**o găleţică şi o lopăţică**	o gerlet**see**cer shee o lopert**see**cer
building blocks (bricks)	**nişte cuburi**	**neesh**teh **coo**boor^{y}
chess set	**un joc de şah**	oon zhoc deh shah
colouring book	**o carte de colorat**	o **car**teh deh colo**rat**
doll	**o păpuşă**	o per**poo**sher
electronic game	**un joc electronic**	oon zhoc elec**tro**neec
playing cards	**nişte cărţi de joc**	**neesh**teh cerrts^{y} deh zhoc
roller skates	**nişte patine cu rotile**	**neesh**teh pa**tee**neh coo ro**tee**leh
snorkel	**un tub de scafandru**	oon toob deh sca**fan**droo
teddy bear	**un ursuleţ**	oon oorsoo**lets**
toy car	**o maşină jucărie**	o ma**shee**ner zhoocer**ree**-eh

NUMBERS see page 147

Your Money: Banks—Currency

The Romanian unit of currency is the *leu*—le^{oo} (plural: *lei*) divided into *bani*—ban^{y}

In July, 2005, the Romanian leu was revalued. Currency names did not change, but new bills and coins were issued.

Coins: 1, 5, 10, 50 bani

Notes: 1, 5, 10, 50, 100, 500 lei

Banks are open from Monday until Friday between 8:30am and 6pm. Some, such as BRD and BCR also open on Saturday between 9am and 1pm.

Foreign currency can be changed at airports, banks and in most hotels, but exchange bureaus will generally offer the best rate.

Personal cheques are usually accepted in Romania, but you should always ask to be sure. Big hotels accept payment by credit card, though you will not get the best exchange rate.

Traveller's cheques are easy to cash at the National Tourist Office (ONT) or in most hotels.

Where's the nearest bank	**Unde se află o bancă în apropiere?**	**oon**deh seh **a**fler o **ban**cer uhn apropee-**e**reh
Where's the nearest currency exchange office?	**Unde se află un birou de schimb prin apropiere?**	**oon**deh seh **a**fler oon bee**ro^{oo}** deh skeemb preen apropee-**e**reh

At the bank *La bancă*

I want to change some dollars/ pounds.	**Vreau să schimb nişte dolari/ lire sterline.**	vra^{oo} ser skeemb **neesh**teh do**lar^{y}**/ **lee**reh ster**lee**neh

I want to cash a traveller's cheque.	**Vreau să încasez nişte cecuri de călătorie.**	vra^{oo} ser uhnca**sez** **neesh**teh **cheh**coor^{y} deh cerlerto**ree-**eh
What's the exchange rate?	**Care este cursul de schimb?**	**ca**reh **yes**teh **coor**sool deh skeemb
How much commission do you charge?	**Ce comision reţineţi?**	cheh comeesee-**on** ret**see**nets^{y}
Can you cash a personal cheque?	**Puteţi încasa un cec personal?**	poo**tets**^{y} uhnca**sa** oon chec perso**nal**
Can you telex my bank in London?	**Puteţi trimite un telex la banca mea din Londra?**	poo**tets**^{y} tree**mee**teh oon telex la **ban**ca meh-a deen **lon**dra
I have a/an/some…	**Am…**	am
credit card	**o carte de credit**	o **car**teh deh **cre**deet
Eurocheques	**nişte Eurocecuri**	**neesh**teh e-ooro**che**coor^{y}
letter of credit	**o scrisoare acreditivă**	o scree**swa**reh acredee**tee**ver
I'm expecting some money from New York. Has it arrived?	**Aştept nişte bani din New York. Au sosit cumva?**	ash**tept** **neesh**teh ban^{y} deen new york. a^{oo} so**seet** coom**va**
Please give me… notes (bills) and some small change.	**Vă rog să-mi daţi… bancnote şi ceva bani mărunţi.**	ver rog serm^{y} dats^{y}… banc**no**teh shee che**va** ban^{y} mer**roonts**^{y}
Give me… large notes and the rest in small notes.	**Vă rog să-mi daţi… bancnote mari şi restul în bani mărunţi.**	ver rog serm^{y} dats^{y}… banc**no**teh mar^{y} shee **res**tool uhn ban^{y} mer**roonts**^{y}

Deposits—Withdrawals *Depuneri—Restituiri*

I want to…	**Vreau să…**	vra^{oo} ser
open an account	**deschid un cont bancar**	des**keed** oon cont ban**car**
withdraw… lei	**scot… lei**	scot… lay
Where should I sign?	**Unde trebuie să semnez?**	**oon**deh **tre**booyeh ser sem**nez**
I'd like to pay this into my account.	**Aş vrea să depun aceşti bani în contul meu.**	ash vreh-a ser de**poon** **achesht**^{y} ban^{y} uhn **con**tool me^{oo}

NUMBERS see page 147

Business terms *Termeni de afaceri*

My name is …	**Mă numesc…**	mer noo**mesc**
Here's my card.	**Poftiţi cartea mea de vizită.**	pof**teets**y **car**teh-a meh-a deh **vee**zeeter
I have an appointment with…	**Am o întâlnire cu…**	am o uhntuhl-**nee**reh coo
Can you give me an estimate of the cost?	**Puteţi să-mi numiţi un preţ estimativ?**	poo**tets**y sermy nu**meets**y oon prets esteema**teev**
What's the rate of inflation?	**Care este rata inflaţiei?**	**ca**reh **yes**teh **ra**ta een**fla**tsee-ey
Can you provide me with an interpreter/ a personal computer/ a secretary?	**Puteţi să-mi puneţi la dispoziţie un translator/ un computer/ o secretară?**	poo**tets**y sermy **poo**netsy la deespo**zee**tsee-eh oon trans**la**tor/ oon com**pyoo**ter/ o secre**ta**rer
Where can I make photocopies?	**Unde pot face nişte fotocopii?**	**oon**deh pot **fa**cheh **neesh**teh foto**co**pee

amount	**cantitate**	cantee**ta**teh
balance	**balanţă**	ba**lan**tser
capital	**capital**	capee**tal**
cheque	**cec**	chec
contract	**contract**	con**tract**
discount	**reduceri**	re**doo**chery
expenses	**cheltuieli**	keltoo**yel**y
interest	**dobândă**	do**buhn**der
investment	**investiţie**	eenves**teet**see-eh
invoice	**factură**	fac**too**rer
loss	**pierderi**	**pyer**dery
mortgage	**ipotecă**	eepo**te**cer
payment	**plată**	**pla**ter
percentage	**procentaj**	prochen**tazh**
profit	**profit**	pro**feet**
purchase	**achiziţii**	akee**zee**tsee
sale	**vânzare**	vuhn**za**reh
share	**acţiuni**	actsee-**oon**y
transfer	**transfer**	trans**fer**
value	**valoare**	val**wa**reh

NUMBERS see page 147

At the post office

The sign PTTR indicates a post office in Romania. Post offices provide telegram and telephone facilities as well as postal services. They do not usually have fax facilities, for which you will have to locate a private shop offering this service.

Post offices are usually open between 8am and 6pm. If you want to send a parcel overseas you should go to a special post office where you will be required to complete a customs declaration form. Take your passport with you when you go to collect a parcel or registered letter as you will need to show identification.

To avoid the inevitable long queues in post offices, buy your stamps from tobacconists or at the hotel reception desk.

Post boxes are yellow and some have a separate box for local mail only (marked *loco*).

Where's the nearest post office?	**Unde se află o poştă prin apropiere?**	**oon**deh seh **a**fler o **posh**ter preen apropee-**ereh**
What time does the post office open/close?	**La ce oră deschide/ închide la poştă?**	la cheh **o**rer des**kee**deh/ uhn**kee**deh la **posh**ter
A stamp for this letter/ postcard, please	**Un timbru pentru această scrisoare/ vedere, vă rog.**	oon **teem**broo **pen**troo **achas**ter scree**swa**reh/ ve**de**reh ver rog
A… -lei stamp, . please	**Un timbru de… lei, vă rog.**	oon **teem**broo deh… lay ver rog
What's the postage for a letter to London?	**Cât costă timbrul pentru o scrisoare la Londra?**	cuht **cos**ter **teem**brool **pen**troo o scree**swa**reh la **lon**dra
What's the postage for a postcard to Los Angeles?	**Cât costă un timbru pentru o vedere la Los Angeles?**	cuht **cos**ter oon **teem**broo **pen**troo o ve**de**reh la los angeles
Where's the letter box (mailbox)?	**Unde este cutia poştală?**	**oon**deh **yes**teh coo**tee**a posh**ta**ler

I want to send this parcel.	**Vreau să expediez coletul acesta.**	vra^{oo} ser expedee-**ez** co**le**tool a**ches**ta
I'd like to send this (by)…	**Aş vrea să expediez asta (prin) …**	ash vreh-a ser expedee-**ez as**ta (preen)
airmail	**avion**	avee-**on**
express (special delivery)	**expres (de urgenţă)**	ex**pres** (deh oor**jen**tser)
registered mail	**scrisoare recomandată**	scree**swa**reh recoman**da**ter
At which counter can I cash an international money order?	**La ce ghiseu pot încasa un mandat internaţional?**	la cheh gee**she**^{oo} pot uhnca**sa** oon man**dat** eenternatsee-o**nal**
Where's the poste restante (general delivery)?	**Unde este ghişeul pentru post restant?**	**oon**deh **yes**teh gee**she**ool **pen**troo post res**tant**
Is there any post (mail) for me? My name is…	**Am vreo scrisoare? Numele meu este…**	am vro scree**swa**reh **noo**meleh me^{oo} **yes**teh

TIMBRE	STAMPS
COLETE	PARCELS
MANDAT POSTAL	MONEY ORDER

E-mail Fax *E-mail (Poştă electronică) Fax*

Where's the nearest Internet Cafe®?	**Unde se află pe aici un Internet-Cafe®?**	**oon**deh seh **af**ler pe a**eetch**^{y} uhn eenter**net** cafe
What are the charges per hour?	**Cât costă o oră de folosire?**	cuht **cos**ter o **o**rer deh folo**see**re
How much does it cost to print?	**Cât costă printarea?**	cuht **cos**ter preen**ta**reh-a
I'd like to send a fax.	**Aş dori să trimit un fax.**	ash doree ser tree**meet** un fax.
How much will this fax cost?	**Cât o să coste fax-ul acesta?**	cuht o ser **cos**teh **fax**ool a**ches**ta

Telephoning *La telefon*

There are public card phones from which one can make national and international calls. Phone cards are available from post offices or kiosks.

Where's the telephone?	**Unde este un telefon?**	**oon**deh **yes**teh oon tele**fon**
I'd like a telephone token.	**Aş vrea o fisă (pentru telefon).**	ash vreh-a o **fee**ser (**pen**troo tele**fon**)
Where's the nearest telephone booth?	**Unde este un telefon prin apropiere?**	**oon**deh **yes**teh oon tele**fon** preen apropee-ereh
May I use your phone?	**Îmi permiteţi să folosesc telefonul dumneavoastra?**	uhm^{y} per**mee**tets^{y} ser folo**sesc** tele**fo**nool doomna**vwas**trer
Do you have a telephone directory for Bucharest?	**Aveţi un anuar telefonic pentru Bucureşti?**	a**vets**^{y} oon anoo-**ar** tele**fo**neec **pen**troo boocoo**resht**^{y}
I'd like to call…	**Aş vrea să telefonez la numărul…**	ash vreh-a ser telefo**nez** la **noo**merrool…
What's the dialling (area) code for…?	**Care este prefixul pentru…?**	**ca**reh **yes**teh pre**fee**xool **pen**troo
I'd like a... lei phonecard.	**Aş dori o cartelă de telefon**	asch do**ree** o car**te**ler deh tele**fon**
I'd like a pre-paid mobile (cell) phone.	**Aş dori un celular/ telefon mobile cu cartelă reactivabilă.**	asch do**ree oon cheloo**-lar/tele**fon** mo**beel** coo car**te**ler reacteeva**bee**ler
I'd like to buy some minutes for my mobile (cell) phone.	**Aş dori să-mi reactivez cartelă pentru câteva minute de convorbire.**	asch do**ree** serm^{y} reactee**vez** car**te**la **pen**troo căte**va** mee**nu**te deh convor**bee**re

Operator *Centrala*

I'd like Bucharest 23 45 67	**Aş vrea o linie cu Bucureşti, numărul 23 45 67**	ash vreh-a o **lee**nee-eh coo boocoo**resht**^{y} **noo**merrool 23 45 67
Can you help me get this number	**Mă puteţi ajuta să obţin acest număr?**	mer poo**tets**^{y} azhoo**ta** ser ob**tseen** a**chest** **noo**merr
I'd like to place a personal (person-to-person) call.	**Aş vrea să dau un telefon.**	ash vreh-a ser da^{oo} oon tele**fon**

NUMBERS see page 147

I'd like to reverse the charges (call collect).	**Aş vrea să telefonez cu taxă inversă.**	ash vreh-a ser telefo**nez** coo **ta**xer **een**verser

Speaking *Convorbirea*

Hello. This is …	**Alo, … la telefon.**	**alo** … la tele**fon**
I'd like to speak to …	**Aş vrea să vorbesc cu …**	ash vreh-a ser vor**besc** coo
Extension …	**Interior …**	eenteree-**or**
Speak louder/ more slowly, please.	**Vorbiţi mai tare/ Nu vorbiţi atât de repede, vă rog.**	vor**beets**ʸ migh **tare**h/ noo vor**beets**ʸ a**tuht** de **re**pede ver rog

Bad luck *Ghinion*

Would you try again later, please?	**Puteţi încerca din nou, mai târziu, vă rog?**	poo**tets**ʸ uhncher**ca** deen noᵒᵒ migh tuhr**zee**ᵒᵒ ver rog
Operator, you gave me the wrong number.	**Centrala, mi-aţi dat un număr greşit.**	chen**tra**la myatsʸ dat oon **noo**merr gre**sheet**
Operator, we were cut off.	**Alo, centrala, s-a întrerupt convorbirea.**	**alo** chen**tra**la sa uhntre**roopt** convor**bee**reh-a

Telephone alphabet *Codul telefonic de enunţare*

A	**Ana**	ana	O	**Olga**	olga
B	**Barbu**	**bar**boo	P	**Petre**	petreh
C	**Constantin**	constan**teen**	Q	**qu**	kyoo
D	**Dumitru**	doo**mee**troo	R	**Radu**	**ra**doo
E	**Elena**	elena	S	**Sandoo**	**san**doo
F	**Florea**	**flo**reh-a	T	**Tudor**	**too**dor
Ţ			Ţ	**Ţară**	**tsa**rer
G	**Gheorghe**	**geor**geh	U	**Udrea**	**oo**dreh-a
H	**Haralambie**	hara**lam**bee-eh	V	**Vasile**	va**see**leh
I	**Ion**	ee-on	W	**dublu V**	**doo**bloo veh
J	**Jiu**	zheeᵒᵒ	X	**Xenia**	**xe**nya
K	**kilogram**	keelo**gram**	Y	**I grec**	ee grec
L	**Lazăr**	**la**zer	Z	**zahăr**	**za**herr
M	**Maria**	ma**ree**-a			
N	**Nicolae**	neeco**la**-eh			

Not there *Nu-i aici, lipseşte*

When will he/ she be back?	**Când se întoarce?**	cuhnd seh uhn**twar**cheh
Will you tell him/ her I called?	**Vreţi să-i spuneţi că am sunat?**	vrets^{y} sery **spoo**nets^{y} cer am soo**nat.**
My name is…	**Numele meu este…**	**noo**meleh me^{oo} **yes**teh
Would you ask him/her to call me?	**Vreţi să-i spuneţi să mă sune?**	vrets^{y} sery **spoo**nets^{y} ser mer **soo**neh.
My number is…	**Numărul meu de telefon este…**	**noo**merrool me^{oo} deh tele**fon yes**teh
Would you take a message, please?	**Pot să las un mesaj, vă rog?**	pot ser las oon me**sazh** ver rog

Charges *taxe*

What was the cost of that call?	**Cât a costat convorbirea aceasta?**	cuht a cos**tat** convor**bee**reh-a **achas**ta
I want to pay for the call.	**Vreau să plătesc convorbirea telefonică.**	vra^{oo} ser pler**tesc** convor**bee**reh-a tele**fo**neecer

YOU MAY HEAR:

Vă caută cineva la telefon.	There's a telephone call for you.
Ce număr aţi format?	What number are you calling?
Linia este ocupată.	The line's engaged.
Nu răspunde.	There's no answer.
Aţi greşit numărul.	You've got the wrong number.
Telefonul este deranjat.	The phone is out of order.
Un moment.	Just a moment.
Aşteptaţi, vă rog.	Hold on, please.
Nu este aici.	He's/She's out at the moment.

Doctor

If you fall ill during your stay in Romania, ask for a *policlinică cu plată* (paying clinic); these are relatively inexpensive and can give you immediate attention by very good doctors. For minor complaints you can get advice from any pharmacy.

General *Expresii de uz general*

Can you get me a doctor?	**Puteţi să chemaţi un doctor, vă rog?**	poo**tets**^{y} ser ke**mats**^{y} oon **doc**tor ver rog
Is there a doctor here?	**Este un doctor aici?**	**yes**teh oon **doc**tor a-**eech**^{y}
I need a doctor, quickly.	**E nevoie de un doctor, repede.**	yeh nev**o**yeh deh oon **doctor re**pedeh
Where can I find a doctor who speaks English?	**Unde pot găsi un doctor care vorbeşte englezeşte?**	**oon**deh pot ger**see** oon **doctor car**eh vor**besh**teh engle**zesh**teh
Where's the surgery (doctor's office)?	**Unde este cabinetul medical?**	**oon**deh **yes**teh cabee**ne**tool medee**cal**
What are the surgery (office) hours?	**Care sunt orele de program?**	**car**eh soont **o**releh deh pro**gram**
Could the doctor come to see me here?	**Poate doctorul să vină să mă vadă aici?**	**pwa**teh **doc**torool ser **vee**ner ser mer **va**der a-**eech**^{y}
What time can the doctor come?	**La ce oră poate să vină doctorul?**	la cheh **o**rer **pwa**teh ser **vee**ner **doc**torool
Can you recommend a/an…?	**Puteţi să-mi recomandaţi…?**	poo**tets**^{y} serm^{y} recoman**dats**^{y}
general practitioner	**un doctor de medicină generală**	oon **doc**tor deh medee**chee**ner gene**ra**ler
children's doctor	**un medic pediatru**	oon **me**deec pedee-**a**troo
eye specialist	**un medic oculist**	oon **me**deec ocoo**leest**
gynaecologist	**un ginecolog**	oon jeeneco**log**
Can I have an appointment…?	**Puteţi să-mi daţi un bon pentru o vizită la doctor … ?**	poo**tets**^{y} serm^{y} dats^{y} oon bon **pen**troo o **vee**zeeter la **doc**tor
tomorrow	**mâine**	**muhy**neh
as soon as possible	**cât de curând posibil**	cuht deh coo**ruhnd** po**see**beel

CHEMIST'S see page 107

Parts of the body *Corpul uman*

appendix	**apendice**	a**pen**deecheh
arm	**braţ**	brats
back	**spate**	**spa**teh
bladder	**vezica urinară**	ve**zee**ca ooreen**na**rer
bone	**os**	os
bowel	**intestin**	eentes**teen**
breast	**sân**	suhn
chest	**piept**	pyept
ear	**ureche**	oo**re**keh
eye(s)	**ochi**	ok^{y}
face	**faţă**	**fa**tser
finger	**deget**	**de**jet
foot	**picior**	pee**chor** (**la**ba pee**cho**roolоo^{y})
genitals	**organe genitale**	or**ga**neh jenee**ta**leh
gland	**glandă**	**glan**der
hand	**mână**	**muh**ner
head	**cap**	cap
heart	**inimă**	**ee**neemer
jaw	**maxilar**	maxee**lar**
joint	**încheietură**	uhnke-ye**too**rer
kidney	**rinichi**	ree**neek**^{y}
knee	**genunchi**	je**noonk**^{y}
leg	**picior**	pee**chor**
ligament	**ligament**	leega**ment**
lip	**buză**	**boo**zer
liver	**ficat**	fee**cat**
lung	**plămîn**	pler**muhn**
mouth	**gură**	**goo**rer
muscle	**muschi**	mooshk^{y}
neck	**gât**	guht
nerve	**nerv**	nerv
nose	**nas**	nas
rib	**coastă**	**cwas**ter
shoulder	**umăr**	**oo**mer
skin	**piele**	**pye**leh
spine	**coloana vertebrală**	col**wa**na verte**bra**ler
stomach	**stomac**	sto**mac**
tendon	**tendon**	ten**don**
thigh	**coapsă**	**cwap**ser
throat	**gâtlej**	guht**lezh**
thumb	**degetul mare**	**de**jetool **ma**reh
toe	**deget de la picior**	**de**jet deh la pee**chor**

tongue	**limbă**	**leem**ber
tonsils	**amigdale**	ameeg**da**leh
vein	**venă**	**ve**ner

Accident—Injury *Accident—Persoane rănite*

There's been an accident.	**A fost un accident.**	a fost oon acchee**dent**
He/She has hurt his/ her head.	**El/ea s-a lovit la cap.**	yel/ya sa lo**veet** la cap
He's/She's unconscious.	**El/ea şi-a pierdut cunoştinţa.**	yel/ya shya pyer**doot** coonosh**teen**tsa
He's/She's bleeding (heavily).	**El/ea sângerează (puternic).**	yel/ya suhnje**ra**zer (poo**ter**neec)
He's/She's seriously injured.	**El/ea e grav rănit(ă).**	yel/ya yeh grav rer**neet**(**er**)
His/Her arm is broken.	**Si-a rupt braţul.**	shya roopt **brat**sool
His/Her ankle is swollen.	**Are genunchiul umflat.**	areh je**noon**kee-ool oom**flat**
I've been stung.	**M-a înţepat ceva.**	ma uhntse**pat** che**va**
I've got something in my eye.	**Am ceva în ochi.**	am che**va** uhn oky
I've got a/an…	**Am…**	am
blister	**o băşică**	o ber**shee**cer
boil	**un furuncul**	oon foo**roon**cool
bruise	**o vânătaie**	o vuhner**ta**yeh
burn	**o arsură**	o ar**soo**rer
cut	**o tăietură**	o terye**too**rer
graze	**o julitură**	o joolee**too**rer
insect bite	**o înţepătură de insectă**	o uhntseper**too**rer deh een**sec**ter
lump	**o umflătură**	o oomfler**too**rer
rash	**o egzemă**	o eg**ze**mer
sting	**o înţepătură**	o uhntseper**too**rer
swelling	**o umflătură**	o oomfler**too**rer
wound	**o rană**	o **ra**ner
Could you have a look at it?	**Vreţi să vă uitaţi la ea?**	vrets^{y} ser ver ooy**tats**^{y} la ya
I can't move my…	**Nu pot să-mi mişc…**	noo pot serm^{y} meeshc
It hurts.	**Mă doare.**	mer **dwa**reh

You May Hear:

Unde vă doare?	Where does it hurt?
Ce fel de durere este?	What kind of pain is it?
slabă/acută/cu zvâcnituri	dull/sharp/throbbing
continuă/întreruptă	constant/on and off
Este…	It's…
rupt/luxat	broken/sprained
dislocat/rupt	dislocated/torn
Trebuie să faceţi o radiografie.	I'd ike you to have an X-ray
Trebuie pus în gips.	We'll have to put it in plaster.
Este infectat.	It's infected.
Aţi făcut vaccin antitetanos?	Have you been vaccinated against tetanus?
O să vă dau un calmant.	I'll give you a painkiller.

Illness *Boală*

I'm not feeling well.	**Nu mă simt bine.**	noo mer seemt **bee**neh
I'm ill.	**Sunt bolnav(ă).**	soont bol**nav**(**er**)
I feel…	**Mă simt…**	mer seemt
dizzy	**ameţit(ă)**	amet**seet**(**er**)
nauseous	**mi-e greaţă**	myeh **gra**tser
shivery	**am frisoane**	am free**swa**neh
I have a temperature/ fever.	**Am temperatură/ febră.**	am tempera**too**rer/ **fe**brer
My temperature is 38 degrees.	**Am 38 de grade.**	am **tray**zhctsc^{y} shi opt deh **grad**eh
I've been vomiting.	**Am vărsat.**	am verr**sat**
I'm constipated/ I've got diarrhoea.	**Sunt constipat/ Am diaree.**	soont constee**pat**/ am dee-**are**-eh
My … hurt(s).	**Mă doare…**	mer **dwa**reh
I've got (a/an)…	**Am…**	am
asthma	**astmă**	**ast**mer
backache	**o durere de spate**	o doo**re**reh deh **spa**teh
cold	**o răceală/gripă**	o rer**cha**ler/**gree**per

cough	**o tuse**	o **too**seh
cramps/ stomach cramps	**cârcei/ crampe la stomac**	cuhr**tschay**/ **cram**peh la sto**mac**
earache	**o durere de ureche**	o doo**re**reh deh oo**re**keh
hay fever	**alergie la polen**	aler**jee-**eh la po**len**
indigestion	**indigestie**	eendee**jes**tee-eh
palpitations	**palpitaţii**	palpee**ta**tsee
rheumatism	**reumatism**	re-ooma**teesm**
sore throat	**o durere în gât**	o doo**re**reh uhn guht
stiff neck	**o durere de ceafă**	o doo**re**reh deh **cha**fer
stomach ache	**o durere de burtă**	o doo**re**reh deh **boor**ter
sunstroke	**insolaţie**	eensol**a**tsee-eh
I have a headache.	**Am o durere de cap/ Mă doare capul.**	am o doo**re**reh deh cap/ mer **dwa**reh **ca**pool
I have a nosebleed.	**Îmi curge sânge din nas.**	uhm^{y} **coor**jeh **suhn**jeh deen nas
I have difficulties breathing.	**Respir greu.**	res**peer** gre^{oo}
I have chest pains.	**Mă doare pieptul.**	mer **dwa**reh **pyep**tool
I had a heart attack… years ago.	**Am avut un atac de cord… cu ani în urmă.**	am av**oot** oon a**tac** deh cord… coo an^{y} uhn **oor**mer
My blood pressure is too high/ too low.	**Am tensiunea prea mare/ prea mică.**	am tensee-**oo**neh-a preh-a **ma**reh/ preh-a **mee**cer
I'm allergic to…	**Sunt alergic la…**	soont a**ler**jeec la
I'm diabetic.	**Sunt diabetic(ă).**	soont dee-a**be**teec(er)

Women's section *Pentru femei*

I have period pains.	**Am dureri la ciclu.**	am doo**rer**^{y} la **chee**cloo
I have a vaginal infection.	**Am o infecţie vaginală..**	am o een**fec**tsee-eh vajee**na**ler
I'm on the pill.	**Iau anticoncepţionale.**	ya^{oo} anteeconcheptsee- -o**na**leh
I haven't had a period for 2 months.	**Nu mi-a venit ciclul de două luni.**	noo mya ve**neet chee**- clool deh **do-**wer loon^{y}
I'm (3 months') pregnant.	**Sunt gravidă (în luna a treia).**	soont gra**vee**der (uhn **loo**na a **tre**ya)

YOU MAY HEAR:

De când vă simţiţi aşa?	How long have you been feeling like this?
E prima dată când aveţi asta?	Is this the first time you've had this?
Vă iau temperatura/pulsul.	I'll take your temperature/ blood pressure.
Suflecaţi mâneca, vă rog.	Roll up your sleeve, please.
Vă rog dezbracaţi-vă (până la brâu).	Please undress (down to the waist).
Vă rog să vă întindeţi aici.	Please lie down over here.
Deschideţi gura.	Open your mouth.
Respiraţi adînc.	Breathe deeply.
Tuşiţi, vă rog.	Cough, please.
Unde vă doare?	Where does it hurt?
Aveţi…	You've got (a/an)…
apendicită	appendicitis
cistită	cystitis
gastrită	gastritis
gripă	flu
o imflamaţie a…	inflammation of…
o intoxicaţie alimentară	food poisoning
hepatită	hepatitis
icter	jaundice
o boală venerică	venereal disease
pneumonie	pneumonia
pojar	measles
Nu este contagioasă.	It's (not) contagious.
Este o alergie.	It's an allergy.
O să vă fac o injecţie.	I'll give you an injection.
Vreau o recoltare de sânge/ scaun/urină.	I want a specimen of your blood/stools/urine.
Trebuie să staţi în pat… zile.	You must stay in bed for… days.
Vreau să vă vadă un specialist.	I want you to see a specialist.
Trebuie să mergeţi la spital pentru un examen general.	I want you to go to the hospital for a general check-up.

Prescription—Treatment Reţete—Tratament

This is my usual medicine.	**Acesta este medicamentul meu obişnuit.**	a**ches**ta **yes**teh medeeca**men**tool me^{oo} obeeshnoo-**eet**
Can you give me a prescription for this?	**Puteţi să-mi daţi o reţetă pentru acest medicament?**	poo**tets**^{y} serm^{y} dats^{y} o ret**se**ter **pen**troo a**chest** medeeca**ment**
Can you prescribe a/an/some…?	**puteţi să-mi prescrieţi…**	poo**tets**^{y} serm^{y} pres**cree**-ets^{y}
antidepressant	**nişte antidepresive**	**neesh**teh anteedepre**see**veh
sleeping pills	**nişte somnifere**	**neesh**teh somnee**fe**reh
tranquillizer	**nişte tranchilizante**	**neesh**teh trankelee**zan**teh
I'm allergic to certain antibiotics/penicillin.	**Sunt alergic la anumite antibiotice/ penicilină.**	soont a**ler**jeec la anoo**mee**teh anteebee-**o**teecheh/ peneechee**lee**ner
I don't want anything too strong.	**Nu vreau ceva prea puternic.**	noo vra^{oo} che**va** preh-a poo**ter**neec
How many times a day should I take it?	**De câte ori pe zi trebuie să iau acest medicament?**	deh **cuh**teh or^{y} peh zee **tre**boo-yeh ser ya^{oo} a**chest** medeeca**ment**
Must I swallow them whole?	**Trebuie să le înghit întregi?**	**tre**booyeh ser leh uhn**geet** uhn**trej**^{y}

YOU MAY HEAR:

Ce tratement urmaţi?	What treatment are you having?
Pe cale injectabilă sau orală?	By injection or orally?
Luaţi … linguriţe din acest medicament…	Take… teaspoons of this medicine…
Luaţi o pastilă cu un pahar de apă…	Take one pill with a glass of water…
la … ore	every … hours
de … ori pe zi	… times a day
înainte/după fiecare masă	before/after each meal
dimineaţa/seara	in the morning/at night
dacă aveţi dureri	if there is any pain
timp de… zile	for… days

CHEMIST'S see page 107

Fee *Plata*

How much do I owe you?	**Cât vă datorez?**	cuht ver dato**rez**
May I have a receipt for my health insurance?	**Pot să am o chitanţă pentru asigurăre?**	pot ser am o kee**tan**tser **pen**troo aseegoo**ra**reh
Can I have a medical certificate?	**Pot să am un certificat medical?**	pot ser am oon cherteefee**cat** medee**cal**
Would you fill in this health insurance form, please?	**Vreţi să completaţi formularul de asigurări, vă rog?**	vrets^y ser comple**tats^y** formoo**la**rool deh aseegoo**rerr^y** ver rog

Hospital *Spital*

Please notify my family.	**Vă rog anunţaţi-mi familia.**	ver rog anoon**tsats^y-m^y** fam**ee**lee-a
What are the visiting hours?	**Care sunt orele de vizită?**	**ca**reh soont **o**releh deh **vee**zeeter
When can I get up?	**Când mă pot da jos din pat?**	cuhnd mer pot da zhos deen pat
When will the doctor come?	**Când vine doctorul?**	cuhnd **vee**neh **doc**torool
I'm in pain.	**Am dureri.**	am doo**rer^y**
I can't eat/ sleep.	**Nu pot mânca/ dormi.**	noo pot muhn**ca**/ dor**mee**
Where is the bell?	**Unde este soneria?**	**oon**deh **yes**teh sone**ree**-a

nurse	**soră (medicală)**	**so**rer (medee**ca**ler)
patient	**pacient**	pa**chee**-ent
anaesthetic	**anestetic**	anes**te**teec
blood transfusion	**transfuzie de sânge**	trans**foo**zee-eh deh **suhn**jeh
injection	**injecţie**	eenz**hec**tsee-eh
operation	**operaţie**	ope**ra**tsee-eh
bed	**pat**	pat
bedpan	**oală de noapte/ ploscă**	**wa**ler deh **nwap**teh/ **plos**cer
thermometer	**termometru**	termo**me**troo

Dentist *Dentist*

If you need to see the dentist while in Romania ask for a *cabinet dentar* at the *policlinică cu plată*. You will normally be able to get a quick appointment.

Can you recommend a good dentist?	**Puteţi să-mi recomandaţi un dentist bun?**	poo**tets**^{y} serm^{y} recoman**dats**^{y} oon den**teest** boon
Can I make an (urgent) appointment to see Dr…?	**Puteţi să-mi faceţi o programare de urgenţă pentru doctorul…**	poo**tets**^{y} serm^{y} **fa**chets^{y} o progra**ma**reh deh oor**jen**tser **pen**troo **doc**torool
Couldn't you make it earlier?	**Nu puteţi să o faceţi mai devreme?**	noo poo**tets**^{y} ser o **fa**chets^{y} migh de**vre**meh
I have a broken tooth.	**Am un dinte spart.**	am oon **deen**teh spart
I have toothache.	**Mă doare dintele/ măseaua.**	mer **dwa**reh **deen**teleh/ mer**sa**wa
I have an abscess.	**Am un abces.**	am oon ab**ches**
This tooth hurts.	**Mă doare dintele acesta.**	mer **dwa**reh **deen**teleh a**ches**ta
at the top	**sus**	soos
at the bottom	**jos**	zhos
at the front	**în faţă**	uhn **fa**tser
at the back	**în spate**	uhn **spa**teh
Can you fix it temporarily?	**Puteţi să-l trataţi provizoriu?**	poo**tets**^{y} serl tra**tats**^{y} provee**zo**ree-oo
I don't want it pulled out.	**Nu vreau să-l extrageţi.**	noo vra^{oo} serl ex**tra**jets^{y}
Could you give me an anaesthetic?	**Puteţi să-mi faceţi anestezie?**	poo**tets**^{y} serm^{y} **fa**chets^{y} aneste**zee**-eh
I've lost a filling.	**Mi-a căzut o plombă.**	mya cer**zoot** o **plom**ber
My gums…	**Gingia…**	jeen**jee**a
are very sore	**mă doare**	mer **dwa**reh
are bleeding	**sângerează**	suhnje**ra**zer
I've broken my dentures.	**Mi s-a rupt proteza.**	mee sa roopt pro**te**za
Can you repair my dentures?	**Puteţi să-mi reparaţi proteza?**	poo**tets**^{y} serm^{y} repa**rats**^{y} pro**te**za
When will they be ready?	**Când va fi gata?**	cuhnd va fee **ga**ta

Reference section

Where do you come from? *De unde veniţi?*

Africa	**Africa**	afreeca
Asia	**Asia**	asee-a
Australia	**Australia**	a-ooostralee-a
Europe	**Europa**	e-ooropa
North America	**America de Nord**	amereeca deh nord
South America	**America de Sud**	amereeca deh sood
Belgium	**Belgia**	beljee-a
Belorus	**Bielorusia**	byeloroosee-a
Bulgaria	**Bulgaria**	boolgaree-a
Canada	**Canada**	canada
China	**China**	keena
Czech Republic	**Republica Cehă**	repoobleeca cheher
Denmark	**Danemarca**	danemarca
England	**Anglia**	anglee-a
Finland	**Finlanda**	feenlanda
France	**Franţa**	frantsa
Germany	**Germania**	jermanee-a
Great Britain	**Marea Britanie**	mareh-a breetanee-eh
Greece	**Grecia**	grechee-a
India	**India**	eendee-a
Ireland	**Irlanda**	eerlanda
Italy	**Italia**	eetalee-a
Japan	**Japonia**	zhaponee-a
Luxembourg	**Luxemburg**	looxemboorg
Netherlands	**Olanda**	olanda
New Zealand	**Noua Zeelandă**	no-wa zeelander
Norway	**Norvegia**	norvejee-a
Romania	**România**	romuhneea
Russia	**Rusia**	roosee-a
Scotland	**Scoţia**	scotsee-a
Slovakia	**Slovacia**	slovachee-a
South Africa	**Africa de Sud**	afreeca deh sood
Spain	**Spania**	spanee-a
Sweden	**Suedia**	soo-edee-a
Switzerland	**Elveţia**	elvetsee-a
Transylvania	**Transilvania**	transeelvanee-a
Turkey	**Turcia**	toorchee-a
Ukraine	**Ucraina**	oocrayna
United States	**Statele Unite**	stateleh ooneeteh
Wales	**Ţara Galilor**	tsara galeelor

Numbers *Numere*

0	**zero**	**ze**ro
1	**unu**	**oo**noo
2	**doi**	doy
3	**trei**	tray
4	**patru**	**pa**troo
5	**cinci**	cheench^{y}
6	**şase**	**sha**seh
7	**şapte**	**shap**teh
8	**opt**	opt
9	**nouă**	**no-**wer
10	**zece**	**ze**cheh
11	**unsprezece**	**oon**sprezecheh
12	**doisprezece**	**doy**sprezecheh
13	**treisprezece**	**tray**sprezecheh
14	**paisprezece**	**pigh**sprezecheh
15	**cincisprezece**	**cheench^{y}**sprezecheh
16	**şaisprezece**	**shigh**sprezecheh
17	**şaptesprezece**	**shap**tesprezeceh
18	**optsprezece**	**opt**sprezecheh
19	**nouăsprezeche**	**no-**wersprezecheh
20	**douăzeci**	do-wer**zech^{y}**
21	**douăzeci şi unu**	do-wer**zech^{y}** shee **oo**noo
22	**douăzeci şi doi**	do-wer**zech^{y}** shee doy
23	**douăzeci şi trei**	do-wer**zech^{y}** shee tray
24	**douăzeci şi patru**	do-wer**zech^{y}** shee **pa**troo
25	**douăzeci şi cinci**	do-wer**zech^{y}** shee cheench^{y}
26	**douăzeci şi şase**	do-wer**zech^{y}** shee **sha**seh
27	**douăzeci şi şapte**	do-wer**zech^{y}** shee **shap**teh
28	**douăzeci şi opt**	do-wer**zech^{y}** shee opt
29	**douăzeci şi nouă**	do-wer**zech^{y}** shee **no-**wer
30	**treizeci**	tray**zech^{y}**
31	**treizeci şi unu**	tray**zech^{y}** shee **oo**noo
32	**treizeci şi doi**	tray**zech^{y}** shee doy
40	**patruzeci**	patroo**zech^{y}**
41	**patruzeci şi unu**	patroo**zech^{y}** shee **oo**noo
42	**patruzeci şi doi**	patroo**zech^{y}** shee doy
50	**cincizeci**	cheench^{y}**zech^{y}**
51	**cinzeci şi unu**	cheench^{y}**zech^{y}** shee **oo**noo
52	**cinzeci şi doi**	cheench^{y}**zech^{y}** shee doy
60	**şaizeci**	shigh**zech^{y}**
61	**şaizeci şi unu**	shigh**zech^{y}** shee **oo**noo
62	**şaizeci şi doi**	shigh**zech^{y}** shee doy

70	**şaptezeci**	shapteh**zech**^{y}
71	**şaptezeci şi unu**	shapteh**zech**^{y} shee **oo**noo
72	**şaptezeci şi doi**	shapteh**zech**^{y} shee doy
80	**optzeci**	opt**zech**^{y}
81	**optzeci şi unu**	opt**zech**^{y} shee **oo**noo
82	**optzeci şi doi**	opt**zech**^{y} shee doy
90	**nouăzeci**	no-wer**zech**^{y}
91	**nouăzeci şi unu**	no-wer**zech**^{y} shee **oo**noo
92	**nouăzeci şi doi**	no-wer**zech**^{y} shee doy
100	**o sută**	o **soo**ter
101	**o sută unu**	o **soo**ter **oo**noo
102	**o sută doi**	o **soo**ter doy
110	**o sută zece**	o **soo**ter **ze**cheh
120	**o sută douăzeci**	o **soo**ter do-wer**zech**^{y}
130	**o sută treizeci**	o **soo**ter tray**zech**^{y}
140	**o sută patruzeci**	o **soo**ter patroo**zech**^{y}
150	**o sută cincizeci**	o **soo**ter cheench^{y}**zech**^{y}
160	**o sută saizeci**	o **soo**ter shigh**zech**^{y}
170	**o sută şaptezeci**	o **soo**ter shapteh**zech**^{y}
180	**o sută optzeci**	o **soo**ter opt**zech**^{y}
190	**o sută nouăzeci**	o **soo**ter no-wer**zech**^{y}
200	**două sute**	**do**-wer **soo**teh
300	**trei sute**	tray **soo**teh
400	**patru sute**	**pa**troo **soo**teh
500	**cinci sute**	cheench^{y} **soo**teh
600	**şase sute**	**sha**seh **soo**teh
700	**şapte sute**	**shap**teh **soo**teh
800	**opt sute**	opt **soo**teh
900	**nouă sute**	**no**-wer **soo**teh
1000	**o mie**	o **mee**-eh
1100	**o mie o sută**	o **mee**-eh o **soo**ter
1200	**o mie două sute**	o **mee**-eh **do**-wer **soo**teh
2000	**două mii**	**do**-wer mee
5000	**cinci mii**	cheench^{y} mee
10,000	**zece mii**	**ze**cheh mee
50,000	**cincizeci de mii**	cheench^{y}**zech**^{y} deh mee
100,000	**o sută de mii**	o **soo**ter deh mee
1,000,000	**un milion**	oon meelee-**on**
1,000,000,000	**un miliard**	oon meelee**ard**

first	**primul (prima)**	**pree**mool (**pree**ma)
second	**al doilea (a doua)**	al **do**-eeleh-a (a **do**-wa)
third	**al treilea (a treia)**	al **tre**-eeleh-a (a **tre**-ya)
fourth	**al patrulea (a patra)**	al **pa**trooleh-a (a **pa**tra)
fifth	**al cincilea (a cincea)**	al **cheen**cheeleh-a (a **cheen**cheh-a)
sixth	**al şaselea (a şasea)**	al **sha**seleh-a (a **sha**seh-a)
seventh	**al şaptelea (a şaptea)**	al **shap**teleh-a (a **shap**teh-a)
eighth	**al optulea (a opta)**	al **op**tooleh-a (a **op**ta)
ninth	**al nouălea (a noua)**	al **no**-werleh-a (a **no**-wa)
tenth	**al zecelea (a zecea)**	al **ze**cheleh-a (a **ze**cheh-a)
once/twice	**o dată/de două ori**	o **da**ter/deh **do**-wer or^y
three times	**de trei ori**	deh tray or^y
a half	**o jumătate**	o zhoomer**ta**teh
half a…	**jumătate…**	zhoomer**ta**teh
half of…	**jumătate de…**	zhoomer**ta**teh deh
a quarter/one third	**un sfert/o treime**	oon sfert/o tre-**ee**meh
a pair of	**o pereche de**	o pe**re**keh deh
a dozen	**o duzină**	o doo**zee**ner
one per cent	**unu la sută**	**oo**noo la **soo**ter
3.4%	**trei virgulă patru la sută**	tray **veer**gooler **pa**troo la **soo**ter

Date and time *Data şi anul*

1993	**o mie nouă sute nouă zeci şi trei**	o **mee**-eh **no**-wer **soo**teh **no**-wer zech^y she tray
2005	**două mii cinci**	**do**-wer mee cheench^y

Year and age *Anul şi vârsta*

year	**an**	an
leap year	**an bisect**	an bee**sect**
decade	**deceniu**	de**cheh**-nee-oo
century	**secol**	**se**col
this year	**anul acesta**	**a**nool a**ches**ta
last year	**anul trecut**	**a**nool tre**coot**
next year	**anul viitor**	**a**nool vee-ee**tor**
each year	**în fiecare an**	uhn **fee**-ecareh an
two years ago	**acum doi ani**	a**coom** doy an^y
years ago	**cu ani în urmă**	coo an^y uhn **oor**mer
in one year	**într-un an**	uhntr-oon an
in the eighties	**în anii optzeci**	uhn **a**nee opt**zech**^{y}
in the nineties	**în anii nouăzeci**	uhn **a**nee no-wer**zech**^{y}

the 16th century	**în secolul al şaisprezecelea**	uhn **se**colool al **shigh**sprezecheleh-a
in the 20th century	**în secolul douăzeci**	uhn **se**colool do-wer**zech**^{y}
How old are you?	**Ce vârstă aveţi?/ Câţi ani ai?**	cheh **vuhr**ster a**vets**^{y}/ cuhts^{y} an^{y} igh
I'm 30 years old.	**Am treizeci de ani.**	am tray**zech**^{y} deh an^{y}
He/She was born in 1960.	**El/Ea s-a născut în o mie nouă sute şaizeci.**	yel/ya s-a ners**coot** uhn o **mee**-eh **no**-wer **soo**teh shigh**zech**^{y}
What is his/her age?	**Ce vârsta are el/ea?**	cheh **vuhr**ster **a**reh yel/ya

Seasons *Anotimpurile*

spring/summer	**primăvară/vară**	**pree**mervarer/**va**rer
autumn/winter	**toamnă/iarnă**	**twam**ner/**yar**ner
in spring	**primăvara**	**pree**mervara
during the summer	**în timpul verii**	uhn **teem**pool **ve**ree
in autumn	**toamna**	**twam**na
during the winter	**în timpul iernii**	uhn **teem**pool **yer**nee
high season	**în sezon**	uhn se**zon**
low season	**în afara sezonului**	uhn a**fa**ra se**zo**noolo^{y}

Months *Lunile anului*

January	**ianuarie**	yanoo-**a**ree-eh
February	**februarie**	febroo-**a**ree-eh
March	**martie**	**mar**tee-eh
April	**aprilie**	a**pree**lee-eh
May	**mai**	migh
June	**iunie**	**yoo**nee-eh
July	**iulie**	**yoo**lee-eh
August	**august**	**a**^{oo}goost
September	**septembrie**	sep**tem**bree-eh
October	**octombire**	oc**tom**bree-eh
November	**noiembrie**	no**yem**bree-eh
December	**decembrie**	de**chem**bree-eh
in September	**în septembrie**	uhn sep**tem**bree-eh
since October	**din octombrie**	deen oc**tom**bree-eh
the beginning of January	**la începutul lunii ianuarie**	la uhnche**poo**tool **loo**nee yanoo-**a**ree-eh
the middle of February	**la mijlocul lunii februarie**	la **meezh**locool **loo**nee febroo-**a**ree-eh
the end of March	**la sfârşitul lui martie**	la sfuhr**shee**tool loo^{y} **mar**tee-eh

Days and date *Zilele şi data*

What day is it today?	**ce zi este azi?**	cheh zee **yes**teh az^{y}
Sunday	**duminică**	doo**mee**neecer
Monday	**luni**	loon^{y}
Tuesday	**marţi**	marts^{y}
Wednesday	**miercuri**	**myer**coor^{y}
Thursday	**joi**	zhoy
Friday	**vineri**	**vee**ner^{y}
Saturday	**sâmbătă**	**suhm**berter
It's…	**Este…**	**yes**teh
July 1	**întâi iulie**	uhn**tuhy yoo**lee-eh
March 10	**zece martie**	**ze**cheh **mar**tee-eh
in the morning	**dimineaţa**	deemee**na**tsa
during the day	**în timpul zilei**	uhn **teem**pool **zee**lay
in the afternoon	**după amiaza**	**doo**per a**mya**za
in the evening	**seara**	**sa**ra
at night	**noaptea**	**nwap**teh-a
the day before yesterday	**alaltăieri**	a**lal**teryer^{y}
yesterday	**ieri**	yer^{y}
today	**azi**	az^{y}
tomorrow	**mâine**	**muhy**neh
the day after tomorrow	**poimâine**	**poy**muhyneh
the day before	**cu o zi înainte**	coo o zee uhna**een**teh
the next day	**ziua următoare**	**zee**wa oormer**twa**reh
two days ago	**acum două zile**	a**coom do**-wer **zee**leh
in three days' time	**peste trei zile**	**pes**teh tray **zee**leh
last week	**săptămâna trecută**	serpter**muh**ner tre**coo**ter
next week	**săptămâna viitoare**	serpter**muh**ner vee-ee**twa**reh
birthday	**zi de naştere**	zee deh **nash**tereh
day off	**zi liberă**	ze **lee**berer
holiday	**sărbătoare legală**	serber**twa**reh le**ga**ler
holidays/vacation	**concediu/vacanţă**	con**che**dyoo/va**can**tser
week	**saptamână**	serpter**muh**ner
weekend	**sfârşit de săptămână**	sfuhr**sheet** deh serpter**muh**ner
working day	**zi lucrătoare**	zee loocrer**twa**reh

Public holidays *Sărbători legale*

1 January/ New Year's Day and 2 January	**Întâi Ianuarie/ Anul Nou şi 2 Ianuarie**	uhn**tuhy** yanoo-**aree**-eh/ **a**nool no shi doy yanoo-**aree**-eh
1 May	**Întâi Mai**	uhn**tuhy** migh
Christmas Day	**Crăciun**	crer**choon**
Second Christmas Day	**Ziua a doua de Crăciun**	**zee**-wah a **do**-wah de crer**choon**
MOVEABLE DAYS		
Easter	**Paşte**	**pash**teh

Greetings and wishes *Salutări şi urări*

Merry Christmas!	**Sărbători fericite!**	serber**tor**y fere**echee**teh
Happy New Year!	**An Nou Fericit!**	an nooo fe**ree**cheet
Happy Easter!	**Cristos a Înviat!**	crees**tos** a uhnvee-**at**
Happy birthday!	**La mulţi ani!**	la mooltsy any
Best wishes!	**Noroc, şi numai bine!**	no**roc** shee **noo**migh **bee**neh
Congratulations!	**Felicitări!**	feleechee**terr**y
Good luck/ All the best!	**Noroc/ Toate cele bune!**	no**roc**/ **twa**teh **che**leh **boo**neh
Have a good trip!	**Călătorie plăcută!**	cerlerto**ree**-eh pler**coo**ter
Have a good holiday!	**Vacanţă plăcută!**	va**can**tser pler**coo**ter
Best regards from…	**Sincere salutări de la…**	**seen**chereh saloo**terr**y deh la
My regards to…	**Toate cele bune lui…/ Complimente lui…**	**twa**teh **che**leh **boo**neh looy/ complee**men**teh looy

What time is it? *Cât e ceasul?*

The 24-hour clock is generally used in timetables and often in everyday conversation too, for example when fixing appointments.

Excuse me. Can you tell me the time?	**Fiţi amabil, puteţi să-mi spuneţi cât este ceasul?**	feetsy a**ma**beel poo**tets**y sermy **spoo**netsy cuht **yes**teh **cha**sool

It's …	**Este…**	**yes**teh
five past one	**ora unu şi cinci minute**	ora **oo**noo shee cheench^{y} mee**noo**teh
ten past two	**ora două şi zece minute**	ora **do-**wer shee **ze**cheh mee**noo**teh
a quarter past three	**trei şi un sfert**	tray shee oon sfert
twenty past four	**patru şi douăzeci**	**pa**troo shee do-wer**zech^{y}**
twenty-five past five	**cinci şi douăzeci şi cinci**	cheench^{y} shee do-wer**zech^{y}** shee cheench^{y}
half past six	**şase şi jumătate**	**sha**seh shee zhoomer**ta**teh
twenty-five to seven	**şapte fără douăzeci şi cinci**	**shap**teh **fer**rer do-wer**zech^{y}** shee cheench^{y}
twenty to eight	**opt fară douăzeci**	opt **fer**rer do-wer**zech^{y}**
a quarter to nine	**nouă fară un sfert**	**no-**wer **fer**rer oon sfert
ten to ten	**zece fară zece**	**ze**cheh **fer**rer **ze**cheh
five to eleven	**unsprezece fară cinci**	**oon**sprezecheh **fer**rer cheench^{y}
twelve o'clock (noon/ midnight)	**ora douăsprezece/ zero**	ora **do-**wersprezecheh/ **ze**ro
at noon	**la amiază**	la a**mya**zer
at midnight	**la miezul nopţii**	la **mye**zool **nop**tsee
in the morning	**dimineaţa**	deemeena**t**sa
in the afternoon	**după-amiaza**	**doo**per-a**mya**za
in the evening	**seara**	**sa**ra
The train leaves at…	**Trenul pleacă la ora…**	**tre**nool **pla**cer la **o**ra
13.04 (1.04pm)	**treisprezece zero patru/ unu şi patru minute**	**tray**sprezecheh **ze**ro **pa**troo/ **oo**noo shee **pa**troo mee**noo**teh
0.40 (0.40am)	**ora zero şi patruzeci de minute**	ora **ze**ro shee patroo**zech^{y}** deh mee**noo**teh
in five minutes	**în cinci minute**	uhn cheench^{y} mee**noo**teh
in a quarter of an hour	**într-un sfert de oră**	uhntr-oon sfert deh **o**rer
half an hour ago	**acum jumătate de oră**	a**coom** zhoomer**ta**teh deh **o**rer
about two hours	**vreo două ore**	vro **do-**wer **o**reh
more than 10 minutes	**mai mult de zece minute**	migh moolt deh **ze**cheh mee**noo**teh
less than 30 seconds	**mai puţin de treizeci de secunde**	migh poo**tseen** deh tray**zech^{y}** deh se**coon**deh

Common abbreviations *Abrevieri*

a.c.	**anul curent**	the current year
ACR	**Automobil Club Român**	Romanian Automobile Club
ap.	**apartamentul**	apartment
bd.	**bulevardul**	avenue/boulevard
BRCE	**Banca Româna de Comerţ Exterior**	Romanian Bank for Foreign Trade
BRD	**Banca Româna pentru Dezvoltare**	Romanian Bank for Development
BTT	**Biroul de Turism pentru Tineret**	Youth Travel Agency
CATT	**Compania Autonomă de Turism pentru Tineret**	Company for Youth Travel
CP	**cai putere**	horsepower
de ex.	**de exemplu**	for example
dl.	**domnul**	Mr
dlui.	**dumnealui**	he (formal)
dna.	**doamna**	Mrs
dşoara	**domnişoara**	Miss
dvs.	**dumneavoastră**	you (formal)
ONT	**Oficiul Naţional de Turism**	National Toursit Office
PTTR	**Poşta, Telegraf, Telefon, Radio**	Post Office
Pţa	**piaţa**	square
RATB	**Regia Autonomă de Transporturi Bucureşti**	Bucharest Public Transport Company
SA	**Societate Anonimă**	Incorporated (Inc.)
Sf.	**sfântul**	Saint
SNCFR	**Societatea Naţională a Căilor Ferate Române**	Romanian National Railways
SRL	**Societate cu Răspundere Limitată**	Public LImited Company (plc)
str.	**strada**	street
ş. a. m. d.	**şi aşa mai departe**	and so on
TAROM	**Transporturile Aeriene Române**	Romanian Airlines
TVR	**Televizunea Română**	Romanian Television

Signs and notices *Semne şi anunţuri*

Aşteptaţi, vă rog	Please wait
Atenţie	Caution
Bărbaţi	Gentlemen
Casa	Cash desk
Câine rău	Beware of the dog
De închiriat	For hire/To let
Deschis	Open
De vânzare	For sale
Femei	Ladies
Fierbinte	Hot
Frig	Cold
Fumatul interzis	No smoking
Ieşire de incendiu	Emergency exit
Ieşire	Exit
Împingeţi	Push
Informaţii	Information
…interzis	…forbidden
Intraţi fără să bateţi (la uşă)	Enter without knocking
Intrare	Entrance
Intrarea interzisă	No admittance
Intrarea gratuită	Free admittance
Jos	Down
Liber	Vacant
Lift	Lift
Nu atingeţi	Do not touch
Nu avem locuri	No vacancies
Nu blocaţi intrarea	Do not block entrance
Nu deranjaţi	Do not disturb
Nu funcţionează	Out of order
Ocupat	Occupied
Păstraţi curăţenia	No littering
Pericol (de moarte)	Danger (of death)
Proaspăt vopsit	Wet paint
Rezervat	Reserved
Solduri	Sale
Sunaţi, vă rog	Please ring
Sus	Up
Trageţi	Pull
Vândut	Sold out

Emergency *Urgenţă*

Call the police	**Chemaţi poliţia**	ke**mats**^{y} po**lee**tsee-a
Consulate	**Consulat**	consoo**lat**
DANGER	**PERICOL**	pe**ree**col
Embassy	**Ambasadă**	amba**sa**der
FIRE	**FOC**	foc
Gas	**Gaz**	gaz
Get a doctor	**Chemaţi un doctor**	ke**mats**^{y} oon **doc**tor
Go away	**Pleacă de aici**	**pla**cer deh a-**eech**^{y}
HELP	**AJUTOR**	azhoo**tor**
Get help quickly	**Chemaţi pe cineva repede**	ke**mats**^{y} peh chee**ne**va **re**pedeh
I'm ill	**Sunt bolnav(a)**	soont bol**nav**(**a**)
I'm lost	**M-am rătăcit**	mam rerter**cheet**
Leave me alone	**lăsaţi-mă/lasă-mă în pace**	ler**sa**tseemer/ **la**sermer uhn **pa**cheh
LOOK OUT	**ATENȚIE**	a**ten**tsee-eh
Poison	**Otravă**	o**tra**ver
POLICE	**POLIȚIA**	po**lee**tsee-a
Stop that man/ woman	**Opriţi omul acela/ femeia aceea**	o**preets**^{y} omool a**che**la/ fe**me**ya a**che**-a
STOP THIEF	**HOȚUL**	**ho**tsool

Emergency telephone numbers *Numere utile*

Here are some important emergency telephone numbers:

961 Ambulance	955 Police	981 Fire

Lost property—Theft *Obiecte pierdute—Furt*

Where's the …?	**Unde este …?**	**oon**deh **yes**teh
lost property (lost and found) office	**biroul de obiecte pierdute**	bee**ro**-ool deh o**byec**teh pyer**doo**teh
police station	**centrul de poliţie**	**chen**trool de po**lee**tsee-eh
I want to report a theft.	**Vreau să raportez un furt.**	vra^{oo} ser rapor**tez** oon foort
My … has been stolen.	**Mi s-a furat …**	mee sa foo**rat**
I've lost my …	**Am pierdut …**	am pyer**doot**
handbag	**poşeta/geanta**	po**she**ta/**jan**ta
passport	**paşaportul**	pasha**por**tool
wallet	**portmoneul**	portmo**ne**-ool

CAR ACCIDENTS see page 78

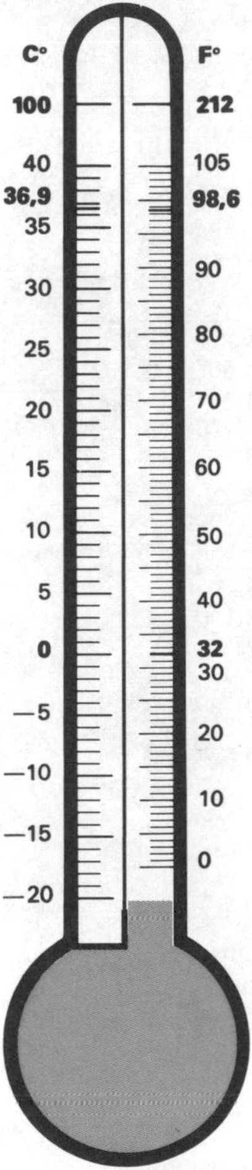

Conversion tables

Centimetres and inches

To change centimetres into inches, multiply by .39.

To change inches into centimetres, multiply by 2.54.

	in.	feet	yards
1 mm	0.039	0.003	0.001
1 cm	0.39	0.03	0.01
1 dm	3.94	0.32	0.10
1 m	39.40	3.28	1.09

	mm	cm	m
1 in.	25.4	2.54	0.025
1 ft.	304.8	30.48	0.304
1 yd.	914.4	91.44	0.914

(32 metres = 35 yards)

Temperature

To convert Centigrade into degrees Fahrenheit, multiply Centigrade by 1.8 and add 32.

To convert degrees Fahrenheit into Centigrade, subtract 32 from Fahrenheit and divide by 1.8.

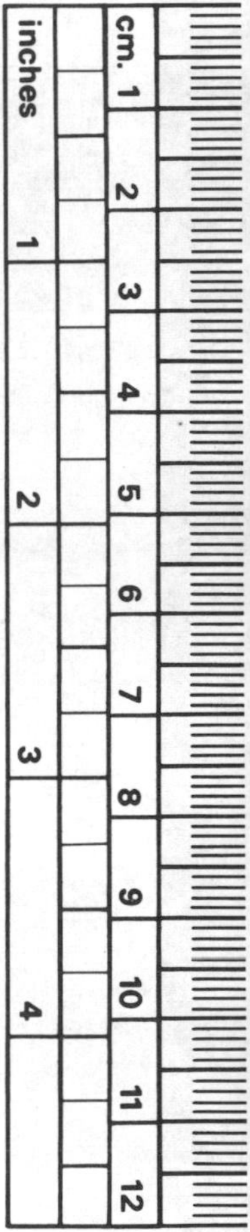

Kilometres into miles

1 kilometre (km.) = 0.62 miles

km.	10	20	30	40	50	60	70	80	90	100	110	120	130
miles	6	12	19	25	31	37	44	50	56	62	68	75	81

Miles into kilometres

1 mile = 1.609 kilometres (km.)

miles	10	20	30	40	50	60	70	80	90	100
km.	16	32	48	64	80	97	113	129	145	161

Fluid measures

1 litre (l.) = 0.88 imp. quart or 1.06 U.S. quart

1 imp. quart = 1.14 l. 1 U.S. quart = 0.95 l.

1 imp. gallon = 4.55 l. 1 U.S. gallon = 3.8 l.

litres	5	10	15	20	25	30	35	40	45	50
imp. gal.	1.1	2.2	3.3	4.4	5.5	6.6	7.7	8.8	9.9	11.0
U.S. gal.	1.3	2.6	3.9	5.2	6.5	7.8	9.1	10.4	11.7	13.0

Weights and measures

1 kilogram or kilo (kg.) = 1000 grams (g.)

100 g. = 3.5 oz. 1/2 kg. = 1.1 lb.

200 g. = 7.0 oz. 1 kg. = 2.2 lb.

1 oz. = 28.35 g.

1 lb. = 453.60 g.

Basic Grammar

Nouns and articles

In Romanian, nouns belong to three genders: masculine, feminine and neuter. Nouns ending in a consonant are usually masculine or neuter, and nouns that end in a vowel are generally feminine. Although there are many exceptions in the plural form, masculine nouns usually end in **-i**; feminine nouns end in **-i**, and neuter nouns end in **-e** or **-uri.**

pom – pomi	tree – trees	(masc.)
excursie – excursii	trip – trips	(fem.)
scaun – scaune	chair – chairs	(neut.)

1. **Indefinite article** (a)
The indefinite article is **un** for masculine nouns, **o** for feminine nouns and **un** for neuter nouns. With plural forms, the invariable article **nişte** "some" is used.

(masc.)	**un călător**	a traveller	**nişte călători**	some travellers
(fem.)	**o piesă**	a play	**nişte piese**	some plays
	o librărie	a bookshop	**nişte librării**	some bookshops
	o carte	a book	**nişte cărţi**	some books
(neut.)	**un spectacol**	a show	**nişte spectacole**	some shows
	un taxi	a taxi	**nişte taxiuri**	some taxis

2. **Definite article** (the)
In Romanian, there is no separate word for the definite article; instead a particle is placed at the end of the noun, depending on its gender and number; the definite articles for singular nouns are **ul, -a, -ul,** and for plural are **-i,** and **-le.**

(masc.)	**copac**	tree	**copacul**	the tree	**copacii**	the trees
(fem.)	**casă**	house	**casa**	the house	**casele**	the houses
(neut.)	**hotel**	hotel	**hotelul**	the hotel	**hotelurile**	the hotels
	birou	office	**biroul**	the office	**birourile**	the offices

Adjectives

The adjective agrees in number, case and gender with the noun it describes. It usually follows the noun but certain common adjectives precede the noun. The table below shows the declension of nouns, adjectives and indefinite articles.

	masc. a good doctor	fem. a good map	neut. a good hotel
SINGULAR			
subject direct object }	**un doctor bun**	**o hartă bună**	**un hotel bun**
possessive object indirect object }	**unui doctor bun**	**unei hărţi bune**	**unui hotel bun**
PLURAL			
subject direct object }	**nişte doctori buni**	**nişte hărţi bune**	**nişte hoteluri bune**
possessive object indirect object }	**unor doctori buni**	**unor hărţi bune**	**unor hoteluri bune**

Each case is illustrated in the examples below. Note the different forms of the possessive object (of … *or* …'s) and the indirect object (to …).

***Un doctor bun* este foarte ocupat.**	*A good doctor* is very busy.
Puteţi să chemaţi *un doctor bun?*	Can you get me *a good doctor?*
Biroul *unui doctor bun* est curat.	*A good doctor's* office is clean.
El a împrumutat cartea lui *unui doctor bun.*	He lent his book *to a good doctor.*

Demonstrative adjectives

	masc.	fem.	neut.
this	**acest(a)**	**această (aceasta)**	**acest(a)**
these	**aceşti(a)**	**aceste(a)**	**aceste(a)**
that	**acel(a)**	**acea/aceea**	**acel(a)**
those	**acei(a)**	**acele(a)**	**acele(a)**

These adjectives can be placed either before or, for particular emphasis, after the noun. When placed after the noun, they take the endings of the definte article form (shown in brackets).

Possessive adjectives and pronouns

	singular			plural		
	masc.	fem.	neut.	masc.	fem.	neut.
pronoun particle	**al**	**a**	**al**	ai	**ale**	**ale**
my	**meu**	**mea**	**meu**	mei	**mele**	**mele**
your	**tău**	**ta**	**tău**	tăi	**tale**	**tale**
his/her/its	**său**	**lui/sa/ei**	**lui/ei/său**	săi/lui/ei	**lui/sale/ei**	**sale**
our	**nostru**	**noastră**	**nostru**	noştri	**noastre**	**noastre**
your	**vostru**	**voastră**	**vostru**	voştri	**voastre**	**voastre**

Invariable adjectives are used for "their" – **lor**, and the formal form of "you" – **dumneavoastră.** When they are not the subject of the sentence, **ei** "her" and **lui** "his" replace the forms of **său.**

The possessive pronoun is formed by preceding the possessive adjective with the pronoun particle.

pâinea noastră our bread **cărţile sunt ale mele** the books are mine

Personal pronouns

	Subject	Direct Object	Indirect Object	Reflexive
I	**eu**	**mă**	**îmi**	**mă**
you (sing.)	**tu**	**te**	**îţi**	**te**
he, it	**el**	**îl**	**îi**	**se**
she	**ea**	**o**	**îi**	**se**
we	**noi**	**ne**	**ne**	**ne**
you (plur.)	**voi/ dumneavoastră**	**vă**	**vă**	**vă**
they (masc.)	**ei**	**ii**	**le**	**se**
they (fem.)	**ele**	**le**	**le**	**se**

Romanian has four forms for the word "you".

tu for adressing a close friend or child (singular)

dumneata (d-ta) for addressing a colleague (singular)

voi for addressing close friends (plural)

dumneavoastră (dvs.) for addressing one or more strangers or people older than yourself; this is the most respectful term and should be used when in doubt

Verbs

There are five main conjugations of verbs in Romanian language. They are distinguished by the ending of the infinitive: **-a, -ea, -e, -i** and **î.**

The **present tense**:

	a învăţa (to learn)	**a vedea** (to see)	**a face** (to make, do)	**a vorbi** (to speak)
eu	**învăţ**	**văd**	**fac**	**vorbesc**
tu	**înveţi**	**vezi**	**faci**	**vorbeşti**
el/ea	**învaţă**	**vede**	**face**	**vorbeşte**
noi	**învăţăm**	**vedem**	**facem**	**vorbim**
voi	**învăţaţi**	**vedeţi**	**faceţi**	**vorbiţi**
ei/ele	**învaţă**	**văd**	**fac**	**vorbesc**

Here are three common irregular verbs:

	a fi (to be)	**a avea** (to have)	**a lua** (to take)
eu	**sunt**	**am**	**iau**
tu	**eşti**	**ai**	**iei**
el/ea	**este**	**are**	**ia**
noi	**suntem**	**avem**	**luăm**
voi	**sunteţi**	**aveţi**	**luaţi**
ei/ele	**sunt**	**au**	**iau**

Note: Verbs often appear in Romanian without a personal pronoun because the ending of the verb is sufficient to indicate the subject. Personal pronouns precede the verb only for emphasis.

The **perfect tense** is formed with the help of the auxilliary verb **a avea** "to have" followed by the past participle of the verb used.

Verbs with infinitives ending in **-a, -i** and **-î** form the past participle by adding **-t**; those with an **-ea** ending replace it with **-ut**; others ending in **-e** replace it with either **-ut** or **-s**:

infinitive	past participle		
a invita	**invitat**	**am invitat**	I (have) invited
a vedea	**văzut**	**a vazut**	he/she/it say (has seen)
a face	**făcut**	**aţi făcut**	you did (have done)
a se duce	**dus**	**s-au dus**	they went (have gone)

The **future tense** is formed in two main ways:

1. by using the colloquial **o să** plus the subjunctive (similar to the present tense in all forms except the third person).

O să stau o lună	I'll be staying a month.
O să venim la ora opt.	We'll come at eight.

2. by using the auxiliary forms **voi, vei, va, vom, veţi** and **vor** placed in front of the infinitive form of the verb without **a.**

eu voi pleca	I shall leave	**noi vom pleca**	we shall leave
tu vei pleca	you shall leave	**voi veţi pleca**	you shall leave
el/ea va pleca	he/she shall leave	**ei vor pleca**	they shall leave

The negative

The negative is formed by putting the negation **nu** in front of the verb; eg:

eu nu locuiesc aici	I do not live here
eu nu am locuit aici	I did not live here
eu nu voi locui aici	I will not live here

With the verb **a avea** "to have", the negative is often reduced to **n-**:

n-am	I don't have	**n-aveţi**	you don't have

Dictionary

English—Romanian

f feminine *m* masculine *nt* neuter *pl* plural

A
abbey mânăstire *f*
abbreviation abreviere *nt*
about *(approximately)* vreo, cam
above deasupra
abscess abces *nt*
absent nu-i aici
absorbent cotton vată *f*
accept, to a accepta
accessories accesorii *nplt*
accident accident *nt*
account cont *nt* bancar
ache durere *f*
adaptor adaptor *nt*
address adresă *f*
address book agendă *f* de adrese
adhesive colant
adhesive tape scoci *nt*
admission intrare *f*
admitted admis
Africa Africa *f*
after după
after-shave lotion loţiune *f* după ras
afternoon, in the după-amiaza *f*
again din nou
age vârstă *f*
ago *(two years)* în urmă cu; acum *(doi ani)*
air bed saltea *f* pneumatică
air conditioning aer *nt* condiţionat
air mattress saltea *f* pneumatică
airmail par avion
airplane avion *nt*
airport aeroport *nt*
aisle seat loc *nt* la culoar
alarm clock radio-ceas *nt*
alcohol alcool *nt*
alcoholic alcoolic
all tot
allergic alergic
almond migdală *f*
alphabet alfabet *nt*
also de asemenea
alter, to *(garment)* a modifica
altitude sickness rău *nt* de altitudine
amazing uluitor
amber chihlimbar *nt*
ambulance salvare *f*
American american *m*
American plan pensiune *f* completă
amethyst ametist *nt*
amount sumă *f*
amplifier amplificator *nt*
anaesthetic anestetic *nt*
analgesic calmant *nt*
and şi
animal animal *nt*
aniseed anason *nt*
ankle genunchi *m*
anorak hanorac *nt*
another altul *m*; alta *f*
answer răspuns *nt*
antibiotic antibiotic *nt*
antidepressant antidepresiv *nt*
antique shop magazin *nt* de antichităţi
antiques antichitaţi *fpl*
antiseptic cream cremă *f* antiseptică
any nici un
anyone cineva
anything ceva; nimic
anywhere pe undeva
apartment apartament *nt*
aperitif aperitiv *nt*
appendicitis apendicită *f*
appendix apendice *nt*
appetizer antreu *nt*
apple măr *nt*
appliance aparatură *f*

appointment programare *f;* întâlnire *f*
apricot caisă *f*
April aprilie *m*
archaeology arheologie *f*
architect arhitect *m*
area code prefix *nt*
arm braţ *nt*
around *(approximately)* în jur de
arrangement *(set price)* tarif *nt*
arrival sosiri *fpl*
arrive, to a ajunge; a veni; a sosi
art artă *f*
art gallery galerie *f* de artă
artichoke anghinare *f*
article obiect *nt*
artificial artificial
artificial light lumină *f* artificială
artist artist *m*
ashtray scrumieră *f*
Asia Asia
ask for, to a spune; a comanda
asparagus sparanghel *m*
aspirin aspirină *f*
asthma astmă *f*
astringent loţiune *f* astringentă
at la
at least cel puţin
at once imediat
aubergine vânătă *f*
August august *m*
aunt mătuşă *f*
Australia Australia
Austria Austria
automatic automat *nt*
autumn toamnă *f*
average în medie
awful groaznic; urât

B
baby copil *m*
babysitter îngrijitoare *f* de copii, babysitter *f*
back spate *nt*
back, to be/to get a se întoarce
backache durere *f* de spate
backpack rucsac *nt*
bacon şuncă *f*
bacon and eggs şuncă şi ouă
bad rău
bag sac *m;* pungă *f*
baggage bagaj *nt*
baggage cart cărucior *nt* de bagaje
baggage check birou *nt* de bagaje; înregistrarea *f* bagajelor
baggage locker cabină *f* de bagaje; birou *nt* de bagaje
baked copt
baker's brutărie *f*
balance *(finance)* balanţă *f*
balcony balcon *nt*
ball-point pen pix *nt* cu pastă
ball *(inflated)* minge *f*
ballet balet *nt*
banana banană *f*
Band-Aid® pansamente *ntpl*
bandage bandaj *nt*
bangle brăţară *f*
bangs breton *nt*
bank *(finance)* bancă *f*
banknote bancnotă *f*
bar *(room)* bar *nt*
barber's frizer *m*
basil busuioc *nt*
basketball baschet *nt*
bath baie *f*
bath salts săruri de baie *fpl*
bath towel prosop *nt* de baie
bathing cap cască *f* de înot
bathing hut cabină *f* de schimb
bathing suit costum *nt* de baie
bathrobe halat *nt* de baie
bathroom baie *f*
battery baterie *f*
be, to a fi
beach plajă *f*
beach ball minge *f* de plajă
bean fasole *f*
beard barbă *f*
beautiful frumos
beauty salon salon *nt* de cosmetică
bed pat *nt*
bed and breakfast cazare şi micul dejun
bedpan oală *f* de noapte
beef vacă *f*
beer bere *f*
beet(root) sfeclă *f* roşie
before *(time)* înainte
beginner începător *m*
beginning început *nt*
behind înapoi; în spate
beige bej
Belgium Belgia

bell *(electric)* sonerie *f*
Belorus Bielorusia *f*
below dedesubt
belt curea *f*
bend *(road)* curbă *f*
berth cuşetă de dormit *f*
better mai bine
between între
bicycle bicicletă *f*
big mare
bilberry afină *f*
bill nota *f* de plată; *(banknote)* bancnotă *f*
billion *(Am.)* bilion *nt*
binoculars binoclu *nt*
bird pasăre *f*
birth naştere *f*
birthday zi *f* de naştere
biscuit *(Br.)* biscuit *nt*
bitter amar
black negru
black and white *(film)* alb-negru
black coffee cafea *f* neagră *(turcească)*
blackberry mură *f*
blackcurrant coacăz *nt* negru
bladder vezică *f* urinară
blade lamă *f*
blanket pătură *f*
bleach decolorant *nt*
bleed, to a sângera
blind *(window shade)* jaluzea *f*
blister băşică *f*
blocked înfundat
blood sânge *nt*
blood pressure tensiune *f* arterială; puls *nt*
blood transfusion transfuzie *f* de sânge
blouse bluză *f*
blow-dry un pieptănat *nt*
blue albastru
blueberry afină *f*
blusher ruj *nt* de obraz
boat barcă *f*
bobby pin agrafă *f*
body corp *nt*
boil furuncul *m*
boiled fiert
boiled egg ou fiert *nt*
bone os *nt*
book carte *f*
booking office agenţie *f* de voiaj
booklet (of tickets) carnet *nt* de bilete
bookshop librărie *f*
boot cizmă *f*
born născut
botanical gardens grădină *f* botanică
botany botanică *f*
bottle sticlă *f*
bottle-opener deschizător *nt* de sticle
bottom jos *nt*
bow tie papion *nt*
bowel intestin *nt*
box cutie *f*
boxing box *nt*
boy băiat *m*
boyfriend prieten *m*
bra sutien *nt*
bracelet brăţară *f*
braces *(suspenders)* bretele *fpl*
braised fiert înăbuşit
brake frână *f*
brake fluid lichid *nt* de frână
brandy ţuică *f*
bread pâine *f*
break, to a sparge; a rupe
break down, to a avea o pană de motor
breakdown pană *f*
breakdown van maşină *f* de depanare
breakfast micul dejun *nt*
breast sân *m*
breathe, to a respira
bridge pod *nt*
bring down, to a aduce
bring, to a aduce
British britanic *m*
broken defect; spart, rupt
brooch broşă *f*
brother frate *m*
brown maro
bruise vânătaie *f*
Brussels sprouts varză *f* de Bruxelles
bubble bath spumă *f* de baie
bucket găleată *f*
buckle cataramă *f*
build, to a construi
building clădire *f*
building blocks/bricks cuburi *ntpl*
bulb *(light)* bec *nt*
Bulgaria Bulgaria *f*
bump *(lump)* umflătură *f*
burn arsură *f*

burn out, to *(bulb)* a se arde
bus autobuz *nt*
bus stop staţie *f* de autobuz
business afaceri *fpl*
business class clasa *f* business
business district zona *f* băncilor
business trip scop *nt* de serviciu
busy ocupat
but dar
butane gas gaz *nt* butan; butelie *f* de gaz
butcher's măcelărie *f*
butter unt *nt*
button nasture *m*
buy, to a cumpăra

C

cabana cabană *f*
cabbage varză *f*
cabin *(ship)* cabină *f*
cable legătură *f*
cable car teleferic *nt*
cable release declanşator *nt*
café cafe-bar *nt*
cake prăjitură *f*
calculator calculator *nt*
calendar calendar *nt*
call *(phone)* apel *nt* telefonic
call, to *(give name)* a se zice; *(phone)* a telefona
call, to *(summon)* a da; a chema
call back, to a suna înapoi
calm liniştit
cambric batist *nt*
camel-hair păr *nt* de cămilă
camera aparat *nt* de filmat; aparat de fotografiat
camera case port-aparat *nt*
camera shop magazin *nt* de aparate foto
camp site camping *nt*; loc *nt* de campare
camp, to a campa
campbed pat de camping *nt*
camping camping *nt*
camping equipment echipament *nt* de camping
can opener deschizător *n* de conserve *t*
can *(be able to)* a putea să
can *(container)* cutie *f* de conservă
Canada Canada *f*
Canadian canadian *m*
cancel, to a anula
candle lumânare *f*
candy dropsuri *ntpl*
cap şapcă *f*
capers capere fpl
capital *(finance)* capital *nt*
car maşină *f*
car hire închirieri *fpl* auto
car mechanic mecanic *m* auto
car park parcare *f*
car racing raliu *nt*
car radio radio *nt* de maşină
car rental agenţie *f* de închiriat maşini
carafe carafă *f*
carat carat *nt*
caravan rulotă *f*
caraway chimen *m*
carbon paper hârtie *f* indigou
carbonated *(fizzy)* apă *f* gazoasă
carburettor carburator *nt*
card carte *f* de joc *f*; carte *f* de visita
card game joc de cărti *nt*
cardigan jachetă *f*
carp crap *m*
carpet carpetă *f*
carrot morcov *m*
cart cărucior *nt*
carton *(of cigarettes)* cartuş *nt* de ţigări; pachet *nt* de ţigări
cartridge *(camera)* încărcător *nt* de film
case port-aparat *nt*
cash desk casă *f*
cash, to a încasa
cassette casetă *f*
cassette recorder casetofon *nt*
castle castel *nt*
catalogue catalog *nt*
cathedral catedrală *f*
Catholic catolic
cauliflower conopidă *f*
caution atenţie *f*
cave peşteră *f*
celery ţelină *f*
cemetery cimitir *nt*
centimetre centimetru *m*
centre centru nt
century secol *nt*
ceramics ceramică *f*
cereal cereală *f*
certain sigur

certificate certificat *nt*
chain *(jewellery)* lănţişor *nt*
chain bracelet brăţară *f* lănţişor
chair scaun *nt*
chamber music muzică *f* de cameră
change, to a schimba; bani *ntpl* mărunţi
chapel capelă *f*
charcoal cărbune *nt* pentru grătar
charge cost *nt*; tarif *nt*; taxă *f*
charge, to a plăti; a reţine
charm bracelet brăţară *f* cu talismanuri
charm *(trinket)* talisman *nt*
cheap ieftin
check *(Am.)* cec *nt*
check *(restaurant)* nota *f* de plată
check, to a verifica; a controla; *(luggage)* a înregistra
check-up *(medical)* examen *nt* medical
check in, to *(airport)* a înregistra bagajele
check out, to a pleca, a părăsi
cheers! noroc *nt*
cheese brânză *f*
chemist's farmacie *f*
cheque cec *nt*
cherry cireşe *fpl*
chess şah *nt*
chess set joc *nt* de şah
chest piept *nt*
chestnut castană *f*
chewing gum gumă *f* de mestecat
chewing tobacco tutun *nt* de mestecat
chicken pui *m*
chicken breast piept *nt* de găină
chicory andive *fpl*
chiffon şifon *nt*
child copil *m*
children's doctor doctor pediatru *m*
China China *f*
chips cartofi *mpl* prăjiţi
chives arpagic *nt*
chocolate ciocolată *f*
chocolate bar baton *nt* de ciocolată
chop *(meat)* cotlet *nt*
Christmas Crăciun *nt*
chromium crom *nt*
church biserică *f*
cigar trabuc *nt*
cigarette ţigară *f*
cigarette case tabacheră *f*
cigarette holder port-ţigaret *nt*
cigarette lighter brichetă *f*
cine camera cameră *f* de filmat
cinema cinema *nt*
cinnamon scorţişoară *f*
circle *(theatre)* balcon *nt*
city oraş *nt*
city centre centrul *nt* oraşului
classical clasic
clean curat
clean, to a spăla
cleansing cream lapte demachiant *nt*
cliff stâncă *f*
clip clamă *f*
cloakroom garderoba *f*
clock ceas *nt*
clock-radio radio-ceas *nt*
close, to a închide
clothes haine *fpl*
clothes peg/pin cârlig *nt* de rufe
clothing îmbrăcăminte *f*
cloud nor *m*
clove cuişoare *fpl*
coach *(bus)* autocar *nt*
coat haină *f*
coconut nucă *f* de cocos
coffee cafea *f*
coins numismatica *f*
cold rece; frig
cold *(illness)* răceală *f*; gripă *f*
cold cuts salamuri *npl*
collar guler *nt*
collect call convorbire *f* cu taxă inversă
colour culoare *f*; color
colour chart paletă *f* de culori
colour rinse şampon *nt* colorant
colour shampoo şampon *nt* colorant
colour slide diapozitiv *nt* color
colourfast nu iese la spălat
comb pieptene *m*
comedy comedie *f*
commission *(fee)* comision *nt*
common *(frequent)* curent
compact disc compact disc *nt*
compartment *(train)* loc *nt*
compass busolă *f*
complaint reclamaţie *f*
concert concert *nt*
concert hall sală de concert *f*
condom preservativ *m*
conductor *(orchestra)* dirijor *m*

conference room sală *f* de conferinţe
confirm, to a confirma
confirmation confirmare *f*
congratulation felicitări *fpl*
connection *(transport)* legătura *f* de tren
constipation constipaţie *f*
consulate consulat *nt*
contact lens lentile *fpl* de contact
contagious contagios
contain, to a conţine
contraceptives anticoncepţionale *ntpl*
contract contract *nt*
control control *nt*
convent mănăstire *f*
cookie fursec *n*
cool box geantă *f* frigorifică
copper cupru *nt*
coral coral *m*
corduroy velur *nt*
corkscrew tirbuşon *nt*
corn plaster leucoplast *nt* pentru bătături
corn *(sweet)* porumb *nt*
corn *(foot)* bătătură *f*
corner colţ *nt*
cost preţ *nt*; cost *nt*
cost, to a costa
cot pătuţ *nt*
cotton bumbac *nt*
cotton wool vată *f*
cough tuse *f*
cough drops picături *fpl* de tuse
cough, to a tuşi
counter ghişeu *nt*
country ţară *f*
countryside la ţară
courgette dovlecel *m*
court house tribunal *nt*
cousin văr *m*
crab crab *m*
cramp cârcel *m*
crayfish *(river)* rac *m*
crayon creion *nt*
cream frişcă *f*
cream *(toiletry)* cremă *f*
crease resistant nu se şifonează
credit credit *nt*
credit card carte *f* de credit
crepe crep
crisps cartofi *mpl* cipşi
crockery veselă *f*
cross cruce *f*
crossing *(maritime)* traversare *f*
crossroads intersecţie *f*
cruise croazieră *f*
crystal cristal *nt*
cucumber castravete *m*
cuff link buton *nt* de manşetă
cuisine mâncăruri *fpl*
cup ceaşcă *f*
curler bigudiu *nt*
currants stafide *fpl*
currency schimb *nt*
currency exchange office birou *n* de schimb
current curent *nt* de apă
curtain perdea *f*
curve *(road)* curbă *f*
customs vamă *f*
cut *(wound)* tăietură *f*
cut, to *(with scissors)* a tunde
cut off, to *(interrupt)* a întrerupe
cut glass sticlă *f* şlefuită
cutlery tacâmuri ntpl
cutlet cotlet *nt*
cycling ciclism *nt*
cystitis cistită *f*
Czech Republic Republica Cehă *f*

D

dairy magazin *nt* de brânzeturi şi lactate
dance dans *nt*
dance, to a dansa
danger pericol *nt*
dangerous periculos
dark întuneric; închis
date *(appointment)* întâlnire *f*
date *(day)* dată *f*
date *(fruit)* curmale *fpl*
daughter fată *f*
day zi *f*
day off zi liberă *f*
daylight lumină *f* de zi
decade deceniu *nt*
decaffeinated decofeinizat
December decembrie *m*
decision decizie *f*
deck chair şezlong *nt*
deck *(ship)* punte *f*
declare, to *(customs)* a declara
deep adânc

degree *(temperature)* grad *nt*
delay întârziere *f*
delicatessen magazin *nt* de delicatese
deliver, to a livra
delivery livrare *f*
denim doc *nt*
Denmark Danemarca *f*
dentist dentist *m*
denture proteză *f*
deodorant deodorant *nt*
department store magazin universal *nt*
department *(museum)* departament *nt*; *(shop)* raion *nt*
departure plecări *fpl*
deposit *(down payment)* depunere *f*; avans *nt*
dessert desert *nt*
detour *(traffic)* deviere *f*
develop, to a developa
diabetic diabetic
dialling code prefix *nt* telefonic
diamond diamant *nt*
diaper scutec *nt* de unică folosinţă
diarrhoea diaree *f*
dictionary dicţionar *nt*
diesel motorină *f*
diet regim *n* alimentar
difficult greu
difficulty dificultate *f*
digital ceas *nt* digital
dill mărar *nt*
dining car vagon restaurant *nt*
dining room sufragerie *f*; sala de mese *f*
dinner *(have)* a cină *f*; a lua masa de seară
direct direct
direct, to a îndruma
direction directie *f*
director *(theatre)* regizor *m*
directory *(phone)* anuar *nt*
disabled persoane *fpl* invalide
disc disc *nt*
discotheque discotecă *f*
discount reducere *f*
disease boală *f*
dish mâncare *f*
dishwashing detergent detergent *nt* de vase
disinfectant desinfectant *nt*
dislocated dislocat
dissatisfied nemulţumit
disturb, to a deranja
diversion *(traffic)* deviere *f*
dizzy ameţit
do, to a face
doctor doctor *m*
doctor's office cabinet *nt* medical
dog câine *m*
doll păpuşă *f*
dollar dolar *m*
double bed pat *nt* dublu
double room cameră *f* de două persoane
down jos
downtown centru *nt*
dozen duzină *f*
drawing paper hârtie *f* de desenat
drawing pins pioneze *fpl*
dress rochie *f*
dressing gown capot *nt*
drink băutură *f*
drink, to a bea
drinking water apă *f* potabilă
drip, to a curge
drive, to a conduce
driving licence carnet *nt* de conducere
drop *(liquid)* picătură *f*
drugstore farmacie *f*
dry uscat; sec
dry cleaner's curăţătorie *f*
dry shampoo şampon *nt*
duck raţă *f*
dummy *(baby's)* suzetă *f*
during în timpul
duty *(customs)* vamă *f*
dye vopsea *f*

E

each fiecare
ear ureche *f*
earache durere *f* de urechi
early devreme
earring cercel *m*
east est *nt*
Easter Paşte *m*
easy uşor
eat, to a mânca
eel ţipar *m*
egg ou *nt*
eggplant vânătă *f*
eight opt

eighteen optsprezece
eighth al optulea
eighty optzeci
elastic bandage bandaj *nt* elastic
electrical appliance aparatură *f* electrică
electrical goods shop magazin *nt* de aparate electrice
electricity electricitate *f*
electric(al) electric(e)
electronic electronic
elevator lift *nt*
eleven unsprezece
embarkation point punct *nt* de îmbarcare
embassy ambasadă *f*
embroidered brodat
embroidery broderie *f*
emerald smarald *nt*
emergency urgenţă *f*
emergency exit ieşire *f* de incendiu
emery board pilă *f*
empty gol
enamel email *nt*
end sfârşit *nt*
engaged *(phone)* ocupat
engagement ring inel *nt* de logodnă
engine *(car)* motor *nt*
England Anglia *f*
English englez; englezesc
enjoy oneself, to a se distra
enjoyable minunat
enlarge, to a mări
enough destul
entrance intrare *f*
entrance fee intrare *f*
envelope plic *nt*
equipment echipament *nt*
eraser gumă *f*
escalator escalator *nt*; lift *nt*
estimate *(cost)* cost *nt* aproximativ; preţ *nt* estimativ
Eurocheque eurocec *nt*
Europe Europa *f*
evening seară *f*
evening dress ţinută obligatorie *f*; *(woman's)* rochie de seară *f*
evening, in the seara
everything tot, toate
exchange, to a schimba
exchange rate curs *nt* de schimb
excursion excursie *f*
excuse me pardon
exercise book caiet *nt*
exhaust pipe ţeavă *f* de eşapament
exhibition expoziţie *f*
exit ieşire *f*
expect, to a aştepta
expenses cheltuieli *fpl*
expensive scump
exposure *(photography)* expunere *f*
exposure counter dispositiv *nt* de numărătoare
express expres (tren) *nt*
expression expresie *f*
expressway autostradă *f*
extension *(phone)* interior *nt*
extension cord/lead prelungitor *nt*
extra în plus
eye ochi *m*
eye drops picături *fpl* de ochi
eye shadow fard *nt* de pleope
eye specialist medic *m* oculist
eyebrow pencil creion *nt* de sprâncene
eyesight vedere *f*

F

fabric *(cloth)* pânzeturi *fpl*
face faţă *f*
face pack mască *f*
face powder pudră *f* de obraz
factory uzina *f*
fair târg *nt*
fall *(autumn)* toamnă *f*
fall, to a cădea
family familie *f*
fan belt curea *f* de ventilator
far departe
fare *(ticket)* costul *nt* (biletului)
farm fermă *f*
fast rapid (tren) *nt*
fat *(meat)* gras
father tată *m*
faucet robinet *nt*
fax fax *nt*
February februarie *m*
fee *(doctor's)* plată *f*
feeding bottle biberon *nt*
feel, to *(physical state)* a simţi
felt fetru *nt*
felt-tip pen cariocă *nt*
ferry bac *nt*

fever febră *f*
few puţini; *(a few)* câţiva
field câmp *nt*
fifteen cincisprezece
fifth al cincilea
fifty cincizeci
fig smochină *f*
file *(tool)* pilă *f*
fill in, to a completa
filling *(tooth)* plombă *f*
filling station staţie *f* de benzină
film film *nt*
film winder maneta *f* de rulat filmul
filter filtru *nt*
filter-tipped cu filtru
find, to a găsi
fine *(OK)* bine
fine arts arte *fpl* frumoase
finger deget *nt*
Finland Finlanda *f*
fire foc *nt*
first primul
first-aid kit trusă *f* de prim ajutor
first class clasa *f* întâi
first name prenume *nt*
fish peşte *m*
fishing a pescui
fishing tackle unelte *ntpl* de pescuit
fishmonger's pescărie *f*
fit, to a proba
fitting room cabină *f* de probă
five cinci
fix, to a trata
fizzy (mineral water) (apă minerală) gazoasă *f*
flannel flanelă *f*
flash *(photography)* blitz *nt*
flash attachment legătură *f* de blitz
flashlight lanternă *f*
flat *(apartment)* apartament *nt*
flat *(shoe)* pantofi *mpl* plaţi (fără toc)
flat tyre roată *f* dezumflată
flea market talcioc *nt*
flight zbor *nt*
floor palier *nt*
floor show spectacol *nt* în mijilocul publicului
florist's florărie *f*
flour făină *f*
flower floare *f*
flu gripă *f*
fluid lichid *nt*
foam rubber mattress saltea *f* de burete de cauciuc
fog ceaţă *f*
folding chair scaun *nt* pliant
folding table masă *f* pliantă
folk music muzică *f* populară
follow, to a urma
food mâncare *f*
food poisoning intoxicaţie *f* alimentară
foot laba *f* piciorului, picior *nt*
foot cream cremă *f* de picioare
football fotbal **n**
footpath potecă *f*
for pentru
forbidden interzis
forecast prevedere *f*
forest pădure *f*
forget, to a uita
fork furculiţă *f*
form *(document)* formular *nt*
fortnight două săptămâni
fortress cetate *f*
forty patruzeci
foundation *cosmetic* fond de ten *nt*
fountain fântână *f*
fountain pen stilou *nt* cu cerneală
four patru
fourteen paisprezece
fourth al patrulea
fowl pasăre *f*
frame *(glasses)* ramă *f*
France Franţa *f*
free liber; gratuit
French bean fasole *f* fideluţa
Friday vineri *f*
fried prăjit
fried egg ou *nt* prăjit
friend prieten *m*
fringe breton *nt*
from de la
frost ger *nt*
fruit fruct *nt*
fruit cocktail cocteil *nt* de fructe
fruit juice suc *nt* de fructe
fruit salad salată *f* de fructe
frying pan tigaie *f*
full plin
full board pensiune *f* completă
full insurance asigurare *f* casco
furniture mobilă *f* stil
furrier's blănărie *f*

G

gabardine gabardină *f*
gallery galerie *f* de artă
game joc *nt*
game *(food)* vânat
garage garaj *nt*; servis *nt*
garden grădină *f*
gardens grădina *f* publică
garlic usturoi *m*
gas gaz *nt*
gasoline benzină *f*
gastritis gastrită *f*
gauze tifon *nt*
gem piatră *f* prețioasă
[illegible]
[illegible]nt *nt*
general practitioner d[illegible]or *m* de medicină generală; generalist *m*
genitals organe genitale *ntpl*
gentlemen bărbați *mpl*
geology geologie *f*
Germany Germania *f*
get, to *(find)* a lua
get off, to a coborî
get past, to a face loc
get to, to a ajunge
get up, to a se da jos din pat
gherkin castravete *m* murat
gift cadou *nt*
gin gin *nt*
gin and tonic gin cu apă tonică
ginger ghimber *m*
girdle centură *f*
girl fată *f*
girlfriend prietenă *f*
give, to a da; a pune
give way, to *(traffic)* a ceda (trecerea)
gland glandă *f*
glass pahar *nt*
glasses ochelari *npl*
gloomy sumbru
glove mănușă *f*
glue lipici *nt*
go, to a merge
go away! pleacă de aici
go back, to a se întoarce
go out, to a ieși
gold aur *nt*
gold plated aurit
golden auriu
golf golf *nt*
golf course teren *nt* de golf
good bun
good afternoon bună ziua
good-bye la revedere
good evening bună seara
good morning bună dimineața
good night noapte bună
goose gâscă *f*
gooseberries agrișe *fpl*
gram(me) gram *nt*
grammar gramatică *f*
grammar book carte *f* de gramatică
grapes struguri mpl
grapefruit grepfrut *nt*
grapefruit juice suc *nt* de grepfrut
gray gri
graze julitură *f*
greasy *(păr)* gras
Great Britain Marea Britanie *f*
Greece Grecia *f*
green verde
green bean fasole verde *f*
greengrocer's aprozar *nt*
greeting salut *nt*
grey gri
grilled grătar *nt*
grocery (grocer's) băcănie *f*
groundsheet folie *f* de mușama
group grup *nt*
guesthouse hotel-pensiune *nt*
guide ghid *nt*
guidebook ghid *nt*
guinea fowl bibilică *f*
gum *(teeth)* gingie *f*
gynaecologist ginecolog *m*

H

hair păr *nt*
hair dryer uscător *nt* de păr
hair gel gel *nt* de păr
hair lotion loțiune *f* de păr
hair spray fixativ *nt* de păr
hairbrush perie *f* de păr
haircut tunsoare *f*
hairdresser coafor *nt*
hairgrip clamă *f*
hairpin ac de păr *nt*
half jumătate *f*
half an hour jumătate *f* de oră
half board demipensiune *f*
half price jumătate *f* de preț

hall porter valet *m*
ham şuncă *f*
ham and eggs şuncă şi ouă
hammer ciocan *nt*
hammock hamac *nt*
hand mână *f*
hand cream cremă *f* de mâini
hand washable de spălat de mână
handbag geantă *f*; poşeta *f*
handicrafts artizanat *nt*
handkerchief batistă *f*
handmade lucrat de mână
hanger umeraş *nt*
happy fericit
harbour port *nt*
hard dur
hard-boiled (egg) ou *n* (fiert) tare
hare iepure *m*
hat pălărie *f*
have, to a avea
have to, to *(must)* a trebui, a fi necesar
hay fever alergie *f* la polen
hazelnut alune *fpl* de pădure
he el
head cap *nt*
head waiter ospătar *m* şef
headache durere de cap *f*
headphones căşti *fpl*
health insurance form formular *nt* de asigurare
heart inimă *f*
heart attack atac *nt* de cord
heat, to a încălzi
heavy greu; puternic
heel toc *nt*
height înălţime *f*
helicopter helicopter *nt*
hello bună; *(telephone)* alo
help! ajutor
help, to a ajuta
her a ei
herb tea ceai *nt* de plante medicinale
herbs mirodenii *fpl*
here aici
hi bună
high înalţime *f*; mare
high season în sezon
hill deal *nt*
hire închiriere *f*
hire, to a închiria
his a lui
history istorie *f*
hitchhike, to a face autostop
hold on! *(phone)* aşteptaţi
hole gaură *f*
holiday vacanţă *f*
holidays vacanţă; concediu *nt*
home casă *f*
home address adresa *f* de acasă
home town oraşul *nt*
honey miere *f*
hope, to a spera
horse racing curse *fpl* de cai
horseback riding călărie *f*
hospital spital *nt*
hot water apă *f* caldă
hot-water bottle buiotă *f* cu apă fierbinte
hot cald; *(boiling)* fierbinte
hotel hotel *nt*
hotel directory/guide ghid *nt* al hotelurilor
hotel reservation rezervare *f* la hotel
hour oră *f*
house casă *f*
household article articol *nt* de uz casnic
how far cât de departe
how long cât timp
how many câţi *mpl*, câte *fpl*
how much cât
hundred o sută
hungry foame *f*
hunting vânătoare *f*
hurry, to be in a a se grăbi
hurt *(to be)* (a fi) rănit
hurt, to a durea
husband soţ *m*
hydrofoil navă *f* cu aripi portante

I

I eu
ice gheaţă *f*
ice cream îngheţată *f*
ice cube cuburi *ntpl* de gheaţă
ice pack pungă *f* cu cuburi de gheaţă
iced tea ceai *nt* rece
icon icoană *f*
if dacă
ill bolnav *m*, bolnavă *f*
illness boală *f*
important important
imported importat

impressive impresionant
in în
include, to a include
included inclus
India India *f*
indigestion indigestie *f*
inexpensive nu prea scump
infected infectat
infection infecţie *f*
inflammation inflamaţie *f*
inflation inflaţie *f*
inflation rate rata *f* inflaţiei
influenza gripă *f*
information informaţie *f*
injection injecţie *f*
injure, to a (se) răni
injured rănit
injury rană *f*
ink cerneală *f*
inquiry informaţie *f*
insect bite înţepătură *f* de insectă
insect repellent spray *nt* contra insectelor
insect spray insecticid *nt*
inside înăuntru
instrument (musical) instrument *nt* muzical
insurance asigurare *f*
insurance company companie *f* de asigurări
interest *(finance)* dobândă *f*
interested, to be a fi interesat
interesting interesant
international internaţional
interpreter interpret *m*
intersection intersecţie *f*
introduce, to a prezenta
introduction *(social)* prezentare *f*
investment investiţie *f*
invitation invitaţie *f*
invite, to a invita
invoice factură *f*
iodine iod *nt*
Ireland Irlanda *f*
Irish irlandez *m*
iron *(for laundry)* fier *nt* de călcat
iron, to a călca
ironmonger's fierărie *f*
it acest
Italy Italia *f*
its al său, a sa, ai săi, ale sale
ivory fildeş *nt*

J

jacket jachetă *f*
jade jad *nt*
jam *(preserves)* gem *nt*
jam, to a se bloca
January ianuarie *m*
Japan Japonia *f*
jar *(container)* borcan *nt*
jaundice icter *nt*
jaw maxilar *nt*
jazz jazz *nt*
jeans blugi *mpl*
jersey jerseu *nt*
jewel box cutie *f* de bijuterii
jeweller's magazin *nt* de bijuterii; bijuterie *f*
joint încheietură *f*
journey călătorie *f*
juice suc *nt*
July iulie *m*
jumper pulover *nt*
June iunie *m*
just *(only)* doar

K

keep, to a ţine
kerosene gaz *nt*
key cheie *f*
kidney rinichi *mpl*
kilo(gram) kilogram *nt*
kilometre kilometru *m*
kind amabil
kind *(type)* fel *nt*
knee genunchi *m*
kneesocks şosete lungi fpl
knife cuţit *nt*
knock, to a ciocăni
know, to a şti

L

label etichetă *f*
lace dantelă *f*
ladies femei *fpl*
lake lac *nt*
lamb *(meat)* miel *m*
lamp lampă *f*
landscape peisaj *nt*
language limbă *f*
lantern felinar *nt*

large mare
last ultimul; trecut
last name numele *nt* de familie
late târziu
late, to be a rămâne în urmă
laugh, to a râde
launderette spălătorie *f* Nufărul
laundry service servicii *ntpl* de spălătorie
laundry *(clothes)* rufe *fpl* de spălat
laundry *(place)* spălătorie *f*
laxative laxativ *nt*
lead *(metal)* plumb *nt*
lead *(theatre)* rol *nt* principal
leap year an bisect *m*
leather piele *f*
leave, to a pleca; *(deposit)* a lăsa
leeks praz *nt*
left stânga
left-luggage office birou *nt* de bagaje
leg picior *nt*
lemon lămâie *f*
lemonade limonadă *f*
lens *(camera)* obiectiv *nt*
lens *(glasses)* lentilă *f*
lentils linte *f*
less mai puţin
lesson lecţie *f*
let, to *(hire out)* a închiria
letter scrisoare *f*
letter box cutie *f* poştală
letter of credit scrisoare *f* acreditivă
lettuce salată *f* verde
library bibliotecă *f*
licence *(driving)* carnet *nt* de conducere
lie down, to a se întinde
life belt colac *nt* de salvare
life boat barcă *f* de salvare
life guard *(beach)* salvamar *m*
lift *(elevator)* lift *nt*
light uşor; *(colour)* deschis
light *(lamp)* lumină *f*
light *(for cigarette)* foc *nt*
light meter celulă *f* fotoelectrică
lighter brichetă *f*
lighter fluid/gas gaz *nt* de brichetă
lightning fulger *nt*
like ca
like, to a vrea; *(please)* a plăcea
linen *(cloth)* in *nt*
lip buză *f*
lipsalve strugurel *nt* de buze
lipstick ruj *nt* de buze
liqueur lichior *nt*
listen, to a asculta
litre litru *nt*
little *(a little)* puţin
live, to a locui
liver ficat *m*
lobster homar *m*
local local *nt*
long lung
long-sighted prezbit *m*
look, to a se uita
look for, to a căuta
look out! atentie
loose *(clothes)* largi
lose, to a pierde
loss pierdere *f*
lost rătăcit
lost and found/lost property office birou *nt* de obiecte pierdute
lot *(a lot)* mult
lotion loţiune *f*
loud *(voice)* *(cu voce)* tare
lovely frumos
low mic
low season în afara sezonului
lower de jos
luck noroc *nt*
luggage bagaj *nt*
luggage locker cabină de bagaje *f*; birou *nt* de bagaje
luggage trolley cărucior *nt* de bagaje
lump *(bump)* umflătură *f*
lunch dejun *nt*; masa *f*
lung plămân *nt*

M

machine (washable) (care se spală la) maşină
mackerel macrou *n*
magazine revistă *f*
magnificent magnific
maid cameristă *f*
mail poşta *f*
mail, to a pune la poştă
mailbox cutie *f* de scrisori
main important; principal
make, to a face
make up, to *(prepare)* a face
make-up machiaj *nt*

make-up remover pad tampon *nt* pentru demachiat
mallet ciocan *nt*
man bărbat *m;* om *m*
manager director *m*
manicure manichiură *f*
many mulţi *m,* multe *f*
map hartă *f*
March martie *m*
marinated marinat(ă)
marjoram măghiran *nt*
market piaţă *f*
marmalade marmeladă *f*
married căsătorit
mass *(church)* slujbă *f* religioasă
matt *(finish)* mat
match *(matchstick)* chibrit *nt,*
match *(sport)* meci *nt*
match, to *(colour)* a potrivi
material *(cloth)* material *nt*
matinée matineu *nt*
mattress saltea *f*
May mai *m*
may *(can)* a permite
meadow pajişte *f*
meal masă *f*
mean, to a însemna
means miljoace *npl*
measles pojar *nt*
measure, to a măsura
meat carne *f*
meatball chiftele *fpl*
mechanic mecanic *m*
mechanical pencil creion *nt* mecanic
medical certificate certificat *nt* medical
medicine medicină *f; (drug)* medicament *nt*
medium-sized de capacitate medie
medium *(meat)* bine făcut, potrivit
meet, to a întâlni
melon pepene *m* galben
memorial monument *nt* comemorativ
mend, to a repara
menthol (cigarettes) ţigări *fpl* mentolate
menu meniu *nt*
merry fericit
message masaj *nt*
metre metru *m*
mezzanine *(theatre)* balcon *nt*
middle mijloc
midnight miezul nopţii *nt*
mild *(light)* slab
mileage kilometraj *nt*
milk lapte *nt*
milliard miliard *nt*
million milion *nt*
mineral water apă *f* minerală
minister *(religion)* pastor *m*
mint mentă *f*
minute minut *nt*
mirror oglindă *f*
miscellaneous diverse
Miss domnişoară *f*
miss, to a lipsi
mistake greşeală *f*
moccasin mocasini *mpl*
modified American plan demipensiune *f*
moisturizing cream cremă *f* hidratantă
moment moment *nt*
monastery mănăstire *f*
Monday luni
money bani *mpl*
money order mandat *nt*
month lună *f*
monument monument *nt*
moon lună *f*
moped motoretă *m*
more mai mult
morning, in the dimineaţa
mortgage ipotecă *f*
mosque moschee *f*
mosquito net plasă *f* contra ţânţarilor
motel motel *nt*
mother mamă *f*
motorbike motocicletă *f*
motorboat barcă *f* cu motor
motorway autostradă *f*
mountain munte *m*
mountaineering alpinism *nt*
moustache mustaţă *f*
mouth gură *f*
mouthwash apă *f* de gură
move, to a mişca
movie film *m*
movie camera cameră *f* de filmat
movies filme *ntpl*
Mr. domnul *m*
Mrs. doamna *f*
much mult
mug cană *f*

muscle muşchi *m*
museum muzeu *nt*
mushroom ciupercă *f*
music muzică *f*
musical comedie *f* muzicală
must *(have to)* a trebui; avea nevoie; a crede
mustard muştar *nt*
my al meu

N

nail *(human)* unghie *f*
nail brush periuţă *f* de unghii
nail clippers foarfece *nt* de unghii cu arc
nail file pilă *f* de unghii
nail polish ojă *f* de unghii
nail polish remover acetonă *f*
nail scissors foarfece *nt* de unghii
name nume *nt*
napkin şerveţel *nt*
nappy scutec *nt*
narrow strâmt
nationality naţionalitate *f*
natural natural
natural history ştiinţele *fpl* naturale
nausea greaţă *f*
near aproape; lângă
nearby în apropiere
nearest cel mai aproape
neat (drink) (băutură) *f* simplă
neck gât *nt*
necklace colier *nt*
need, to a avea nevoie de
needle ac *nt*
negative negativ *nt*
nephew nepot *m*
nerve nerv *m*
Netherlands Olanda *f*
never niciodată
new nou
New Year Anul Nou *m*
New Zealand Noua Zeelandă *f*
newsagent's chioşc *nt* de ziare
newspaper ziar *nt*
newsstand chioşc *nt* de ziare
next următorul; viitor
next to lângă
nice *(beautiful)* frumos
niece nepoată *f*
night noapte *f*
night, at la noapte
night cream cremă *f* de noapte
nightclub club *nt* de noapte
nightdress/-gown pijama *f*
nine nouă
nineteen nouăsprezece
ninety nouăzeci
ninth al nouălea
no nu
noisy zgomotos
nonalcoholic nealcoolic
none niciunul *m*; niciuna *f*
nonsmoker nefumător *m*
noodles tăiţei *mpl*
noon la amiază *f*
normal normal
north nord *nt*
North America America de Nord *f*
Norway Norvegia *f*
nose nas *nt*
nose drops picături de nas *fpl*
nosebleed a curge sânge din nas
not nu
note paper hârtie *f* de scris
note *(banknote)* bancnotă *f*
notebook carnet *nt*
nothing nimic
notice *(sign)* anunţ *nt*
notify, to a înştiinţa
November noembrie *m*
now acum
number număr *nt*
nurse soră (medicală) *f*
nutmeg nucşoară *f*

O

o'clock oră *f*
occupation *(profession)* ocupaţia *f*
occupied ocupat
October octombrie *m*
office birou *nt*
oil ulei *nt*
oily *(greasy)* gras
old vechi, bătrân
old town oraş *nt* vechi
olive măslin *m*
on pe
on foot pe jos
on request staţie *f* facultativă
on time la timp
once o dată

one unu
one-way *(traffic)* sens unic *nt*
one-way ticket un (bilet) dus *nt*
onion ceapă *f*
only numai; doar
onyx onix *nt*
open deschis
open, to a deschide
open-air în are liber
opera operă *f*
opera house operă *f*
operation operaţie *f*
operator centrala *f*
opposite vis-a-vis
optician optician *m*
or sau
orange *(fruit)* portocală *f*
orange *(colour)* portocaliu
orange juice suc *nt* de portocale
orchestra orchestră *f*
orchestra *(seats)* stal *nt*
order *(goods, meal)* comandă *f*
order, to *(goods, meal)* a comanda
oregano sovârv *m*
ornithology ornitologie *f*
other alt
our al nostru
out of order deranjat; nu funcţionează
out of stock stoc *nt* terminat
outlet *(electric)* priză *f*
outside afară
oval oval
overalls salopete *fpl*
overdone *(meat)* prea prăjită
overheat, to *(engine)* a încălzi peste măsură
overtake, to a depăşi
owe, to a datora

P

pacifier *(baby's)* suzetă *f*
packet pachet *nt*
pail găleţică *f*
pain durere *f*
painkiller calmant *nt*
paint vopsea *f*
paint, to a picta
paintbox cutie *f* de culori
painter pictor *m*
painting pictură *f*; tablou *nt*
pair pereche *f*
pajamas pijama *f*
palace palat *nt*
palpitations palpitaţii *fpl*
panties chiloţi *mpl*
pants *(trousers)* pantaloni *mpl*
panty girdle burtieră *f*
panty hose ciorapi *mpl* cu chilot
paper hârtie *f*
paper napkin şerveţel *nt* de hârtie
paperback carte *f*
paperclip agrafă *f* pentru hârtie
paraffin *(fuel)* paratina *f*
parcel colet *nt*
pardon, I beg your poftim/poftiţi
parents părinţi *mpl*
park parc *nt*
park, to a parca
parking parcare *f*
parking lot parcare *f*
parliament building clădirea *f* parlamentului
parsley pătrunjel *m*
partridge potârniche *f*
party *(social gathering)* petrecere *f*
pass *(mountain)* trecătoare *f*
pass, to *(driving)* a trece
pass through, to a trece
passport paşaport *nt*
passport photo fotografie *f* de paşaport
pasta paste făinoase *fpl*
paste *(glue)* clei *nt*
pastry shop plăcintărie *f*
patch, to *(clothes)* a pune un petec
path potecă *f*
patient pacient *m*
pattern model *nt*
pay, to a plăti
payment plată *f*
pea mazăre *f*
peach piersică *f*
peak vârf *nt*
peanut arahidă *f*
pear pară *f*
pearl perla *f*
pedestrian pieton *m*
peg *(tent)* cârlig *nt* de cort
pen stilou *nt*
pencil creion *nt*
pencil sharpener ascuţitoare *f*
pendant pandantiv *m*

penicillin penicilină *f*
penknife briceag *m*
pensioner pensionar *m*
people oameni *mpl*
pepper piper *m*
per cent procent *nt*
per day pe zi
per hour pe oră
per night pe noapte
per person de persoană
per week pe săptămână
percentage procentaj *nt*
perch biban *m*
perform, to *(theater)* a juca
perfume parfum *nt*
perhaps poate
period pains dureri *fpl* la ciclu
period *(monthly)* ciclu *nt*
permanent wave permanent *nt*
permit permis *nt*
person persoană *f*
personal personal
personal call/person-to-person call a da un telefon
personal cheque cec *nt* personal
petrol benzină *f*
pewter aliaj *nt* cu cositor
pharmacy farmacie *f*
pheasant fazan *m*
photo poză *f*; fotografie *f*
photocopy fotocopie *f*
photographer atelier *nt* de fotografiat
photography fotografie *f*
phrase frază *f*
pick up, to *(person)* a lua
picnic picnic *nt*
picnic basket coş *nt* de picnic
picture *(painting)* tablou *nt*
picture *(photo)* poză *f*
pig porc *m*
pigeon porumbel *m*
pike ştiucă *f*
pill somnifer *nt*
pillow pernă *f*
pin ac *nt*; agrafă *f*
pineapple ananas *m*
pink roz
pipe pipă *f*
pipe cleaner instrument *nt* pentru curăţat pipa
pipe tobacco tutun *nt* de pipă
pipe tool dispozitiv *nt* de curăţat pipă
place, to a da
place loc *nt*
place of birth locul *nt* naşterii
plain *(colour)* simplă
plane avion *nt*
planetarium planetar *m*
plaster gips *nt*
plastic plastic
plastic bag pungă *f* de plastic
plate farfurie *f*
platform *(station)* peron *nt*
platinum platină *f*
play *(theatre)* piesă *f*
play, to a cânta; a juca
playground teren *nt* de joc
playing card cărţi *fpl* de joc,
please vă rog
plimsolls tenişi *mpl*
plug *(electric)* ştecher *nt*
plum prună *f*
pneumonia pneumonie *f*
poached fiert în apă
pocket buzunar *nt*
pocket calculator calculator *nt* de buzunar
pocket watch ceas *nt* de buzunar
point of interest *(sight)* obiectiv *nt* turistic important
point, to a arăta
poison otravă *f*
poisoning intoxicaţie *f* (alimentară)
pole *(ski)* prăjină *f*
pole *(tent)* stâlp *m* de cort
police poliţie *f*
police station post *nt* de poliţie; centru *nt* de poliţie
pond iaz *nt*
poplin poplin *nt*
pork porc *m*
port port *nt*
portable portabil
porter hamal *m*; portar *m*
portion porţie *f*
Portugal Portugalia *f*
possible, (as soon as) (cât de curând) posibil
post office poşta *f*
post *(mail)* poşta *f*
post, to a pune la poştă
postage costul *nt* prin poştă
postage stamp timbru *nt*
postcard vedere *f*

poste restante post restant *nt*
potato cartof *m*
pottery olărit *nt*
poultry păsări *fpl*
pound liră *f* sterlină
powder pudră *f*
powder compact pudră *f* compactă
powder puff puf *nt* de pudră
pregnant gravidă *f*
premium *(gasoline)* benzină *f* super
prescribe, to a prescrie
prescription reţetă *f*
present cadou *nt*
press stud capsă *f*
press, to *(iron)* a călca
pressure presiune *f*; tensiune *f*
pretty drăguţ
price preţ *nt*; cost *nt*; tarif *nt*
priest preot *m*
print *(photo)* poză *f*
private particular
processing *(photo)* developat
profession *(occupation)* ocupaţie *f*
profit profit *nt*
programme program *nt*
pronounce, to a pronunţa
pronunciation pronunţie *f*
propelling pencil creion *nt* mecanic
Protestant protestant *m*
provide, to a puna la dispoziţie
prune prune *fpl* uscate
public holiday sărbătoare *f* legală
pull, to a trage; *(tooth)* a extrage
pullover pulovăr *nt*
pump pompă *f*
puncture *(flat tyre)* pană *f* de cauciuc
purchase achiziţie *f*
pure pur
purple roşu-închis, purpuriu
push, to a împinge
put, to a pune
pyjamas pijama *f*

Q

quail prepeliţă *f*
quality calitate *f*
quantity cantitate *f*
quarter sfert *nt*
quarter of an hour sfert *nt* de oră
quartz cuarţ *nt*
question întrebare *f*
quick(ly) repede
quiet linişte *f*

R

rabbi rabin *m*
rabbit iepure *m*
race course/track hipodrom *nt*
racket *(sport)* rachetă *f*
radiator *(car)* radiator *nt*
radio radio *nt*
radish ridiche *f*
railway cale ferată *f*
railway station gară *f*
rain ploaie *f*
rain, to a ploua
raincoat haină *f* de ploaie
raisin stafidă *f*
rangefinder telemetru *nt*
rare *(meat)* crudă; în sânge
rash egzemă *f*
raspberry zmeură *f*
rate *(inflation)* rată *f*
rate *(price)* cost *nt*
razor aparat *nt* de ras
razor blades lamă *f* de ras
reading lamp lampă *f* de citit
ready gata
real *(genuine)* veritabil
rear coada *f*
receipt chitanţă *f*
reception recepţie *f*
receptionist recepţionist *m*
recommend, to a recomanda
record *(disc)* disc *nt*
record player pick-up *nt*
rectangular rectangular(ă)
red roşu; *wine* vin *nt* roşu
reduction reduce *f*
refill *(pen)* rezervă *f* de stilou
refund *(to get a)* (a primi) banii *mpl* înapoi
regards salutări *fpl*
register, to *(luggage)* a înregistra
registered mail (scrisoare) *f* recomandată *f*
registration înregistrare *f*
registration form formular *nt* de înregistrare
regular (petrol) (benzină) *f* normală
religion religie *f*
religious service slujbă *f* religioasă

rent, to a închiria
rental închiriere *f*
repair a repara
repair, to a repara
repeat, to a repeta
report, to *(a theft)* a raporta
request staţie *f* facultativă
required cerut
reservation rezervaţie *f*
reservations office birou *nt* de rezervări
reserve, to a rezerva
reserved rezervat
rest rest *nt*
restaurant restaurant *nt*
return, to *(come back)* a se întoarce; *(give back)* a înapoia
return ticket bilet *nt* dus-întors
rheumatism reumatism *nt*
rib coastă *f*
ribbon panglică *f*
rice orez *nt*
right *(correct)* bine
right *(direction)* dreapta
ring *(jewellery)* inel *nt*
ring, to *(doorbell)* a suna
river râu *nt*
river trip croazieră *f*
road drum *nt*
road assistance asistenţă *f* rutieră
road map harta *f* drumurilor
road sign semn *nt* de circulaţie
roast beef friptură *f* de vacă
roasted prăjit
roll chiflă *f*
roll-neck pulover *nt* cu guler pe gât
roll film bobină *f* de film
roller skate patine *fpl* cu rotile
Romania România *f*
Romanian *(language)* româneşte
room cameră *f*
room number numărul *nt* camerei
room service serviciu *nt* de cameră
room *(space)* spaţiu *nt*
rope frânghie *f*
rosary rozariu *nt*
rosemary rozmarin *m*
rouge ruj *nt*
round rotund
round-neck pulover *nt* cu guler în jurul gâtului
round-trip ticket bilet *nt* dus-întors
round up, to a rotunji
route traseu *nt*
rowing boat barcă *f* cu rame
rubber *(eraser)* gumă *f*
rubber *(material)* cauciuc *nt*
ruby rubin *nt*
rucksack rucsac *nt*
ruin ruină *f*
ruler *(for measuring)* linie *f*
rum rom *nt*
running water apă *f* curentă
Russia Rusia *f*

S

safe seif *n*
safe *(free from danger)* nu este periculos
safety pin ac *nt* de siguranţă
saffron şofran *m*
sage salvie *f*
sailing navigaţie *f*
sailing boat barcă *f* cu pânze
salad salată *f*
sale *(bargains)* solduri *ntpl; (commerce)* vânzare *f*
salt sare *f*
salty sărat
same acelaşi
sand nisip *nt*
sandals sandale *fpl*
sandwich sendvici *nt;* sandviş *nt*
sanitary napkin/towel tampon *nt* extern
sapphire safir *nt*
sardines sardele *fpl*
satin satin *nt*
Saturday sâmbătă *f*
sauce sos *nt*
saucepan cratiţă *f*
saucer farfurioară *f*
sauerkraut varză *f* acră
sausage cârnaţi *mpl*
scarf fular *nt*
scarlet roşu-aprins; stacojiu
scenery peisaj *nt*
scenic route traseu *nt* turistic (spre)
scissors foarfece *nt;* foarfecă *f*
scooter scuter *nt*
Scotland Scoţia *f*
scrambled eggs scrob *nt*
screwdriver şurubelniţă *f*

sculptor sculptor *m*
sculpture sculptură *f*
sea mare *f*
seafood fructe *ntpl* de mare
season anotimp *nt*
seasoning condimente *ntpl*
seat loc *nt*
second al doilea; secundă *f*
second class clasa *f* a doua
second-hand shop consignaţie *f*
second hand *(watch)* secundar *nt*
secretary secretară *f*
section raion *nt*
see, to a vedea; a întâlni
self-service shop magazin *nt* cu autoservire
sell, to a vinde
send, to a trimete; a livra; a expedia
sentence propoziţie *f*
separately separat
September septembrie *m*
seriously grav
service serviciu *nt*
service *(church)* slujbă *f* religioasă
serviette şerveţel *nt*
set menu meniu *nt* fix
set *(hair)* bigudiuri *ntpl*
setting lotion fixativ *nt*
seven şapte
seventeen şaptesprezece
seventh al şaptelea
seventy şaptezeci
sew, to a coase
shade *(colour)* culoare *f*
shampoo şampon *nt*
shampoo and set şampon şi bigudiuri
shape măsură *f*
share *(finance)* acţiune *f*
sharp *(pain)* (durere) acută
shave ras *nt*
shaver aparat *nt* de ras
shaving brush pămătuf *nt* de ras
shaving cream cremă *f* de ras
she ea
shelf raft *nt*
ship vapor *nt*
shirt cămaşă *f*
shivery frisoane *npl*
shoe pantof *m*
shoe polish cremă *f* de pantofi
shoe shop magazin *nt* de încalţaminte
shoelace şiret *nt* de pantofi
shoemaker's cizmar *m*
shop magazin *nt*
shop window vitrină *f*
shopping area centru *nt* comercial
shopping centre centru *nt* comercial
short scurt
short-sighted miop
shorts şort *nt*
shoulder umăr *m*
shovel lopăţică *f*
show spectacol *nt*
show, to a arăta
shower duş *nt*
shrimp crevete *m*
shrink, to a intra la apă
shut închis
shutter *(window)* oblon *nt*; *(camera)* obturator *nt*
sick *(ill)* bolnav m
sickness *(illness)* boaiă *f*
side parte *f*
sideboards/-burns perciuni *mpl*
sightseeing excursie *f*
sightseeing tour traseu *nt*
signs *(notice)* semne *ntpl*
sign, to a semna
signet ring inel *nt* cu sigiliu
silk mătase *f*
silver argint *nt*; *(colour)* argintiu
silver plated argintat
silverware argintărie *f*
simple simplu
since de, din
sing, to a cânta
single cabin cabină *f* pentru o persoană
single room cameră *f* cu un pat
single *(ticket)* un dus
single *(unmarried)* necăsătorit
sister soră *f*
sit down, to a sta jos
six şase
sixteen şaisprezece
sixth al şaselea
sixty şaizeci
size mărime *f*
size *(clothes, shoes)* măsură *f*
skate patină *f*
skating rink patinoar *nt*
ski schi *nt*
ski, to a schia
ski boot ghete *fpl* de schi

ski lift teleschi *nt*
ski run pistă *f*
skiing schi *nt*
skiing equipment echipament *nt* de schi
skiing lessons lecţii *fpl* de schi
skin piele *f*
skin-diving a plonja
skin-diving equipment echipament *nt* de plonjat
skirt fustă *f*
sky cer *nt*
sleep, to a dormi
sleeping bag sac *nt* de dormit
sleeping car vagon *nt* de dormit
sleeping pill somnifer *nt*
sleeve mânecă *f*
sleeveless fără mânecă
slice felie *f*
slide *(photo)* diapozitiv *nt*
slip *(underwear)* jupon *nt*
slipper papuc *m*
Slovakia Slovacia *f*
slow down, to a reduce viteza
slow(ly) mai puţin repede; mai încet; mai rar
small mic
smoke, to a fuma
smoked afumat
smoker fumător *m*
snack gustare *f*
snack bar chioşc *nt* cu gustări
snap fastener capsă *f*
sneaker pantofi *mpl* de tenis
snorkel tub *nt* de scafandru
snow zăpadă *f*
snuff tutun *nt* de prizat
soap săpun *nt*
soccer fotbal *nt*
sock şosetă *f*
socket *(electric)* priză *f*
soft-boiled (egg) (ou) moale
soft drink băutură *f* răcoritoare
soft *(lens)* lentile *fpl* flexibile
sole *(shoe)* talpă *f*
soloist solist *m*
some nişte
someone cineva
something ceva
somewhere undeva
son băiat *m*
song cântec *nt*
soon curând
sore throat durere *f* de gât
sore *(painful)* dureros
sorry scuzaţi; regret
sort *(kind)* fel *nt*
soup supă *f*
south sud *nt*
South Africa Africa de Sud *f*
South America America de Sud
souvenir suvenir *nt*
souvenir shop magazin *nt* de suveniruri
spade lopăţică *f*
Spain Spania *f*
spare tyre roată *f* de rezervă
sparkling (wine) (vin) spumos *nt*
spark(ing) plug bujie *f*
speak, to a vorbi
speaker *(loudspeaker)* difuzor *nt*
special special
special delivery de urgenţă
specialist specialist *m*
speciality specialitate *f*
specimen *(medical)* recoltare *f*
spectacle case port-ochelari *nt*
speed viteză *f*
spell, to a se scrie
spend, to a cheltui
spice condiment *nt*
spinach spanac *nt*
spine coloană *f* vertebrală
sponge burete *m*
spoon lingură *f*
sport sport *nt*
sporting goods shop magazin *nt* cu articole de sport
sprained luxat
spring *(season)* primăvară *f*
spring *(water)* izvor *nt*
square pătrat *nt; (town)* piaţă *f*
stadium stadion *nt*
staff *(personnel)* personal *nt*
stain pată *f*
stalls *(theatre)* stal *nt*
stamp *(postage)* timbru *nt*
staple capsă *f*
star stea *f*
start, to a începe
starter *(meal)* antreu *nt*
station *(railway)* gară *f*
station *(underground, subway)* staţie *f* de metrou; (metrou) *nt*

stationer's papetărie *f*
statue statuie *f*
stay sejur *nt*
stay, to a sta; *(reside)* a locui
steal, to a fura
steamed în aburi
stew tocană *f*
stewed fiert
stiff neck durere *f* de ceafă
still (mineral water) (apă) simplă *f*
sting înţepătură *f*
sting, to a înţepa
stitch, to a coase
stock exchange bursă *f*
stocking ciorap *m*
stomach stomac *nt*
stomach ache durere *f* de burtă
stools scaun *nt*
stop *(bus)* staţie *f* de autobuz
stop, to a opri; a sta
stop! opreşte!
stop thief! hoţii!
store *(shop)* magazin *nt*
straight ahead drept înainte
straight (drink) băutură *f* simplă
strange straniu
strawberry căpşună *f*
street stradă *f*
street map harta *f* străzilor; harta oraşului
streetcar tramvai *nt*
string sfoară *f*
strong tare; puternic
student student *m*
study, to a studia
stuffed umplut
sturdy durabilă
sturgeon sturion *m*
subway *(railway)* metrou *nt*
suede piele *f* de căprioară
sugar zahăr *nt*
suit *(man's)* costum *nt* bărbătesc; *(woman's)* costum *nt* de damă
suitcase valiză *f*
summer vară *f*
sun soare *m*
sun-tan cream cremă *f* de bronzat
sun-tan oil ulei *nt* de bronzat
sunburn arsură *f* de soare
Sunday duminică *f*
sunglasses ochelari *ntpl* de soare
sunstroke insolaţie *f*
super *(petrol)* super
superb superb
supermarket magazin *nt* alimentar
suppository supozitoare *ntpl*
surgery *(consulting room)* cabinet *nt* medical
surname numele *nt* de familie
suspenders *(Am.)* bretele *fpl*
swallow, to a înghiţi
sweater pulover *nt*
sweatshirt bluză *f* de trening din bumbac
Sweden Suedia *f*
sweet dulce
sweet corn porumb *m*
sweet shop magazin *nt* de dulciuri
sweet *(confectionery)* dulciuri *ntpl*
sweetener zaharină *f*
swell, to a (se) umfla
swelling umflătură *f*
swim, to a înota
swimming înot *nt*
swimming pool piscină *f*
swimming trunks costum *nt* de baie
swimsuit costum *nt* de înot
switch *(electric)* buton *nt*, întrerupător *nt*
switchboard operator telefonist(ă) *m/f*
Switzerland Elveţia *f*
swollen umflat
synagogue sinagogă *f*
synthetic sintetic
system sistem *nt*

T

T-shirt cămaşă *f*
table masă *f*
tablet *(medical)* tabletă *f*
tailor's croitor *m*
take, to a lua; a merge; *(time)* a dura
take away, to de luat acasă
taken *(occupied)* liber
talcum powder pudră *f* de talc
tampon tampon *nt* intern
tangerine mandarină *f*
tap (water) (apă de la) robinet *nt*
tape recorder casetofon *nt*
tapestry tapiserie *f*
tarragon tarhon *m*
tart tartă *f*
tax taxă *f*; TVA

taxi taxi *nt*
taxi rank/stand staţie *f* de taxi
tea ceai *nt*
team echipă *f*
teaspoon linguriţă *f*
telegram telegramă *f*
telegraph office birou PTT *nt*
telephone telefon *nt*
telephone, to *(call)* a telefona
telephone booth telefon *nt*
telephone call apel *nt* telefonic
telephone directory anuar *nt* telefonic
telephone number număr *nt* de telefon
telephoto lens teleobiectiv *nt*
television televizor *nt*
telex telex *nt*
telex, to a trimete un telex
tell, to a spune
temperature temperatură *f*
temporary provizoriu
ten zece
tendon tendon *nt*
tennis tenis *nt*
tennis court teren *nt* de tenis
tennis racket rachetă *f* de tenis
tent cort *nt*
tent peg cârlig *nt* de cort
tent pole stâlp *m* de cort
tenth al zecelea
term *(word)* termen *m*
terrace terasă *f*
terrifying îngrozitor
tetanus tetanus *nt*
than decât
thank you mulţumesc
thank, to a mulţumi
that acela
theatre teatru *nt*
theft furt *nt*
their al lor
then atunci
there acolo
thermometer termometru *nt*
these aceştia *mpl*; acestea *fpl*
they ei *mpl*; ele *fpl*
thief hoţ *m*
thigh coapsă *f*
thin subţire
think, to *(believe)* a crede
third al treilea
thirsty, to be a îţi fi sete
thirteen treisprezece
thirty treizeci
this asta; acesta
those acelea
thousand o mie *f*
thread aţă *f*
three trei
throat gât *nt*
throat lozenge pastile *fpl* pentru dureri de gât
through prin
through train tren *nt* direct
thumb degetul *nt* mare
thumbtack pioneză *f*
thunder tunet *nt*
thunderstorm furtună *f*
Thursday joi *f*
thyme cimbru *m*
ticket bilet *nt*
ticket office casă *f* de bilete
tie cravată *f*
tie clip clamă *f* de cravată
tie pin ac *nt* de cravată
tight *(close-fitting)* strâmt
tights dresuri *ntpl*
time oră *f*
time *(occasion)* oră *f*; zi *f*
timetable *(trains)* mersul *nt* trenurilor
tin *(container)* cutie *f* de conserve
tin opener deschizător *nt* de conserve
tint vopsea *f*
tinted fumuriu
tire *(tyre)* roată *f*
tired obosit
tissue *(handkerchief)* batistă de hârtie *f*
to până la
to get *(fetch)* a comanda
to get *(go)* a ajunge
to get *(obtain)* a obţine; a cumpăra
toast pâine *f* prăjită
tobacco tutun *nt*
tobacconist's tutungerie *f*
today azi
toe deget *nt* de la picior
toilet paper hârtie *f* igienică
toilet water apă *f* de toaletă
toiletry parfumerie *f*
toilets toaleta *f*
tomato roşie *f*
tomato juice suc *nt* de roşii
tomb mormânt *nt*

tomorrow mâine
tongue limbă *f*
tonic water apă *f* tonică
tonight deseară; diseară
tonsils amigdale *fpl*
too prea; *(also)* de asemenea
too much prea mult
tools scule *fpl*
tooth dinte *m*
toothache durere *f* de dinţi
toothbrush perie *f* de dinţi
toothpaste pastă de dinţi *f*
top, at the vârf (în vârful capului); sus
torch *(flashlight)* lanternă *f*
torn rupt
touch, to a atinge
tough *(meat)* (carne) tare
tour croazieră *f*; traseu *nt*
tourist office agenţie *f* de voiaj; oficiu *nt* de turism
tourist tax taxă turistică *f*
tow truck maşină *f* de depanare
towards spre
towel prosop *nt*
towelling *(terrycloth)* material *nt* flauşat
tower turn *nt*
town oraş *nt*
town center centru *nt*
town hall primărie *f*
toy jucărie *f*
toy shop magazin de jucării *nt*
tracksuit trening *nt*
traffic trafic *nt*
traffic light semafor *nt*
trailer rulotă *f*
train tren *nt*
tram tramvai *nt*
tranquillizer tranchilizant *nt*
transfer *(finance)* transfer *nt*
transformer transformator *nt*
translate, to a traduce
transport, means of mijloace *ntpl* de transport
Transylvania Transilvania *f*
travel agency agenţie *f* de voiaj
travel guide ghid *nt*
travel sickness rău *nt* de călătorie
travel, to a călători
traveller's cheque cec *nt* de voiaj; cec de călătorie
travelling bag sac *m* de voiaj
treatment tratament *nt*
tree copac *m*
tremendous nemaipomenit
trim, to *(a beard)* a aranja
trip călătorie *f*
trolley cărucior *nt*
trousers pantaloni *mpl*
trout păstrăv *m*
truck camion *nt*
try on, to a proba
tube tub *nt*
Tuesday marţi *f*
tumbler pahar *nt*
turkey curcă *f*
Turkey Turcia *f*
turn, to *(change direction)* a (se) întoarce
turnip nap *m*
turquoise turcoaz; *colour* turcoaz
turtleneck guler *nt* pe gât
tweezers pensetă *f*
twelve doisprezece
twenty douăzeci
twice de două ori
twin beds cu două paturi
two doi
typewriter maşină *f* de scris
typing paper hârtie *f* pentru maşină de scris
tyre cauciuc *nt*

U

ugly urât
Ukraine Ucraina *f*
umbrella umbrelă *f*
umbrella *(beach)* umbrelă *f* de soare
uncle unchi *m*
unconscious (to be) a-şi pierde cunoştinţa
under sub
underdone *(meat)* cu puţin sânge
underground *(railway)* metrou *nt*
underpants chiloţi *mpl*
undershirt maiou *nt*
understand, to a înţelege
undress, to a *(se)* dezbrăca
United States Statele Unite *fpl*
university universitate *f*
unleaded (benzină) *f* fără plumb
until până
up sus
upper de sus

upset stomach *(a avea)* stomacul *nt* deranjat
upstairs la etaj
urgent urgent
urine urină *f*
use, to a folosi
useful util
usually de obicei; obişnuit

V

V-neck cu guler *nt* în formă de V
vacancy liber
vacant liber
vacation vacanţă *f*
vaccinate, to a *(se)* vaccina
vacuum flask termos *nt*
vaginal infection infecţie *f* vaginală
valley vale *f*
value valoare *f*
value-added tax taxă *f* pe valoare adăugată
vanilla vanilie *f*
veal viţel *m*
vegetables legume *fpl*
vegetable store aprozar *nt*
vegetarian vegetarian
vein venă *f*
velvet catifea *f*
velveteen bumbac *nt* pluşat
venereal disease boală *f* venerică
venison căprioară *f*
vermouth vermut *nt*
very foarte
vest *(Am.)* vestă *f*
vest *(Br.)* maiou *nt*
veterinarian veterinar *m*
video camera cameră *f* video
video cassette casetă *f* video
video recorder aparat *nt* video
view *(panorama)* vedere *f*
village sat *nt*
vinegar oţet *nt*
vineyard vie *f*
visit vizită *f*
visit, to a vizita
visiting hours orele *fpl* de vizită
vitamin pill vitamine (tablete) *fpl*
vodka vodcă *f*
volleyball volei *nt*
voltage voltaj *nt*
vomit, to a vărsa

W

waist brâu *nt*
waistcoat vestă *f*
wait, to a aştepta
waiter chelner *m*; ospătar *m*
waiting room sala *f* de aşteptare
waitress chelneriţă *f*
wake, to a se scula
Wales Ţara Galilor *f*
walk, to a merge
wall zid *nt*
wallet portmoneu *nt*
walnut nuc *m*
want, to a dori; a vrea
warm cald; fierbinte
wash, to a spăla
washable care se spală
washbasin chiuvetă *f*
washing-up liquid detergent *nt* de vase
washing powder detergent de rufe
watch ceas *nt*
watchmaker's ceasornicar *m*
watchstrap curea *f* de ceas
water apă *f*
water flask termos *nt*
water melon pepene *m* roşu
watercress măcriş *n*
waterfall cascadă *f*
waterproof antiacvatic
water-skis schi nautic
wave val *nt*
way drum *nt*
we noi
weather vreme *f*
weather forecast (ce vreme se prevede) prevedere *f* meteorologică
wedding ring verighetă *f*
Wednesday miercuri *f*
week săptămână *f*
weekday zi *f* lucrătoare
weekend sfârşit *nt* de săptămână
well bine
well-done *(meat)* bine prăjită
west vest *nt*
what ce
wheel roată *f*
when când
where unde
where from de unde
which care

whipped cream frişcă *f*
whisky whisky *nt*
white alb
who cine
whole întreg
why de ce
wick meşă *f*
wide larg
wide-angle lens obiectiv *nt* superangular
wife soţie *f*
wig perucă *f*
wild boar porc *m* mistreţ
wind vânt *nt*
window fereastră *f*; *(shop)* vitrină *f*
windscreen/shield parbriz *nt*
windsurfer windsurfer *m*
wine vin *nt*
wine list listă de vinuri *f*
wine merchant's magazin *nt* de vinuri
winter iarnă *f*
winter sports sporturi *ntpl* de iarnă
wiper *(car)* ştergătoare *nt* de parbriz
wish urare *f*
with cu
withdraw, to *(from account)* a scoate
withdrawal restituire *f*
without fără
woman femeie *f*
wonderful minunat
wood pădure *f*
wool lână *f*
word cuvânt *nt*
work, to a funcţiona
working day zi *f* lucrătoare
worse mai rău
worsted lână toarsă *f*
wound rană *f*
wrap up, to a împacheta
wrinkle-free neşifonat
wristwatch ceas *nt* de mână
write, to a scrie
writing pad bloc *nt* notes
writing paper hârtie de scris *f*
wrong greşit; rău

X

X-ray radiografie *f*

Y

year an *nt*
yellow galben
yes da
yesterday ieri
yet încă
yoghurt iaurt *nt*
you tu, dumneavoastră
young tînăr *m*
your a ta, al tău, a/al dumneavoastră
youth hostel cămin *nt*; cazare *f*

Z

zero zero
zip(per) fermoar *nt*
zoo grădină *f* zoologică
zoology zoologie *f*
zucchini dovlecel *m*

Indice Român

ROMANIA
HUNGARY
UKRAINE
UKRAINE
MOLDOVA
SERBIA AND MONTENEGRO
BLACK
Carpathian Mts.
Transylvanian Alps
Transylvania
Moldavia
Walachia
Dobruja
Mureş
Siret
Prut
Olt
Danube
Danube
Mouths of the Danube
Iron Gate
Satu Mare
Baia Mare
Oradea
Bistriţa
Cluj-Napoca
Tîrgu Mureş
Arad
Mediaş
Timişoara
Sibiu
Deva
Reşiţa
Drobeta-Turnu Severin
Craiova
Slatina
Piteşti
Giurgiu
Botoşani
Piatra Neamţ
Iaşi
Bacău
Bîrlad
Focşani
Braşov
Galaţi
Buzău
Ploieşti
BUCHAREST
Călăraşi
Tulcea
Constanţa
20°
24°
28°
48°
44°